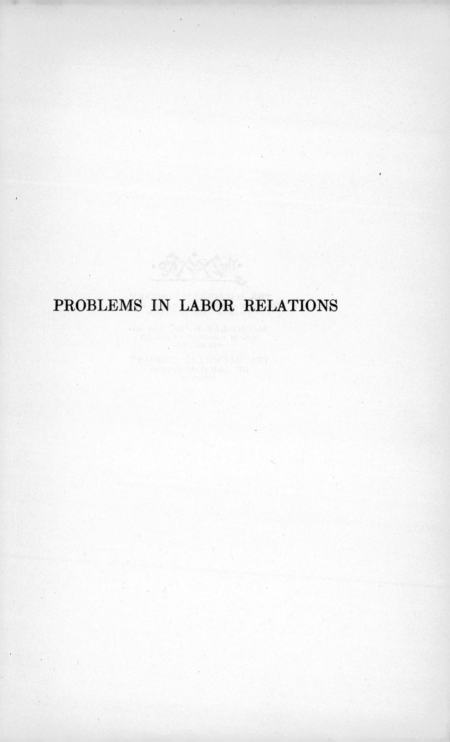

PROBLEMS IN LABOR RELATIONS

THE MACMILLAN COMPANY
NEW YORK · BOSTON · CHICAGO · DALLAS
ATLANTA · SAN FRANCISCO

MACMILLAN & CO., LIMITED
LONDON · BOMBAY · CALCUTTA
MELBOURNE

THE MACMILLAN COMPANY
OF CANADA, LIMITED
TORONTO

PROBLEMS IN LABOR RELATIONS

A Case Book Presenting Some Major Issues in the Relations of Labor, Capital, and Government

BY

HERMAN FELDMAN, Ph.D.

Professor of Industrial Relations
The Amos Tuck School of Administration and Finance
Dartmouth College

NEW YORK

THE MACMILLAN COMPANY

1937

Published April, 1937.

SET UP AND ELECTROTYPED BY T. MOREY & SON

PRINTED IN THE UNITED STATES OF AMERICA

To

WILLIAM R. GRAY

Dean of the Amos Tuck School

PREFACE

This book is intended as an aid to the study and teaching of labor relations. It consists entirely of problems, without "solutions." While it is designed, in part, for courses involving professional training for labor administration or graduate work in labor relations, it has more particularly had in view introductory courses in labor problems conducted in accordance with the modern techniques being developed in progressive teaching.

Each problem outlines a definite situation providing issues requiring decision, instead of immediately supplying the traditional or authoritative ideas concerning it. This objective approach forces the student or thoughtful reader to begin with an attempt to understand labor problems through his own analysis. It encourages the vaguely sociological person to attack a problem more realistically, more precisely, and more independently than by just reading about it. It leads the narrower and more practical individual to view a situation more broadly and socially than by uncritical acceptance of ready-made solutions.

The concrete issues presented are designed to heighten interest by providing tangible contacts with the points at which general problems have their source. The nature of these issues is such as to require responsible thinking in the light of all the circumstances, rather than mere recitation of what has been already said or written about a subject in general.

A problem book is not, however, a substitute for other means of study. The problem method makes the wider use of text and reference assignments not merely desirable but essential. It vitalizes lectures, discussions, and quizzes. In particular, "honors" work, project study, and seminars can be much improved by the advance assignment of problems which require rounded analysis and comprehensive treatment of major issues. There is greatly needed for these purposes an adequate selection of problems dealing with fundamentals in labor relations, both for introductory and applied courses. It is to help fill what is almost a void that the present material has been prepared.

There remains the question of the use of this volume to the general reader. If he is not too "general" a reader, it is hoped that he will get a more realistic feel of many situations and have his curiosity aroused by the method of presentation employed here.

The growing appreciation of the value of this way of studying and teaching labor relations is convincingly shown in the frequent requests received for prepared problems from college and university teachers of labor relations, from directors of training in business and government organizations, and from personnel managers. In response to such requests, much of this material has already been distributed in mimeographed form. In spite of its obvious limitations, it has served to demonstrate the possibilities of the problem method in teaching. This method is the important factor. It is for this reason that an introductory chapter has been prepared telling more about the problems and their use by the reader, student, and teacher. The explanation presented in that chapter and in Appendix A is so important to a comprehension of the purpose and scope of this book that it is hoped both will be carefully read.

Because many employers, personnel managers, labor union officials, teachers, students, wage-earners, and others have contributed information, it would be difficult to make suitable acknowledgment to the institutions and individuals who have cooperated in this project. My obligation must be expressed, however, to Dean William R. Gray, whose patient urging and encouragement stimulated initially my interest in teaching by the problem method, and to Mr. Elliott D. Smith, Professor of Industrial Relations, Yale University, for his especially generous and valuable counsel. I am also grateful for the criticisms of the galley proof and of the suggestions offered by Professors Paul H. Douglas of Chicago University, Sumner H. Slichter of Harvard University, Leo Wolman of Columbia University, Theresa Wolfson of Brooklyn College, Richmond C. Nyman of Yale University, and Joseph L. McDonald of the Tuck School, and by Mr. Harry P. Bell of the Economics Department of Dartmouth College.

In the actual preparation of the material and of the manuscript I am particularly indebted to Miss Margaret D. Pierce, of the Tuck School secretarial staff, for her intelligent, competent, and loyal assistance.

HERMAN FELDMAN

HANOVER, NEW HAMPSHIRE
March 1, 1937

TABLE OF CONTENTS

II. Wage Incentives and Wage Methods

PART THREE: OLD AGE, INSECURITY, AND UNEMPLOYMENT

I. The Older Worker

II. Technological Change

III. Industrial Practices Affecting Employment

APPENDIXES

FOREWORD: AN INTRODUCTION TO THE PROBLEM METHOD OF STUDY

This book consists of approximately three hundred cases in labor relations combined in seventy major problems. These problems are grouped in five main parts, under the titles of—I, Wages, Wage Methods, and Wage Administration; II, Hours, Working Conditions, and Labor Regulations; III, Old Age, Insecurity, and Unemployment; IV, The Personal Environment; V, Group Relations, Unions, and Labor Law. Within these main parts there are normally several subdivisions of allied problems, shown on title pages for these parts.

Various individuals differ in their ideas of the distinction between the terms "case" and "problem." The latter term does not of itself raise many doubts except when compared with the word "case." Perhaps it would be best to use the words interchangeably. There is hardly a need to add much to the discussion of this fairly minor point. But to satisfy those to whom the matter may be of interest, an explanation of the sense in which the terms are in most instances used here is presented.

A case, as written up by various institutions and in various books, seems, in most instances, to be a history of what some enterprise or institution did under stated circumstances. The case history as such may be a subject for criticism, but this is not necessarily called for by its terms. If a question is definitely appended, in order to force the reader to exercise his own judgment in determining what should have been done, or should be done, then it is by that process transformed into a problem. The latter, therefore, is a construction of facts presenting an issue requiring independent solution by the reader or student. The desired effect may be obtained by revealing only part of what was done and requiring the student to proceed from this point, or by preparing a mere digest of the facts which raise the issues and then considering fundamental principles.

Most of the cases used here present issues on problems of labor relations beginning in an individual concern or industry. Both in theory and practice this is a desirable starting point. A labor problem often begins in a case affecting an individual or a number of individuals. Its solution may to a degree be possible within the orbit of a single concern or industry. To the extent that it is not solvable in this manner, the student is forced to see it in larger terms and thereby he is led naturally and easily to those solutions requiring larger viewpoints. As an illustration one may refer to Problem 40, regarding applicants for work.

Form of Problems

In editing the case material received, the attempt has been made to reduce the presentation to the absolute minimum necessary to reveal the main issues of the problem, without depriving the reader of a sense of the underlying circumstances in which it is imbedded. In some instances detail has been sacrificed in the individual case, but with the hope that the problem as a whole will supply something of the realistic background. In this process of editing, cases which began as several long pages of factual material may have emerged as paragraphs. The excess has not been discarded without careful thought. It is felt that in this type of book, aiming only at the fundamentals of policy and procedure, it was not too great a loss to sacrifice the full detail as it would be in cases intended for intensive professional study.

In presentation, a degree of uniformity was attempted. Normally a problem as a whole is intended to cover a wide field, and the individual cases to present typical, special, or puzzling aspects. The cases within a problem are not drawn from the same source, yet they are used in combination because the point of a problem is not so much to solve the issue in any particular situation as to seek a fundamental approach to that type of situation as a whole and then to test its application in given cases.

A few of the cases may leave an unsatisfying feeling of incompleteness. This, although not always the result of design, has, in many instances, been definitely intended. The alternative would be to present facts in so thoroughly digested a form, or the issues in so neat an order, that these would be unlike anything experienced in real life. To have made every problem complete in its presentation of the possible aspects to be considered would be to reduce their value as a group in providing a challenge to independent and imaginative thinking. It is for the student or reader to learn to see a problem in its widest applications, and it is for the teacher to aid him to see how and why he has missed major sectors of attack. Appendixes A and B consider further by what process this result may be secured.

Some of the cases are frankly intended to be provocative—to disturb the conservative in his beliefs and force him to think over his ideas anew; to disturb the progressive and lead him to analyze more closely the basis of his faith. There are some instances, probably, in which an individual problem may seem to be one-sided or biased, but it is hoped it will be recognized that this effect is often pedagogical in intention, and that no such impression is desired for the book as a whole.

It is largely because the student or reader is expected to pursue the issues to the extent of referring to one or more good general texts that the construction of the problems has not aimed at a complete balance of presentation. It is further expected that in any problem which may seem to err in emphasis or direction the instructor will supply a corrective influence.

References to the exact name of a concern have in almost all instances been omitted, to avoid embarrassment to anyone involved. The problem has normally been put in the present tense, to aid in making it more of a challenge to present-day thinking rather than a historical review. However, where the situation would be different today from what it was at the time the problem existed, and there is good reason to mention the date, this has been done.

Sources of Cases Used

While some of the cases, involving broad issues, have been constructed by citing from articles, reports, speeches, statements and letters, or by a review of opposing contentions and a presentation of the basic questions involved, the cases are in the main actual situations drawn from experience. In some of these problems the author has participated personally as consultant or investigator. Others were obtained by plant visits, field observation, and other contacts with industrial and governmental employment. In some instances the circumstances of a case were related by friends engaged in labor union work or in personnel management. Still other problems originated in requests for aid desired by correspondents who found themselves involved in some activity which presented difficulties. Certain of the cases were reported by students and graduates, and others by workers who had observed or experienced them. The cases in Part V are based on a wide survey of available material concerning issues arising under various joint agreements between employers and unions or before government labor boards of one kind or another.

The material used has only rarely been taken from books by individual authors. In view of this and of the fact that the passages selected are presented solely for their value as issues for discussion, it has been expedient in some cases to omit exact references to date and source. Care has been taken to avoid injustice to anyone concerned. The omissions of footnote references, inexcusable in a work intended for documentary purposes, is of little, if any, disadvantage to the reader here and aids the general purpose of the volume in preserving the material as of current significance.

Permanence of Issues Involved

A particular effort has been made to steer between the Scylla of "dated" material and the Charybdis of wholly local issues. Each problem has been scrutinized carefully from the standpoint of whether it involves a purely temporary situation. It is expected that in most cases the issues presented will be just as alive a decade or two from now as they are today. For example, will the question of what is appropriate action regarding retention of the middle-aged worker in industry (Problem 32) be out of date within the next decade?

It is true, however, that some of these problems are connected with, or are the result of, the present capitalistic form of society and that a few others are more especially related to the Federal-state system of government. Neither of these will pass out of the picture very soon. An examination of the problems will reveal that in other countries some of the situations are strikingly similar in character, permitting the use of most of the cases for general study. Moreover, the problems taken from or based upon situations in government-operated activities involve broad issues of civil service personnel.

As Professor Elton Mayo emphasizes, in concluding his book *The Human Problems of an Industrial Civilization* (The Macmillan Company, 1933), labor difficulties involve human and social, rather than economic, problems. Hence in the issues raised here, an attempt has been made to give a proper weight to practice as well as to theory, to procedure as well as to principle. This makes for better theory and practice. For these reasons many of the problems have a strong "how" flavor, and the student or teacher is expected to show in detail the actual sequence of steps applying to the situation.

The best results of the problem method of thinking and of teaching are obtained by means of such a follow-through, because *what* is to be done can only be understood properly when an earnest attempt is made to see *how* it is to be done. This applies even to some broad cases, such as those involving the question whether, in a given instance, there should be state or national regulation. Without these specific "hows," proposed in some detail, thinking is likely to remain superficial.

The Questions Asked

In all instances the problems end with a minimum number of questions, intended to force the student to do more intensive thinking and purposeful reading than normal assignments require. It is expected that the student may reflect upon questions of his own and that the teacher will be free to substitute or append his own suggestions of issues on which to base the assignments. The questions raised have not been put after the individual cases but at the end of the problem, so that often the material will have to be re-read in connection with these questions. This is intentional, as the process is expected to bring both a broader comprehension of the aspects involved in the problem as a whole and a more mature handling of the particular cases.

The questions are not expected to be answerable purely by reflective reasoning. They may require research, facts, conferences, primary or secondary knowledge. In this they are similar issues to those confronting one in actual life. But it is hoped that the student will start in trying to find the answer by reasoning it out "on his own." As he finds that he needs additional information or counsel, he may read assigned texts, consult various sources, or make personal inquiries. He can then formulate the more mature views which constitute the basis of a prepared assignment. The process will serve to start him in the habit of thinking out the issues independently and should prepare his mind for further impressions and understandings. The ordinary text assignment often gives, in addition to one or more obligatory references, a host of optional ones which are, in fact, rarely read. The present method not only stimulates the student to utilize independent sources, but in many instances practically forces him to do so.

The misimpression against which some readers must, however, be warned, is that the problems are simple to solve or answer. Were opportunity afforded to raise a few pertinent questions intended to unsettle the commentator, the simplicity would tend to disappear. Usually when a student finds a problem easy it is because he has not thought through valid objections to his solution or failed to consider modifications justified by more carefully analyzed procedures. The superficial answer often means that the student has applied ready-made a stereotyped dogma which he uncritically accepted as true. The person who has really attempted to solve the problem has realized that it involves much more than appears on the surface.

The question may appropriately be raised here whether the availability of pencilled marginal notes made by previous classes might not in time nullify the thought-provoking possibilities of a question. The answer, in large part, is that in the process of using these problems the teacher will learn a great deal more than the student, and the kinds of issues he will raise in successive years will vary and be far ahead of the previous classes' responses. Moreover, the basic factual information required of many problems will have changed. At the least it may be said that the didactic flavor will never approximate that of the completely informative textbook in which, as far as the student is concerned, the answers are regarded as already being there.

It may be appropriate to mention here that there is no answer book or guide connected with this volume. To do this would in a sense go counter to the very experience and purpose of a problem book in this particular field. As a result it may be that the instructor, who is the only one who would be permitted to obtain such an answer book, will regard it a bit difficult to teach through problems the first year. He will find, however, that after the second or third try the subject opens up in ways that make teaching much more interesting and effective. Instructors who resist the problem method find, after they have used it with some persistence, that they would never go back to an exclusive reliance on what might be called the older and perhaps more omniscient forms.

Range of Problems Selected

In order to have the problem useful in teaching, there is needed a selection of situations based on real experience and therefore giving the student an insight into the human circumstances involved. The reliance should be on significant or typical problems which, though applied in concrete cases, involve fundamental principles of approach, and therefore may be considered of permanent value. The issues should be concentrated on those which are stimulating in the nature of the problem presented, yet within the range of mentality, knowledge, research capacity, or imagination of the student.

The cases which are included in the problems here presented have been selected from a much larger number gathered for class purposes. In the process many cases have been discarded after trial because of their inadequacies in one respect or another, or perhaps because of too technical a nature to include in a first volume. In no instances do any two problems cover exactly the same field, but there is occasionally an overlapping between successive problems, the later ones being provided to permit either a choice of approach or an opportunity for more detailed application of principle.

It should not be regarded as a defect of this volume that every possible labor subject in which one may be interested is not covered by some problem. Even to have attempted to include one for all of the many subjects found in a comprehensive textbook would have required a volume of encyclopedic size. It is expected that the teacher who finds it possible to use some problems already prepared for him will be ready to seek and present others in the fields in which he wishes to extend the method.

Among the sections to which inadequate space is given, but which could have been expanded almost indefinitely without much difficulty, is, for example, that on the law of labor relations. Such important subjects as the injunction, the right to sue labor unions, and similar issues are only incidentally covered. One reason for confining the content of this section is that the teacher who is at all familiar with this field can more easily obtain cases here than in other phases of the labor problem. Actual cases of labor law are everywhere at hand, and all one needs to do for many topics is to select a decision of the Supreme Court or of a state court involving dissenting opinions.

Another reason is that the injunction is an issue from which a short case is not easily made. The validity of an injunction is often derivative in nature, and its wisdom depends upon the types of acts which it enjoins. A judgment regarding it may be made only by weighing alternative effects of a wide sociological nature, and would therefore require a much longer presentation than would be appropriate in this book.

Two other subjects which have been given less space than they deserve are employee representation and social insurance. On these two questions an abundance of material is at hand. But at the moment we are in a transitional stage which may soon make certain issues in these fields out of date, and for this reason it has been expedient to omit several cases of present importance.

Applicability to Introductory as Well as Advanced Courses

A hasty reading of the cases, or a merely passing consideration of the possibilities of the problem method in introductory labor courses, may not take into account the fact that the volume has carefully considered the special needs of such courses. The use of a certain number of practical cases in an introductory course, in order to start from real, tangible situations and work outward to general problems, is the tendency in thoughtful and progressive practice. The old idea is fast losing ground that a general, all-embracing coverage of labor subjects, studied wholly through factual readings and the lecture method, is the way to conduct an introductory course. Those who have considered the matter in the light of developing academic pedagogy tend to emphasize independent thought and the development of basic habits of approach. Such teaching pursues fundamental principles and seeks to make the student stop to reflect, perhaps even to worry, as to whether he is going at a problem in a rounded and responsible way.

The teachers who prefer to rely mainly on lectures will find that the use of the problem method will be an excellent way to prepare the mind of the student for the information and ideas which the instructor presents. A problem which raises puzzling issues will stimulate the student to think about its complexities and make him the more eager to obtain the views of the instructor. Something like the tension of the last ten minutes of a good law school class may be obtained when the points which the instructor has selected for comment have acquired a meaning to the student.

Aside from its other values in introductory courses the problem method, when imaginatively applied, is one which greatly enlivens class assignments and discussion. It provides an exceptional opportunity to encourage preparation through group projects and group reports, and it opens the way to workable, original devices of stimulating student enthusiasm and activity.

Value of the Problem Method in Teaching

Much might be said here, even in an introductory way, of the objectives and technique of the problem method of teaching, as compared with the more customary forms of instruction. This advance in the teaching of the social sciences came, peculiarly enough, in graduate and professional teaching, which in other respects had been considered as lagging. For decades elementary and secondary school education had been alive with experiment and change, and academic institutions had begun to give thought to the revitalizing of collegiate instruction. But the squeaky coach of graduate teaching in the social sciences might have been considered as having budged hardly at all were it not for a notable innovation—the displacement of the lecture method by the case system.

President Nicholas Murray Butler once characterized this change as being an advance from an almost exclusively expository and didactic method, through which the major portion of the thinking is done by the teachers themselves, to a process of conference requiring some mental excitation on the part of the students as well. The Harvard Law School—through the introduction and application of this method by Professor Langdell in his classes in the 70's—was the pioneer in a change which has revolutionized the teaching of law everywhere; and the Harvard Graduate School of Business Administration has made the most general application of the case system to business education.

Teaching by the problem method has as its main aim the development of mental power, through the requirement of analysis, synthesis, and an actual decision in a concrete case. If it is not an aid to the quick acquisition of facts or to the acquiring of a broad field of knowledge in a limited length of time, it is likely to heighten the impression and the usability of the facts which are acquired. Its development can have a most significant influence upon the whole field of teaching.

The problem method is particularly needed, however, in the teaching of labor relations. One of the troubles in this field is that too much is taught in terms of generalities of economic and social principles, irresponsibility or sentimentally applied,[1]

[1] One of the leading teachers in this field, on reading this proof, has privately made the following comment: "I have long felt that the teaching of labor subjects in colleges is irresponsible in that it deals largely with abstractions, proceeds often from a careless and uninformed but reformist point of view, and disregards a wide and fundamental set of factors bearing on actual factory management which determine the quantity and quality of the output of industry."

and that too little is considered with reference to the ways in which human nature expresses itself in actual situations. Forcing the student to apply a principle to concrete cases tends to provide correctives of some common faults in the teaching of labor relations. Such cases put a premium on sound information. They may begin, of course, by requiring the student to discover for himself the general principles or approaches involved, but student and teacher should both have to proceed as though something important depended upon their determinations.

As a result the problem method has value in providing a more realistic understanding of the social and administrative aspects of labor relations; in developing an awareness of the variability of approaches and solutions; in stimulating personal interest and self-expression; in supplying a feeling of responsibility for actually dealing with a problem as a citizen with power, rather than just knowing about it; and, as part of all these, in enforcing more careful thinking and exercise of judgment.

Change in Role of Instructor

A particular merit of a good problem procedure is that it puts the relationship of student and teacher on a different plane. Many solutions are possible to a problem. The instructor becomes not the final authority but a consultant or advisor.

Methods of Assignment

The instructor does not need to assign a whole problem, but merely one or more of the cases in a problem, in accordance with his purpose and the degree of thoroughness with which he wishes the answer or solution to be prepared. He may wish to limit the assignment to some practical cases, or he may wish the assignment to involve a broad question of principle. Another possibility is the assignment of different cases within a problem to different individuals in a class, and thus to some degree to individualize the instruction. This has been done successfully in small seminar groups. The class as a whole has considered the main problem, while different students have contributed especially thorough analyses and solutions of individual cases.

It is expected that the instructor will provide a reference and reading list in connection with each problem assigned. Aid may be obtained in this connection from the discussion and suggestions in Appendix B. It should be mentioned here, however, that the problem method provides what is perhaps the only practical method for parcelling out different text assignments to members of the same class, if the instructor is so inclined, because the students are intent on applying themselves to a problem and not in reciting from a specific text.

Those who have not been accustomed to teach by the problem method should not permit initial difficulties, normal to any change, to discourage them. The experience of many teachers has been that once these initial obstacles have been overcome, the use of the problem method, even in part of the course, is seen as superior to didactic instruction. Many of the difficulties found in first applying the problem method are easily overcome through early experience; others will be found to have been illusory.

Among the seeming disadvantages of the problem method, which will be seen in new perspective once the change is made: is the lament that it becomes hard to "cover the ground." But observations of outlines of courses and of classroom procedure in the social sciences will support the view that some teachers cover far too much ground. The teacher who first is troubled because, through the problem method, he does not discuss as many facts and topics relating to the subjects in the course as he could when he used the lecture or quiz-and-answer method, is apt to make a virtue of this after a while. For when he has applied the problem method for a time and has acquired the concrete background for comparing his newer objectives with his former practice, he may come to believe that he used to spread his material too thin. He is likely to find that by the problem approach he is covering more of the fundamentals that will actually "stick," that he is using his class time for more important material, and that much of what he is omitting is of the ephemeral type of information which most students tend to forget anyhow when the course is over.

There are, of course, genuine difficulties in the problem method, as there are in any teaching procedure earnestly applied. To minimize these the teacher would do well to select from the problems in the book those which appear to be easiest to teach, either because they deal with subjects with which he is most familiar or because they seem to lend themselves best to good discussion. In time, as these are found to be an aid to class instruction, he can extend the use of problems until the method becomes the dominant, though not necessarily the exclusive procedure, and its tone communicates itself to the normal attitude in studying labor issues.

Educational Objectives and Techniques

The fundamental question of educational method is, however, whether a course in labor relations or any other subject is for the purpose of teaching truths, facts and principles, or of teaching people to think deeply, clearly, and logically in the presence of new situations. The student of teaching method who has gone beyond the objective of "getting his subject across" will see problems in terms of the particular skills or basic understandings which are to be the objectives of teaching, and will question at every stage which of these a problem is trying to develop. A true problem book will have a sequence of development of these skills or understandings somewhat in the manner of a well conceived book on geometry. The author is aware of the inadequacies of the present problem book from the standpoint of a carefully contrived sequence of such primary objectives.

A discussion of the educational technique which should accompany the instructor's use of the problem method would deal with such matters as, for example, the desirability of enforcing, as the student's preparation, a comprehensive answer in outline form to each of the questions raised. But one would need to analyze the standards which a truly comprehensive outline should meet, and thus be concerned with the processes of analysis, reasoning, and judgment for which teaching methods should strive.

For the possible value or interest which an elementary effort of this sort may have, a memorandum on the subject, distributed to students in connection with the use of these problems, is included here as Appendix A. It was developed as an attempt to introduce some mental discipline into classroom discussion, as compared with the vague and diffuse conversations which sometimes pass for the discussion method. It has already been well received in several quarters and has apparently been of sufficient stimulus to justify presenting it as something which may be helpful in developing this aspect of teaching.

The memorandum is divided into two parts. The first emphasizes the importance of developing certain habits of analysis in thinking through a situation and of style in presenting one's conclusions to others. The second part attempts an application of these and other principles in a specific procedure for attacking problems.

A more thorough discussion of the questions involved in effective teaching, even if within our range of knowledge, would belong more properly in an educational paper, or elsewhere, and is not submitted here. But such appraisal of objectives and technique in the teaching of labor relations is necessary. The author would be glad to exchange correspondence on this subject with those who already feel the need, or who come to feel it by the experience gained in using these problems.

PART ONE: WAGES, WAGE METHODS, AND WAGE ADMINISTRATION

I. Some Major Questions regarding Wages

II. Wage Incentives and Wage Methods

III. Wage Increases and Administration

PROBLEM 1. WAGES IN THEORY AND PRACTICE

Case A. The Determination of "Proper" Wage Levels

Three executives lunch together occasionally to discuss mutual administrative problems. A topic which comes up from time to time is the wage level of clerical and technical employees. One states: "We are in a fog as to the principles and processes involved and would be glad to compare our ideas with those who look upon the subject from the academic heights of economics and ethics."

He is the administrator of a new division of the Federal government, having under his jurisdiction several hundred employees paid out of a lump sum appropriation. The wages of the technical and clerical employees to be hired are not definitely set in the law, and the administrator therefore has considerable range of freedom as to whether a particular grade of employees shall, for example, get $25 a week or $30.

The second official is the comptroller of a philanthropic foundation having a liberal endowment. The institution could set wage scales at any reasonable level it desired. The chief limitation is the realization that the more it spends on its overhead the less it has to distribute for basic services and in support of those whom it is designed to aid. The comptroller therefore feels it necessary to develop sound principles in setting salary levels.

The third executive is the operating vice-president of a business concern which has recently decided to concentrate its headquarters in that city and is gradually transferring certain duties from branch plants in various parts of the country to these central offices. This concern is in a competitive field. Naturally it does not want to load its overhead with any more pay than would be "justified." But what wage is "justified," is not clearly defined in the mind of the vice-president on whom rests the obligation of setting "proper" wage and salary standards for clerical and administrative employees.

The interesting aspect of the problem is that all three men are new to the particular problem of determining wage rates. Being intellectually minded, they are pursuing the additional question of whether there is a justifiable difference in the policies they should apply with regard to remunerating employees. The letter sent by the administrator asks such questions as these:

1. Are there certain general standards of wage payment, from economic and ethical standpoints, to which wages should conform? If so, what are they?
2. Do these standards take into account differences related to the types of industries or establishments in which the workers are employed?
3. How do business concerns actually set wages for jobs, and how *should they* determine them? By what process may the policies you recommend be put into effect?

Case B. **The Basis of Wage Increases**

In 1929 the employees in a textile fiber mill had been working fifty-two hours a week at about 60¢ per hour and had been making an average of about $31 per week. In 1936 these employees were working a full-time week of thirty-six hours, or about a third hours less, and were getting 75¢ per hour, which is 25% more than in 1929, and earning about $27 per week. But the employees said that, regardless of the hourly rate, they were earning less per week than they used to, and that they should be earning more, so as to progress in their scale of living. They demanded $1.00 per hour, but it was understood that they would compromise at 90¢, which would give them $32.40 per week.

The employer wished to avoid a strike and at the same time denied the justice of such a wage. He called it an uneconomic rate. He admitted that in that particular year the concern had been doing well and could pay this additional wage out of surplus, but he feared it might have losses the following year, as it had had in 1931 to 1935, when most of the company surplus had been necessary to maintain its finances in a solvent condition. Moreover, while this particular concern might be able to pay the scale that year, the industry could not do so without substantially raising its prices to the public. This, he asserted, would be unwise even for the workers because it would cut down the volume of orders and therefore of employment.

In private discussions of the matter with an economist whom he has hired as a consultant, he has raised some economic questions which puzzle him. These may be summarized as follows:

1. On what economic basis would it be feasible for a particular employer in an industry to grant a wage increase of this character and under what conditions is he justified in refusing it?

2. On what economic basis would industry as a whole be justified in raising or refusing such increases if demanded nationally?

Case C. Feasibility of a $3600 Family Income

In a statement concerning the future outlook of labor, issued on December 28, 1936, William Green, President of the American Federation of Labor, said: "Before industry can reach capacity production every one who wishes to work must have employment, and every family must have an income of at least $3600." Thus he has set a sort of goal for which labor might be said to be striving.

Public opinion has become confused, however, by contrasting views concerning the feasibility, or even the early desirability, of this level of family income. Ultra-radicals asserted that the amount would be easily attainable if unearned incomes, rents, royalties, and excessive profits and salaries were made available for wages to the masses. Certain conservative spokesmen stated that this income was distant as a practical possibility and that to urge it was, for the moment, dangerous because it might lead to too rapid a raising of wages. This, it was stated, would impair the incentive to enterprise, reduce the rewards of management and, on the assumption that the $3600 was an income to be spent, divert to consumption wealth which should go to capital equipment.

Questions:

1. What answers should be given to the administrators in Case A and to the employer in Case B? Prepare a careful statement, in outline form, designed to present the principles involved in both these questions and their application to the given cases.

2. In the light of actual average family income at present, the trend toward smaller families, and the trend of incomes, how much of an increase would Mr. Green's proposal involve and what are some of the chief steps which would be necessary to hasten its attainment?

PROBLEM 2. ASSERTIONS CONCERNING PRIORITY OF WAGES

Case A. Priority of Wages over Dividends?

During a strike of tool and die makers in automobile plants the general secretary of the union made the following assertion:

> The union refuses to accept the principle that the employers are entitled to profits at all costs. It demands that the men be paid decent wages and work fair hours, and does not worry about the employers. Its function is only to win for the workers; if the employers find their dividends on the down grade, that is their concern.

In another instance the spokesman for a labor union in a wage controversy issued a statement which included the following:

> Labor takes the view that humanity must not pause and wait upon profits on a plea of inability to pay, especially where it is desired to extract full returns on an unwisely capitalized industry. Society cannot tolerate the plea of incapacity to pay just wages. For many years the sweatshop operator has justified his conduct on just such a plea of inability to pay.

Case B. Priority over Interest to Bondholders?

During a depression the income of various groups falls in unequal proportions. In such situations the preferred position of bondholders is usually subject to criticism. For example, in reviewing a government report on income, a well-known writer made the following comparison of the index of relative income:

> It is the year 1930. Wages paid to labor in industry have fallen to about 83. Salaries paid in industry have hardly fallen at all. They are 99.3. Payments to entrepreneurs, which includes farmers,

are 93. Net rents and royalties, which means income from real estate, are about 84.4. Dividends are 97.2. And interest is 102.4. . . .

We now come to 1931. Wages have fallen to 61.4. . . . Only one class of incomes stood up. This was income from interest, which fell only to 99.6.

And now 1932. Labor continued to lead the procession downward. Industrial wages fell to 39.8. Salaries fell to 59.3. Dividends, to 43.4. The income of entrepreneurs, to 59.2; income from real estate, to 44. But interest still stood up remarkably. It was still 96.8. (Walter Lippmann, in the New York *Herald Tribune*, January 30, 1934.)

Under these conditions, it was stated, the distribution of wealth became progressively more and more unequal, taking the greatest toll from those who were already the weakest, and far greater toll from the active producers of wealth than from the recipients of fixed or sheltered incomes.

On this point a spokesman for the railroad labor unions in April, 1934, opposing a 10% cut in wages, made a statement criticizing the disparity in railroad income distribution, and stated:

The railroad funded debt aggregates about 56% of the outstanding capitalization. If profits on such a huge debt are to be given preference over humanity and if employees are to continue to contribute a "dole to idle capital" . . . the breath of life of the worker will have expired in hopeful waiting for the bondholder to receive his final full "pound of flesh."

Case C. Priority over Capital Surplus or Assets?

In a negotiation over a reduction of wages between a concern manufacturing plumbing supplies and their workers, the management indicated its inability to grant the wages involved in the union's terms, on the ground that building was at a standstill and that as the concern had been operating at a loss during the depression, the granting of the terms would mean an additional loss. The union official pointed to the ample surplus that the concern still had, and stated that there was no reason why the loss should not be made up from this source. He said it would be a form of profit sharing in which labor shared in the past profits at a time when such sharing was most likely to be economically beneficial.

The employer replied that a capital surplus representing the earnings of past years was the property of stockholders, and that although it might be used in an emergency to aid employees laid off, it was not a proper basis for ordinary wage negotiation.

Questions:

1. What would be the economic and social effects of each of the asserted priorities if generally adopted?

2. If you believe that the point of view expressed by labor in one or more of these cases should be a basis of industrial wage policy, indicate the manner and extent to which, in each instance favored, it should be applied. If in any case you do not side with labor, show clearly why the contention should be opposed.

PROBLEM 3. THE MARKET WAGE AND ITS CONTROL

Case A. Sweatshop Competition

A shirt manufacturer who describes himself as a liberal, and who wants to live his ideals in practice, wrote, in 1933, as follows:

> I have two plants. One of these is in a Pennsylvania town. The chamber of commerce paid $2500 to bring another shirt factory to a community only about ten miles away. This year I know from reliable sources that that shirt factory's average wages were a bit over $3 a week. The firm nevertheless was persuaded by another community about three counties away to move its plant there for another $2500 and they are now flourishing in that community.
>
> The other plant is in New Jersey. The nature of the competition there is not much different. I have always resisted cut-throat competition with plants in my industry and have in part been able to do so, first because my firm usually got along pretty well and secondly, because my own investments yielded both a feeling of security and profits which made the earnings in the business less important. At present I am attacked from all sides. I have already made two cuts, and I feel inclined to beat my competitors to it by cutting my wages even below their level.

If you were a manufacturer working under these conditions—and it seems that most, if not all, are in this situation this year—and it seemed to you that by reducing wages you would be keeping your employees in your concern, instead of failing and having them unemployed or working at lower wages in another concern, what attention would you pay to the principle of paying at least a living wage?

Case B. A Union's Elimination of Wage Competition

At one time competition in the photo-engraving companies in New York City was practically cut-throat, since prices were set without consideration of the cost of production and almost entirely with the idea of undercutting competitors. The workers are highly skilled and are required to exercise a great deal of personal judgment in their work. When asked for higher wages, the individual concerns in the industry found themselves unable to grant them. The union, according to a business agent, therefore resolved that it had to "force the manufacturers to make money."

Since it was a strong organization which included practically all the workers, the union told the manufacturers quite plainly that the workers wanted higher wages, that the manufacturers would have to make more money in order to give those wages, and that therefore the cut-throat competition would have to stop. There then existed a board of trade for the industry at which the manufacturers got together to discuss policy. The union practically forced the manufacturers to get together on a set of minimum prices.

This agreement lasted several months. In this period exceptional profits were made. The case was brought before the Federal Trade Commission as a violation of the Sherman Anti-Trust Act, and an order was given by the Commission to have the agreement changed. The price scale, as agreed to by the Engravers Board of Trade, was then prefaced and worded in a way that made it less open to legal objection. Under this new agreement, the competition was not regarded as cut-throat. The prices set tended to bear a definite relation to the cost of production and usually allowed for a reasonable profit.

This also meant a great deal in raising the standard of wages, which soon came to be among the highest in the country. The daily wages of some building trade workers were higher, but the work in those trades was not as steady. The concerns were able to give these wages and still make profits, so the union achieved its aim.

Criticisms of the plan came, however, from those paying the prices. They called it a monopoly and asserted that the two sides should not be permitted to make such mutually favorable terms at the expense of the public.

Questions:

1. To what extent can and should such a situation as that indicated in Case A be dealt with by legislation? Discuss the possibilities in terms of economic effects, the types of laws to be instituted and their administrative practicability.

2. Evaluate the possibility and desirability of control of wages in the manner indicated in Case B.

PROBLEM 4. DISPUTED APPLICATION OF THE "MINIMUM WAGE"

Case A. Contested Scope of Minimum Wage Legislation

A proposed leaflet urging minimum wage regulation declares the purposes of such laws to be (1) to end cut-throat competition among employers; (2) to set a bottom limit below which wage rates cannot fall; (3) to assure women fair wages for their services and to help them meet the cost of a healthful standard of living; (4) to sustain and extend advances in wage levels already gained; and (5) thus to establish the purchasing power of the workers necessary to bring about and maintain prosperity. The leaflet was submitted to several people for comment.

An economist invited to serve on a wage board states that he is against minimum wage regulation because "like this pamphlet, it usually combines incompatible aims and confused purposes." He believes that minimum wage regulation, if tried at all, should be limited to a few industries and to workers who are weakest and most exploited, and be "extremely moderate." His memorandum includes the following paragraphs.

> The reformers who supported the National Recovery Administration in 1933 and 1934 desired minimum wage regulation for both men and women in various industries for just these reasons. Did they stop at what might by any meaning of the term be called minimum wages? As a result of their pressure some of the fancy so-called minimum wage rates promulgated as U.S. law included: (1) In clothing, in the Eastern area, a minimum of $1.80 an hour, for machine pressers; (2) in the petroleum industry, a minimum wage for skilled work in derrick and rig building in Texas and New Mexico, $1.50 an hour, with crew foremen to receive a minimum of $1.75 an hour; (3) in the theatrical industry, a minimum of $75 a week for a traveling press representative.

> If minimum wage legislation is given more than a very restricted place the economics of such legislation is questionable. If wages by law are fixed too high, an employer to remain in business must raise the price of his product. In some industries this raises price to the point of reducing demand, which means the discharge of some of his labor, or putting them on part time. From a common-sense point of view, if a woman can earn only $10 a week how can her employer pay her $15? A person is worth only what he or she can earn. Moreover, if the operation is of the type which can be done by machine, or otherwise abolished, there will be every incentive for the employer to do so.

The labor member of the wage board replies that the natural law of supply and demand is not a proper basis of wage fixing. He quotes approvingly a letter published in a newspaper which said, in part:

> Minimum wage laws and price-fixing agreements may be economically impossible as a matter of theory, but they are quite practicable in actual experience. The resale price agreement between manufacturer and retailer has been established practice in many industries, while price-fixing by monopolies no longer is news.

To this the member first quoted retorts that it is bad enough to have price fixing by monopolies and that it will not add to the economic welfare to have the same practice through government action.

This discussion has put the third member, representing the general public, in a quandary. He says he did not realize that all these and other issues would arise in minimum wage regulation, and he does not know what the policy should be.

Case B. Contrasting Bases of Regulation

A state commission appointed to set minimum wages in the laundry industry is considering two alternative principles. One member contends that the task is one of merely discovering the varying amounts which different employers in an industry are actually paying, then fixing the minimum rate somewhere at a point which will eliminate only the lowest wages. Another member contends that the purpose of minimum wage legislation is to fix wages based upon the necessary cost of living; that this should be determined by cost of living surveys; and that a "proper" minimum wage should then be decreed whether the majority of the employers in the industry involved are paying it or not, and "no matter whom it hits."

The member of the commission who supports the former view cites a report on "Variations in Wage Rates under Corresponding Conditions," published in 1935 by the Women's Bureau of the U.S. Department of Labor. This found that in each industry examined the wage payments in the typical sample establishments included showed striking differences from plant to plant, even when other conditions were similar and all possible efforts had been made to select only strictly comparable data. For example, median weekly earnings in the highest-paying were more than double those in the lowest-paying plant among 11 large and 21 small laundries in Ohio, and median weekly rates among 28 large New York laundries also show a difference of 86.5% between lowest- and highest-paying plant.

This member of the commission therefore believes that all that may properly be done is to obtain such wage figures in his state for the industries to be regulated and to lop off the worst ones. He maintains that the other policy is to introduce an idealistic principle which would be without regard to economic effects.

Case C. Perplexities of Legislating a Standard of Living

The Consumers' League of a state is urging that a board appointed to set a minimum wage in the retail trade adopt as a basis what would be necessary for a "minimum cost of proper living." The board has in general accepted the idea of using such a basis, but finds that this has left it with the puzzling problem of determining more definitely what standard to use.

The secretary of the retail stores' association has prepared a strong brief in favor of using as a basis of the cost of living a standard which would be the absolute minimum of subsistence. He argues that minimum wage legislation is considered generally as a sort of health measure, and it is largely on this ground that it is likely to be upheld by the courts; that such laws are intended largely for the unskilled and unprotected wage earners, who would be denied even a minimum necessary for food and lodging if wage levels were absolutely unrestricted; and that if one tried to do much more than that, the legislation would become a general economic regulation of wages and therefore involve much more complicated questions for the board and for society as a whole.

Social workers appearing in behalf of the women involved in the industry state that it would be absurd for a minimum wage to be just enough for a mere animal existence, and that it should provide a "minimum of health and comfort," and thus include an amount for insurance and savings in order to include provision against ordinary risks, some allowance for recreation and education, and recognition of other needs. But the secretary of the retail stores' association cross-examined several of these witnesses as to what should be included in what they considered as the minimum standard of health and comfort and made a list of the items suggested. At the following hearing he brought a financial summary showing that if the items mentioned were taken into account, a minimum wage of $2200 would hardly suffice, and that this was a grotesque notion of what minimum wage regulation was.

This has resulted in protracted discussion of such itemized questions as these: Are cigarettes necessities or luxuries? (It was conceded that they were necessities for men, but there remained a difference of opinion concerning their status among women.) Are silk stockings an extravagance or, under modern urban conditions, essential? Is a water wave or a permanent wave a hairdressing necessity? These and other matters were argued so warmly before the board that it is reopening the matter of a clearer definition of just what standard of living it should use as a basis of wage decrees.

Case D. **Alternatives in Estimating Cost of Living**

A minimum wage commission has adopted tentatively the principle of setting wages upon the basis of "the normal requirements of a woman living in health and decency." It now wishes to take the succeeding step of determining how much money that standard requires. Two different types of budget studies are urged upon it by those who have appeared at its public hearings.

A strong representation has been made in favor of the "minimum quantity budget" procedure, to consist of first establishing in detail a standard list of the amount of food, housing, clothing, and other commodities and services required as a minimum during a year by a woman living in health and decency, and then to price these items in a sample group of localities in order to provide a fair estimate of the wages required to support a woman on such a basis.

This procedure was opposed by another group, including one technical adviser representing the employers' association, on various grounds. It was objected that the standard quantity budget assumes that all people want the same things when, as a matter of fact, there are differences in the kinds of articles consumed in different places; that though the method was appealing in theory, in practice the amount arrived at was likely to be much more than is actually being paid to those for whom a minimum wage is being set; and that when by such a procedure in some states a minimum on this basis for a single woman was estimated to be $20 or more, it was so impractical that it has been cut anyhow to $13, $14, and similar "realistic and actual" amounts. Hence the recommendation made by this group was that a survey be made of the actual expenditures of a representative sampling of women workers in the trade, and with this in hand, to decide among the weekly totals on a figure which would represent the most feasible minimum wage.

The advocates of the minimum quantity budget method retorted that merely to add up what people of a certain class spend does not take into account that the items for which the money was paid may not have been wisely chosen, and that, in any event, what people spend is limited by what they get in pay so that the whole procedure becomes a circular one. The other group replied that it is not for the state to tell working women what is wise for them or unwise, and that the practical method offered as an alternative would at least "keep the commission's feet on the ground."

The commission had previously had the impression that the matter of a cost of living study was a routine technical matter when the basis of liberality had been outlined. It has called a special meeting to consider the question further and to determine the method of study to be authorized.

Case E. **Feasibility of Extra Allowances for Dependents**

A minimum wage board engaged in making a survey of the circumstances of women in an industry in which it is to promulgate a minimum wage has discovered that a substantial proportion of the women in that trade support dependents, including children or invalid husbands, destitute parents, unemployed brothers and sisters, and other relatives. They work alongside girls without any obligations whatever, who may live at home and not even contribute for their own share of the expenses. To set a wage which disregards dependents is to disregard the actual facts of those who are meeting inescapable obligations. But to set a minimum wage adequate for the group with dependents would be to decree an excessive minimum to the other group.

The question before the board is whether it should specify extra allowances for workers for each dependent supported, which would mean a substantially higher minimum wage for those supporting relatives. The justifiability of this as an economic measure and the possible effect of such a differentiation in prejudicing employers against married women and those with dependents are two of the considerations which it believes must be evaluated in the final judgment.

Case F. **Effect on Employment of Low-Grade Workers**

1. During the operation of the textile code in 1934, the minimum wage set for the textile industry was much more than had been previously paid to a substantial proportion of the women employees in a certain plant. The prevailing method of pay was the piece-rate basis. The company increased the piece-rate so as to aid workers to earn the minimum, but it also raised the standards of output. To make it less difficult for the slower workers to produce the higher quotas, the company aided them by better training and supervision.

Nevertheless about 25% of the workers were unable, in spite of the higher piece-rate, to earn the minimum on the basis of this new standard. The management therefore began to displace some of these workers, and in its hiring of new workers was very careful to employ permanently only those who in their trial period showed they were capable of giving much higher production than the average and were therefore worthy of the new minimum pay.

Those displaced, or those who thought they were in danger of being displaced, and others, sent a representative to urge that the minimum wage law be lowered. A spokesman stated that the minimum wage provisions penalized these workers in society who already have most difficulty in getting and holding jobs.

2. A chain store which had been paying many of its girls $8 and $10 has found that it has had to observe a state minimum wage decree of $15. The nature of this chain store's merchandise is such that it can employ people with a minimum of intelligence as long as they are honest, industrious, and in good health. How-

ever, as they are forced to pay a wage for which they can get a much higher type of personnel, the employment department has decided to substitute people with a better education, better personalities, and more experience. A weeding-out process was begun soon after the decree, and requirements for new workers were raised. The company has chosen girls who are older, more personable, and from better families, including in many instances college graduates.

Complaints have therefore come to the minimum wage board that the results of its decree have been to favor those already fortunate, whether because of inheritance, acquired ability, or circumstances, and thus to make harder the lot of those who are less fortunate. The people who are in most need of opportunities for work are stated to be barred by the higher qualifications resulting from the wage decrees. The commission does not know how to meet this complaint, either in theory or in practice.

Questions:

1. If you were the third member of the board in Case A, with which side would you agree, and why?

2. Assume that minimum wage legislation has been adopted in your state and, with reference to the issues considered in Cases A, B, C, and F, indicate what you believe the scope of such laws should be and the standard which should be used as a base.

3. Write a short brief to the commission mentioned in Case D concerning the procedure it should use.

4. What should be the policy regarding dependents in such legislation?

5. What, if anything, can or should be done about such effects as those asserted to have arisen as a consequence of the two wage decrees in Case F?

PROBLEM 5. ISSUES IN WAGE NEGOTIATIONS

Case A. Misunderstanding over Conditions of the Trade

A severe reduction in business was experienced by a New England textile concern, and wage cuts were made in various operations, although resisted by the employees. The reasons for the difficulties included the loss in the market for its main product because of a change in women's styles, severe competition with Southern mills in cost of production, chiefly in labor costs, and the displacement of cotton textiles by rayon.

The union officers, including the president of the State Federation of Labor, asserted that most of the arguments about competition were a subterfuge. They said that the management had closed down part of the plant chiefly to starve the workers into accepting wage cuts. As evidence, they presented the fact that, only a short while before, the company had purchased the factory and site of a large adjoining textile company. They asked: "If the company is doing so poorly, why does it need another large new mill? If they are not just waiting to beat down wages, why do they buy a new plant when they aren't using more than half their existing plant?" The union also questioned the assertions of the company with regard to the unfavorable competitive cost of certain of the items which it produced.

When an interested citizen made inquiries about this matter, the plant officers explained that the adjoining textile mill had failed and that its factory and site were offered at an extremely favorable price, along with valuable water rights that protected the company's own property. The purchase, it was stated, had been made as an investment, and not because of any need for more equipment or factory space.

Case B. Questions regarding Accounting Procedure

In a negotiation concerning terms and conditions of employment between a street railway company and its organized employees, the union demands the continuance of a wage which the company states it cannot afford. In support of this contention the company provides a brief containing items of operating revenue, expenses, and other data of the business, showing that it had had a heavy deficit during the preceding year and that the first six months of the present year would probably show a deficit.

The counsel for the union, however, contends that these excerpts represent merely the company's way of figuring its accounts, as for instance, in the item of depreciation of cars. He asserts that various items in the accounts are questionable and should not be upheld unless accountants hired by the union or by the negotiator are permitted to examine the books and report independently upon them.

Case C. Employees' Right to Criticize Capital Structure

In a wage controversy the spokesman for railroad labor made the following assertions:

> The capitalized structure of the railroads on which full interest payments are being demanded has constantly increased. Through this extravagant "watering" financial policy the railroads are able to make the public believe that they operate at a deficit, when as a matter of fact they enjoy a substantial profit.
>
> The railroads report their earnings in a manner that makes return to the owners largely a "fixed charge," and net income is calculated only after a half-billion dollars have been paid to the owners of the industry.

The two sides were deadlocked for a while over the question of whether this difference in views regarding railroad financing should be injected into an issue of wage adjustment.

Case D. **Wage Adjustments Favoring Non-Strikers**

In a plant employing several hundred workers a misunderstanding at the beginning of a busy season precipitated a strike among some of the younger men. The older workers disapproved of the hasty action and did not go out with the younger men. As a result the strike collapsed. The management was very grateful to the workers who stayed on the job. It therefore decided at the end of the season to pay a bonus which would, in fact, apply only to those workers whose period of service had not been interrupted.

To the company's surprise, the announcement aroused immediate opposition. The bonus was labeled "blood money," and given unprintable titles by the former strikers. Some of the older workers resented the suggestion that they were being paid for not going on strike, and practically agreed to call a strike if the bonus was paid. A spokesman asserted that wage adjustments should not be used to penalize strikers or reward non-strikers.

Questions:

1. Assume that the explanation given by the plant executives in Case A represents the true situation. How can such facts best be made clear to the employees so that misunderstandings will not arise?

2. To what extent should privileges with regard to independent appraisal of the validity of employers' claims regarding competitive costs or conditions of the business be afforded to workers in wage controversies?

3. Should criticisms of capital structure be permitted to play a part in controversies over wages? If your answer is yes, what in the main should be the practices taken into consideration? If not, what protection may be given the worker against misrepresentation of ability to pay through improper financing?

4. In Case D, what would you have done (1) before the issue arose and (2) after the objections became known?

PROBLEM 6. GEOGRAPHICAL DIFFERENTIALS IN WAGES

Case A. Differentials Due to Prevailing Wage Scales

An attempt to set a uniform wage scale in industry on a national basis under the N.R.A. in various industries brought forth the objection from Southern concerns that this would be entirely unwise and unfair in view of the fact that the wages paid in the South were so very much below those paid in the North. The manufacturers cited among their arguments the principle of the prevailing wage as one which had always been regarded important in government contracts. This principle, they asserted, works both ways, and a genuine differential in lower prevailing wage rates should be recognized.

The manufacturers in other centers also objected to equalization on the ground that the lower wage rates made it possible for them to remain in business in spite of Eastern competition and that to remove this wage difference would uproot some of their industries and throw the employees out of work. This, it is said, would decrease the standards of living for the entire community, as well as for the workers involved.

The Northern manufacturers stated that such competition was unfair and should not be encouraged. They argued that no manufacturer should have an advantage over his competitor by reason of lower wage rates. Wages, they said, should be a uniform competitive factor; and competition should be restricted to other factors such as style, quality, nearness to markets, efficiency in production, and the like. Even though this policy might necessitate the relocation of plants which have gone into certain areas because of cheap labor supply, these persons contended, the result would be temporary and would in time lead to the most efficient organization of production.

In many of the wage rates set under the N.R.A., the wage rates for certain areas were set lower, in some cases markedly lower, than the scales applying to other manufacturers under the same industrial codes. A compilation made by the N.R.A. research staff of the minimum wages set for unskilled productive labor in about 500 codes which, with supplemental codes, involved a maximum of 695 instances of possible application of differentials, showed:

in 285 no differentials
in 231 a geographical differential
in 31 a population differential
in 122 both population and geographical differentials
in 26 a differential based on wages formerly paid.

Some of these differentials were small, others substantial, and still others striking. An example of the latter is the rate for common labor in the iron and steel industry, which varied, in the 21 districts for which set, from 40¢ per hour in the North to 25¢, or well over a third less, in a Southern district.

The decision on the extent of the differentials and whether they should be merely temporary or should be a basic assumption in any trade agreements on fair competition, etc., remained an issue in almost every industry. Acquiescence in the differentials was on the basis of not making too great an immediate disturbance, so that the debate as to their justification continued.

One group approached the problem with the assertion that "fair competition" must take into consideration a large number of factors which influence the cost of doing business. Among those mentioned were not merely the cost of living but also nearness to raw materials, nearness to markets, relative productivity of labor, nature of the labor supply, ability of industry to pay, stage of mechanization or development, and competitive nature of the products. It was argued, for example, that if certain Southern manufacturers are distant from the market for their goods, this burden should be equalized by lower wage rates. It was also argued that if certain Western areas suffer from lack of an adequate labor force, their competitive position should be equalized by a lower wage scale.

This proposal was at once attacked as unfair. One of the opponents asked, "Does this involve, for example, penalizing an enterprise which had the intelligence to settle near the source of its supply of materials, by forcing it to pay higher wages than its competitors?"

Case B. Contested Importance of Different Standards of Living

At hearings involving the setting of national scales of wages as minima to be paid in certain trades and occupations, employers appeared from various areas of the country stating that they employed Mexicans, Negroes, "poor whites," and others whose standards of living were so much lower, and therefore whose costs of living were so much less, as to justify lower wages. They stated that it would be absurd to raise the wages of these workers as it would merely encourage them to work fewer days a week.

The opponents of such differentials maintain that the differences in wages enforce lower standards of living. They also state that many of the places where prevailing wages are lower actually provide poorer lodging, much less clothing and food, and generally worse conditions, and that these explain the wages paid. The payment of higher wages, they believe, would in time raise the backward workers to an "American" standard of living.

Case C. Alleged Inequity of Uniform Wage Scales

At a hearing on the salary scales to be paid to post-office clerks a group of employees from a large city requested that they be given more than the standard national rate for their positions. They said that a clerk obtaining a salary of $1500 or

$1700 in a small community might be obtaining a comfortable salary compared to others in that community, whereas in New York City he would be hard pressed to support his family on it. The result of the uniform wage scale, they asserted, was not uniformity, but a gross lack of uniformity in real wages for identical work.

Other workers, including agents of a union of postal clerks, opposed the proposal on the ground that while such differentiation may actually exist, it is impossible to establish it on a basis which would be fair. Two cities or communities may be of the same size, yet one may be overbuilt while the other may be having a housing shortage; one may be in the midst of a farming region, the other the suburb of a large city; one may be prosperous, the other depressed. On this basis, it is stated, no consistent relationship between the size of a community and the cost of housing, clothing, food, and other items can be successfully established.

Postal authorities opposed this largely because of practical difficulties involved. They said it might lead to constant unsettlement of the rates. They pointed out that changes in prices were constantly occurring; that postal clerks in a Florida town with a real estate boom, a Texas town with an oil boom, or in any other locality in which prices suddenly rose, would demand the extras; and further that Congressional wire-pulling would naturally be resorted to by the clerks in other towns to have their wages "equalized."

Case D. Denial of Differences in Costs of Living

An industrial association which has been attempting to eliminate cut-throat competition has a committee which is considering the question of uniform minimum rates throughout the country. The manufacturers representing Southern communities and others in the market who are located in rural areas request a differential on the ground that their localities have lower costs for the same standards of living than would be provided in other areas and that therefore a comparable wage scale should recognize this difference.

The representative of the group of manufacturers who desire the uniform national wage scale denies that there are such differences. He asserts that modern forms of chain store distribution and consumption of mass commodities have very much reduced the differentiation in costs if the same standards of living are taken into account. He quotes among his authorities a study, made by the National Industrial Conference Board, of twelve industrial cities located in Massachusetts, New York, Pennsylvania, and Ohio, the findings of which are illustrated by the following excerpt:

> When the five budget items are combined to form the total cost of living, the differences in cost between the various cities tend to disappear or to diminish to small proportions. This is due to the tendency of high costs for some items in a given city to be balanced by low costs for other items. A further factor which tends to bring about general uniformity in living costs is the fact that differences in costs of food and clothing are reduced to insignificant proportions because of nation-wide competition. Since these two items account for a large proportion of the total cost of living, they exert a strong influence on the total.

The opposing side brought in figures to show instances of living costs of branch factories in isolated sections of Missouri, Kansas, and certain smaller Southern and Western states, which were much lower than the average. To this one Northern liberal manufacturer retorted: "Who would want a twelve-room house free on the Desert of Sahara?" Besides, he maintained, the more rural the location the more likelihood of certain expenses not easily estimated, such as the cost of sending children to boarding schools because of the inadequacy of local facilities, an increase in the cost of medical care, especially in serious illness, because of the distance from competent medical aid, and a greater cost of recreation, such as the expense of long journeys to visit relatives and friends.

A manufacturer representing a large plant in a rural community replied that his company had established a first class school for the people in the community, that its hospital was one of the finest in the state and gave medical advice and some treatment free of charge, and that the employees' association which it had started and encouraged provided more opportunity for amusement than is obtained in most city plants. He argued that a lower direct wage was therefore proper in his case.

Case E. **Extension of American Wages to Workers Abroad?**

1. The American Government is establishing a large new embassy in a foreign country in which wage standards and living standards are very much lower than they are in this country. It employs a number of subordinates, such as clerks and assistants, messengers, and men who take care of the buildings and grounds, who are not American citizens but are, in some cases, expatriates of Canadian and English extraction, and in other instances natives of an oriental race.

The budget for the expenses of the Embassy makes a sharp distinction in the wages to be paid in accordance with these classifications, the American scale of wages to apply only to the chief officials, a much reduced scale to certain "whites" employed, and a greatly reduced rate for the natives to correspond to prevailing wages in that country.

2. A financial corporation has branches in several leading cities of the world. In its offices are cashiers, clerks, and others who are all expected to speak English. Their qualifications otherwise are more or less the same, and they do approximately the same work. The wages paid are, however, variable and correspond to the labor market, the local standard of living, and the prevailing wage. Thus there are sharp differences between the wage scales of comparative jobs performed by people of similar education and training, as among, for example, those employed by the corporation in Bucharest, Florence, and Paris.

Recently the general counsel, one of the directors of the company, took his first trip abroad. He happened to say that he had disregarded the advice of friends to tip porters the prevailing amounts or to haggle with vendors and innkeepers. He said, "Why should I hesitate to give a man a quarter for lugging a couple of heavy bags, merely because a nickel or a dime would have been all that some local person would have given him? Why should I try to pay less than the equivalent of $3.50 or $4.00 a day for a good hotel room and three meals merely because I could beat them down to half the price?"

One of his friends has asked him why his company does not apply the same policy in the wage rates paid to people working in their foreign branches, and cited the Ford Motor Company as having made studies with this end in view. This director has become sufficiently interested in the policy involved to send out a private inquiry to a number of large concerns to see what their practices and views in the matter are.

3. An American manufacturer with a branch plant in a foreign country is considering a wage increase which would yield an "American standard of living" to the employees of that branch, although they are natives who could not otherwise command a wage scale of that sort. The announcement of his intentions has aroused strong opposition from the local manufacturers, who assert that his action would be wrong because it would unsettle the labor market and would be inimical to local trade interests.

Questions:

1. What policies in general should govern with regard to geographical differentials? Indicate specifically what you think should be done in Cases A, C, and E.

2. Discuss fully the validity and importance of the various assertions presented in Cases B and D, adding any significant comment which is applicable to the issues.

PROBLEM 7. WAGE POLICY DURING DEPRESSIONS

Within recent years the economic principle to be applied with regard to wages during a business depression has been the subject of considerable controversy, and a large section of public opinion has apparently reversed itself, some in one direction and some in another. The economic theory held in the past by perhaps the greatest number of authorities and by almost all employers had been that in a time of depression it was best to cut wages. By thus reducing costs and making possible profitable business and the purchase of goods by the consumer, the hope was the sooner to give the basis for widened demand and recovery.

Shortly after the stock market crash in 1929, President Hoover called leading representatives of industry together in a conference and sought to obtain promises that wages would not be cut from the high levels then prevailing. Many industrialists came to his support. Henry Ford suggested that wages should be raised in order to furnish additional purchasing power for the goods which producers were not able to sell. The U.S. Steel Corporation was credited generally, up to the middle of 1930, with having resisted wage cutting and having been an influence in the maintenance of wage scales. Public officials and publicists everywhere proclaimed this as the desirable policy.

Union labor was, of course, prominent in the movement to maintain the wage at its 1929 level. As an example, on November 27, 1930, William Green, President of the American Federation of Labor, declared:

> The Government has committed itself to the maintenance of wage schedules and working standards. It is the duty of all working people to support this policy and to hold fast to the wage levels already established.

Those public enemies among employers who will not willingly subscribe to this humane and sound economic policy should be compelled, through the resisting power of working men and women, and the pressure of sound public opinion, to maintain wages, hours of labor, and conditions of employment which are in accord with American traditions and the American standard of living.

This policy was, in a sense, opposed to what had been the former beliefs of many authorities, but perhaps for the first year of the depression comparatively little dissent was voiced. When, however, the depression deepened, the policy of maintaining high wage rates came under a fire of criticism, as indicated by some of the excerpts to be quoted below.

In April, 1931, at a meeting of the National Metal Trades Association, the president of an employers' research organization called attention to the fact that the cost of living for wage earners had declined much more rapidly than had wages, and stated:

It is, after all, not the money wage, but rather the real wage, represented by the purchasing power of money earnings, that determines whether living standards can be maintained. When, therefore, the cost of living falls, a proportionate reduction in wages need not affect adversely the economic status of the worker.

The question naturally arises whether moderate wage reduction, not larger than the decline in the cost of living, might not permit longer weekly working schedules, with larger payments in the weekly pay envelopes. The reasoning implied in the question is that reduced production costs, on account of the lower wage factor, would result in lower sales prices, and thereby stimulate increased buying, greater industrial activity, and consequent larger employment.

In September, 1931, Mr. Walter Lippmann stated:

After the stock market crash of November, 1929, almost everybody from the President down believed that there was not going to be a real depression and that prices and business activity were going to return within sixty or ninety days to the level of the boom. On that assumption there was good sense in saying that since nothing else was going to be deflated, employers ought to bind themselves not to deflate wages. The assumption was wrong. . . .

> The real interest of a wage-earner today is in the amount of money he has at the end of the week. This is already drastically reduced, and it cannot be restored without a restoration of business activity. The real problem is whether American industry can revive at a lower price level while the costs of production remain at the boom level. (The New York *Herald Tribune*, September 24, 1931.)

Professor Alvin H. Hansen, in his book, *Economic Stabilization in an Unbalanced World*, published in 1932, makes the following comments.

> It is extremely unfortunate that the wholly erroneous theory that depression can be minimized by maintaining wage rates rigidly at the former level, despite the fall in prices, has gained such wide currency. The acceptance of this view precludes the development of schemes of wage adjustment either in trade union agreements or in shop committee plans. The error, as we have seen, lies partly in confusing *wage rates* and *labor incomes*, and partly in overlooking the influence of high wage rates on costs.
>
> The argument that money wages should be maintained in periods of falling prices is sound—within limits. Insofar as the fall in prices can be offset by increased efficiency in the whole field of industry, wages can indeed be maintained. But if there is a drastic fall in prices, only a very small percentage of all industrial concerns can offset the price decline by a proportionate gain in efficiency (pp. 366–367).

Professor Paul H. Douglas, in his book, *Controlling Depressions*, published in 1935, contends:

> When, under the capitalistic system, prices are falling rapidly and output per worker is not advancing correspondingly, it is unwise from the standpoint both of labor and society to rigidly maintain wage rates. For to do so will tend to grind business, operating as it is under the profit system, between the upper and nether millstones respectively of shrinking prices and inflexible wages. In this process, profit margins would rapidly disappear, and in consequence production and employment would greatly decrease. Labor as a whole would, as a matter of fact, tend to lose more from diminished employment than it would gain from the increased real hourly wages of those who were still retained. . . . On the whole, there-

fore, the desirability of preserving labor's *share* of the total product and of increasing this total as much as possible should lead to a flexibility of wage rates in periods of depression as well as in prosperity (pp. 213–214).

Questions:

1. In the light of the contrasting views expressed and of whatever analysis you may be able to make of the economic facts and principles involved, what do you believe should have been the policy to be pursued in the 1929–1935 period by—

a. The Administration?
b. Employers?
c. Trade unions?

2. If in government employment and in certain well-organized trades the wage rates paid had been held up to 1929 levels, while wages in non-unionized industries declined drastically, what would have been the probable economic effects?

PROBLEM 8. PROS AND CONS OF "PREVAILING WAGE" SCALE IN GOVERNMENT CONTRACTS AND ON PUBLIC RELIEF PROJECTS

Case A. The "Prevailing Wage" on Government Work

In many states legislation has been passed to the effect that building and construction contractors doing work for the state should pay the standard prevailing rate of wages of the trade or locality on such work. Among the reasons given for desiring such legislation by those who have urged it are the expectation that it would tend to stabilize bidding conditions between contractors and to place all of them on a parity; would prevent the exploitation of workers and the reduction of wage scales below decent economic levels; would tend to prevent irresponsible contractors from figuring on public work; would protect contractors of greater experience and capital from the irresponsible contractor through the stabilization of wage scales; would tend to improve the general character of the work performed; would tend to maintain purchasing power among the mechanics employed; and would, in consequence, have its effect upon general economic conditions.

Opponents of "prevailing wage" legislation have raised objections regarding the justifiability of its basic principles and its feasibility in practice.

One objection frequently found is the denial of the justice of the principle of "giving legal sanction to whatever happens to be the wage level some group may have extorted in a trade or locality." As one statement words it: "If it is *wrong* for the government to pay an *abnormally low* wage that happens to prevail in a community, why is it *right* to pay an *abnormally high* wage that some all-powerful group of skilled workers may have imposed on the public? Should not government policy be that of determining by its own intelligence, as best it can, a fair or just wage, rather than have some self-seeking minority become, in effect, the government agency?"

An important objection relating to practice rather than to principle is held to be the fact that for many skilled and unionized crafts, the published wage scale is not, in fact, the actual wage scale paid, because of tacit agreements when men are hired. One opponent quoted in a newspaper remarked: "Prevailing wages may not prevail anywhere but with the government. In off-season or in times of depression they may prevail hardly at all in private enterprise. Yet an attempt to undercut the official scale by a government agency at once raises a storm, with the result that government wage scales tend to give a bonus over prevailing wage rates."

Case B. Extension of Principle to Government Purchases

Under the Walsh-Healey Act, which became law on June 30, 1936, all employers contracting with the Federal government "for the manufacture or furnishing of materials, supplies, articles, and equipment in any amount exceeding $10,000" must comply with certain minimum labor standards with respect to the work performed under such contracts. Chief of these standards is that the contractor must pay to the workers employed not less than the prevailing minimum wage paid on similar work in the locality where the articles were manufactured or furnished. The Davis-Bacon Act, passed with certain amendments a little while before, had provided that Government contracts on construction work in excess of $2000 should stipulate that laborers and mechanics employed be paid the wages determined by the Secretary of Labor to be those prevailing in the locality where the work is performed. Before the passage of these two acts, the Federal government had been compelled by law to purchase materials from the lowest responsible bidders.

Regulations made by the Secretary of Labor, including the provision that all work in excess of forty hours a week should be paid for as overtime, were considered too stringent by many manufacturers. They did not want to be under control and inspection because they had sold the Government some goods. In December, 1936, the Navy Department was in the market for 2,600,000 pounds of copper, and twice within that month its advertisements for bids were met without a single offer. Under emergency provisions of the Walsh-Healey Act, the Navy Department finally bought the copper without regard to the compliance of the manufacturers with the Act.

Case C. The "Prevailing Wage" on Relief Work

In recent years there has been great dissension over the question whether wages paid on public work designed to provide employment should be on a relief level, or on a basis of what similar work would be paid if part of the regular activities conducted by national and local governmental agencies.

There are diametrically opposed views on this issue. One group recommends that governments make a careful distinction between their regular activities and those undertaken primarily to relieve unemployment, and that in the latter class the scale be definitely lower. The theory has normally been that work of this character should be paid perhaps one-half, or two-thirds, of the normal pay, in order to reduce the cost of such relief work, or to discourage workers from becoming so satisfied with their government work as not to seek or accept opportunities in private employment.

In connection with a relief bill submitted in 1935, the Federal Relief Administration introduced a memorandum pointing out that to pay the prevailing rate of pay on a full-time basis (130 hours per month) the money would employ only two-thirds as many workers, or the full number only two-thirds of the time, as would be possible at the rate intended by the Administration. If the expedient were adopted of employing the full quota of men, at the prevailing rate of pay, but for fewer hours, as for example, one-half the number of hours (65 hours per month), the amount of work performed would be even less than half of the original quota, because of the inevitable loss in efficiency of working men half time.

A building trades employers' organization, in opposing the prevailing rate on relief work, states: "In many communities where the question of the prevailing rate of wages has arisen, it has been decided by political agencies to be the union scale of wages, whereas the evidence indicates that the large majority of men are not working under union contracts and even the union men who have work are not working at the scale." These employers say that by the device of writing into a contract, or retaining in a contract, a wage scale which, during a depression, is in fact not paid, the union is able to give the impression that the prevailing wage rate is in effect, when actually this would be higher by 20 to 30% than the wage rate being paid to union men themselves.

The A.F. of L. and important craft unions have, however, vigorously stood out for the prevailing rate of pay. The Federation stated that it had no objection to limiting the maximum pay of workers on relief to $50 a month or even less, through reduction of the number of working hours, provided the prevailing rates of wages were paid. It was suggested that the relief workers be rotated so that all would earn at least $50 a month.

A letter of the president of the A.F. of L. to the United States Senate states: "We are of the opinion that a relief wage established on a lower basis than the prevailing rates of pay will tear down our wage standards and, either directly or indirectly, cause reduction in the wages of American working people."

The New York *Times* commented editorially on this assertion as follows:

How much merit is there in the contention that failure to pay "prevailing wages" on the Government's work relief program will "tear down" existing wage standards? When it puts men on work relief, even though it pays them an amount much below the prevailing private wage, it helps—for as long as this program can be continued—to sustain the prevailing wage level even more, because it pays men more than under straight relief, it gives them some employment and reduces still further the competitive pressure for private work.

Case D. Policy if Relief Work Becomes Permanent

Advocates of a regular rather than a relief scale of wages on relief work argue that although formerly such public provision of work was looked upon as a temporary stopgap, with expectation of early abandonment, it has since been regarded in many quarters as a more or less permanent provision by which an industrial society might take care of a varying volume of unemployment.

Regular pay on such projects is, therefore, urged by these advocates, on the ground that no person should be required to live on less than his regular pay on a job held for any considerable time. They say that much of the work would be of a long-time nature, such as a dam, or a flood control project, requiring years to complete; that there would be illogical results if two men doing exactly the same thing on a government job were paid entirely different rates because of an arbitrary difference in their classifications; and that if the individual worker is not responsible for his inability to get a job in private employment, then there is no reason to penalize such a worker by a starvation wage.

Moreover, it is stated that the relief wage scale encourages local government and communities to have some of what would be their regular work done as relief projects paying lower scales of wages, especially when it is possible, by transferring local work to relief projects, to shift all or part of the cost to the state or Federal government. It is asserted that this substitution of relief wages has been done on a widespread scale within the past few years.

Case E. **Controversy over Competition of Private Industry with Government Relief**

Throughout the period of the expanded Federal program for relief and public works, complaints were voiced in many quarters by manufacturers and farmers that the Government's policy was competing unfairly with them and actually making it difficult to obtain labor from among those on the relief rolls. The excerpts below, selected from many items in the press, suggest the nature of the controversy in the summer of 1936.

A publicist writes: "To reabsorb the army of non-producers on public works and relief will not be so easy as long as the government, the labor unions and the public take the view that this army shall be employed only at prevailing hours and wages. For the hard truth is that a considerable part of that army is not efficient enough to produce the goods which the prevailing hours and wages call for."

A Texas newspaper reported:

> Manufacturers have protested to the President that they are unable to hire American labor from relief rolls because of high prevailing Federal relief wages, according to the Texas Manufacturers' Association. Reports from Chamber of Commerce officials indicated that there was a shortage of farm labor. The manager of the Chamber said that he had requests for labor that he could not fill, and that in many places the cotton crop is very sparse. Where it is impossible for cotton pickers to pick over one-hundred pounds of cotton in a day, the wage for such cotton pickers has to be low.
>
> The President made reply that employers who have protested against prevailing Federal relief wages do not want to pay a fair subsistence wage based upon American standards of living. He said that wages paid to Mexican labor along the Mexican border, to French-Canadians on the Canadian border, and to workers in the berry-picking sections of New Jersey were so low that workers would not quit relief jobs to be paid Mexican labor prices in private employment.

Asserting that the prevailing wage paid by the Government was not the wage actually paid by private industry, a Northern newspaper stated that it has received reports of a shortage of cotton pickers in the South and that "even where no scarcity of workers yet exists, the high hourly rates of pay, the easy hours, and the relative pleasantness and security of relief work lead many men to prefer continued WPA jobs to any return to private jobs."

An editorial comment on the relief situation makes the following suggestion:

> Some of the worst evils of the prevailing wage system could be rectified if the local administrators were at least authorized to fix two classifications of workers. To the first they could pay the "prevailing wage," but insist in return on certain standards of work that would be rigidly adhered to. Those who were unable to qualify under these standards would not be dropped, but would be put in a second classification, and receive a smaller rate of payment. The persons in this lower group would then either be less inclined than at present to pass by opportunities for private employment, or they would strive to qualify for the higher group. If those in the higher group were carefully selected on the basis of ability, it would become a normal recruiting market for private industry to draw from.

Questions:

1. Should the principle of the "prevailing wage" be applied on what may be called normal or regular public works construction and government purchases? In your answer indicate the economic and social effects involved, and suggest how the situation in Case B should be met.

2. Which of the policies discussed should be followed regarding the levels of wages to be paid on work undertaken primarily to reduce the volume of unemployment? Outline fully your supporting reasons and indicate, in connection with whichever policy you favor, what protective procedures would minimize the practical disadvantages asserted in the controversy.

PROBLEM 9. CONTROVERSIES OVER PROFIT SHARING WITH EMPLOYEES

Case A. Do Ordinary Employees Deserve Profits?

A specialty manufacturing corporation has a profit-sharing plan by which two-thirds of the profits to be shared go to some four hundred executives and other special personnel whose work requires a "high degree of imagination," and the remaining third of the profits is distributed among about two thousand employees who have been with the concern three years or more.

Since these employees are paid the "going rate" or better, and the concern depends for its success on originality, scientific production, and excellent sales administration, many of the executives have felt that the share given to such employees has been money taken from them. They have raised the issue anew, the matter having been precipitated through the publication of an editorial in a national newspaper on "Who Produces Henry Ford's Wealth?", which stated in part:

> In the strictly literal sense, the workers did produce the motor vehicles sold at a handsome profit. That, however, is not the whole truth. There remains the other and highly important factor of management, both of the production and sale of the millions of cars, with which Mr. Ford must be credited. At about the same time that the Ford Company started operations, some New York and Philadelphia capitalists began the manufacture of cars on a large scale. They employed skilled engineers, and turned out a car that seemed satisfactory, but the cost of production was too high, and in a few years the concern went into bankruptcy. In this case labor produced cars, as it did in the Ford factory, but instead of a fortune, millions of dollars were lost. The difference was in the peculiar ability of Henry Ford to coordinate efficient production

and a wise selling policy, with the results that have astonished the world. Whether productive enterprise shall be a success or a failure depends largely upon the ability of the management.

The dissenting executives made much of this editorial and objected to having the employees' share in profits continued. They believe that the ordinary employees are not responsible for the surplus as they are getting the market wage, or slightly more, for following out certain routine work set for them. If an employee exercises imagination or initiative, or shows executive capacity, he is quite likely to be given promotion and therefore to share in the profits of the executive group. Otherwise, those qualities of origination, planning, and organizing which make the firm a success are not being exercised to any major degree by the employees.

The executives who do believe in the profit-sharing plan state that it is difficult to draw a line properly separating the workers who do exercise imagination in their work from those who do not. An example given is the artist or printer who executes a design along the lines originated by the idea of the sales manager but given actual form by him. Another example is that of personal secretaries to the sales managers, who are intelligent enough to carry a good deal of the load that would otherwise have to be borne by the sales managers themselves. Yet if these secretaries were included in the profit sharing it would be hard to know where to stop in the admission of clerical workers.

To these assertions the dissenting executives retort that if profit sharing is put upon a basis of expediency, that is another matter. Some of them prefer to provide more direct incentives or rewards for good work.

Case B. Contested Bases of Profit Distribution

1. A concern which has decided to distribute profits to its personnel has announced it will give $100 each to a small number of foremen and supervisors, and $50 per employee to the rest. An employee earning $15 a week and one making $40 or more will get the same share in the profits.

The skilled and better paid workers do not like this distribution. At the meeting of the employee-management council their spokesman has stated that if earnings are on an equitable basis, then the relative wages of different employees represent their relative worth to the concern and, therefore, their relative contribution to its profits. The skilled workers and better paid employees desire the money to be distributed pro rata, in accordance with the total earned.

2. The owner of a chemical plant employing approximately one hundred workers decided to give a Christmas gift to his employees which would completely wipe off their debts. He stated that the money was rightfully due to his employees because they had made possible the success of his business. After private inquiries which gave him the facts concerning what each man owed to the bank on his mortgage or to merchants, physicians, dentists, and other debtors, he surprised each man on pay day by handing him a check to cover his complete indebtedness. Some men got several thousands of dollars; others, who had kept out of debt, received merely small presents of $100 or less. This distribution, though recognized as generous, was vigorously disapproved in many quarters as an act penalizing the person who had budgeted his salary and practiced thrift, and rewarding the man who had bought a house or a car without prospect of funds or had borrowed money without repaying.

Questions:

1. Prepare a reasoned discussion of the question whether the rank and file of employees included in profit sharing are entitled to be included in profit sharing.

2. If it is decided that a given profit should be distributed among employees, on what basis should the distribution be made?

PROBLEM 10. PLACE OF PROFIT SHARING IN IMPROVING RELATIONS

A concern manufacturing an extremely low-priced grade of shoes was organized in 1931 by three partners, one of whom took charge of production, the second of sales, and the third of finance. The depression was favorable to its type of shoe, and by 1936 the concern had expanded to a payroll of 260 employees. It had financed its expansion chiefly out of profits and was earning a substantial amount each year. For that reason the question of sharing profits with employees and the matter of employee stock ownership became a frequent subject of discussion among the three partners, each of whom had a different view of what ought to be done.

1. *The partner in charge of production,* who was responsible for the wage rates paid to the employees, was very much interested in the possibility of establishing a profit-sharing plan. He wanted to pay wages well above the average of the community, but feared the danger that, when business conditions changed, there would be the problem of reducing wages, which in his experience had always been a difficult one. He therefore welcomed some form of distribution of profits, whether in cash or stock or both, on the ground that the concern could lose nothing by this, that it would share its profits only when it made them, and that it would be fairer to the employees to pay them as much as they could afford.

He preferred to distribute the profits chiefly in the form of stock rather than in cash, because ownership of stock meant that the interests of employees could be tied up in some degree with the financial standing of the company. He felt that there was less likelihood of approval of a strike by employees whose own property was also at stake.

2. *The sales manager* did not believe that either profit sharing or stock ownership was desirable. He thought that if the amount of cash profit shared at the end of a year proved large, it might tempt employees to unwise expenditures. He felt that profits as such were too largely dependent upon the concern's efficient selling and buying, rather than on extra employee efficiency. In any one year, a single poor purchase of raw materials or any sudden change in prices might completely nullify the hard work of the employees. As for stock ownership, the sales manager argued that as the stock would fall in value at times of poor business and low profits, it would be a source of friction at a time when morale was most needed.

The production manager answered this by stating that he was very hopeful about the firm's ability to hold its own, but that when business depression was general, employees would be giving their best to the job anyhow because of the fear of being laid off. It was during the period of prosperity that profit sharing was particularly desirable as a means of warding off unwise wage increases and of reducing labor turnover.

3. *The treasurer* took a rather hard-headed and conservative attitude on the whole proposition. He said he would rather see the men taken care of through savings plans, group insurance or any other safe way. He felt that the incentives should be such as would be set by improved systems of wage payment. He was willing to see a stock ownership plan which would involve no risk to the employee, such as a special guaranteed, non-transferable stock paying 6% dividend and with a surrender value equal to what was paid in. He regarded this proposition chiefly as a matter of enforcing savings and as a way of making available resources which would aid employees to take care of themselves in case of emergency rather than requiring aid at that time from the concern.

The production manager replied that if $100 worth of stock which the employee purchased would eventually be worth $500, this would give the older employee something substantial, while guaranteed non-transferable stock of unchanging value would have no appreciation in principal. It would be merely a deferred cash payment. The present stage of the company's history, he believed, required adding incentives in the building up of a capable, permanent organization, and he felt that making the employees actual partners in the organization would probably be an important step in morale.

The treasurer precipitated several other issues which proved rather unsettling to the other partners. He asked how "profits" should be defined, and what basis should be used for determining the proportions which should be used for profit sharing. Without a predetermined ratio or schedule of profits to be set aside for sharing, he argued, the management would be inclined to reduce the amount shared in years of small profits, while the employees during those years would probably expect the same ratio as before, or even a higher one, in order to make up for the smaller amount shared. Fearing friction, he also asked the partners to consider what the effects of a year of losses, or a series of such years, might have upon the plan.

Questions:

1. *How would you define "profits"? If profit sharing with employees is desired, what general principles or ratios might be considered in determining the share of the profits distributed to labor?*

2. *What conditions within a company or affecting a company are likely to have a bearing on the effectiveness of profit sharing as a form of incentive?*

3. *Comment on the reasoning of these officials, indicating the place you would assign to profit sharing in employment relations and the policy you would be inclined to follow in this situation.*

PROBLEM 11. WAGE METHODS AS INCENTIVES

Case A. Inadequate Exertion by Time Workers

Almost 60% of the employees in an automobile plant are on piece rates. Their time is money. They keep steadily at work and need little supervision. The nature of the jobs of the remaining 40% tends to make a piece rate system impractical for them. These include such occupations as pattern making, in which it is not desired to have men rush at their work because it might lead to increased spoilage; repetitive jobs done by the conveyor system, in which careful inspection of work takes the place of direct incentives; and certain jobs in which output is difficult to measure or which have not seemed to need the piece-rate basis.

Many of these workers seem to find various means for wasting time. An executive decided to make an observation of conditions and went from one department to another into some of the rest rooms which the company provides. Of the sixty individuals sitting around talking and smoking, fifty-eight were day workers and only two were piece workers.

The company has therefore decided to extend its piece-rate method of payment even further. But a newly formed union, in demands made upon the company, has put in first place the following: "Abolition of all piece work systems of pay, and the adoption of straight hourly rates in their place."

Case B. Effect of Mixing Time Work with Piece Work

In a concern manufacturing office machines and specialties, a good deal of emphasis is laid upon an employee's knowing several different operations in the plant so that when one operation slackens, it will be possible to use the worker elsewhere. Many of the operations are on a piece-rate basis, especially the making of standard parts, but others are repair jobs and special work for which an hourly rate is set because they cannot be put on the piece-rate basis. Hence, a man who is transferred around may be on a piece-rate operation at one time in the day and on an hourly basis later in the day.

Many of these flexible workers have developed certain practices by which they make higher wages at the expense of the firm. This is typified by the case of John T., one of the experienced employees. When he is transferred to a piece-work job for a morning, he works at a killing pace, knowing that he will probably be on an hourly rate for a job later in the day and will be able to work with less pressure. Consequently, he makes $1.40 an hour or more during the morning, and does subnormal work in the afternoon. The concern cannot definitely accuse him of slacking, since a repair job or other work on an hourly basis is inherently capable of no exact measurement, else it would not be on such a basis.

Case C. **Carelessness in Handling Materials**

In certain processes of a lamp company wages are paid on a time basis, with standards of the amount of production expected. The breakage of bulbs, the spoilage of delicate filaments, and other acts of carelessness on the part of the employees are a source of considerable waste. This loss is important since the material constitutes about 50% of the total cost. It is believed that the chief improvement possible is in the care with which material is handled by workers. The speed of work is not regarded as an obstacle.

A careful study was made of the possibilities of reducing breakage, and an estimate attempted of the value of the material that could be saved. The following table shows what might be saved if broken filaments and other wastes were reduced to a smaller percentage.

Division	Total Value of Material in Product per Month	Possible Per Cent of Saving	Value of Possible Amount of Saving per Month
A	$ 50,000	7.1	$ 3,550
B	50,000	6.2	3,100
C	70,000	5.9	4,130
D	150,000	4.4	6,600
E	120,000	3.8	4,560
F	115,000	3.3	3,795
	$555,000		$25,735

The six divisions concerned employ about 1150 workers. The company wants to get across to all of these workers the importance of reducing breakage and to secure within a reasonable time a reduction approximating the estimated possible percentage of savings shown above.

Case D. **Waste of Materials**

In a company making tables, the finishers work on a piece-rate. If economy of lacquer or varnish were stressed too strongly by the management, the quality of work would suffer. On the other hand, as long as their work passes inspection, the finishers have nothing to lose by excessive use of materials. The result is an extravagant use of lacquers, stencils, and varnishes, forcing the company to consider means of reducing such waste.

Questions:

1. What methods of a non-financial character are of possible application in the given cases to meet the problems presented?

2. What methods of wage payment, if any, would you suggest in these cases?

3. Is the prohibition of the piece-rate method of payment a justifiable demand in labor union relations? Support your answer.

PROBLEM 12. THE HUMAN EQUATION IN RATE SETTING

Case A. Difficulty in Selecting Workers to Be Timed

In a concern which has installed a new system of measured production, involving payment by piece-rate, the announcement of the plan states that time-studies will be made on "average workers." The employees who have been resentful of the plan state that this is interpreted by engineers to be an average among "very good workers." The consulting engineers when asked about this stated that it was an average of the "good workers."

There is a widespread conviction among the workers that the engineers regard it to their advantage to select particularly good workers as the ones to be timed, for in that way they will be able to make a much better showing. The employees say this will come about because the other workers will either be forced to work to the utmost or to be content with a lower rate of pay. Thus the effect will be to eliminate many of the workers, in the hope of obtaining those who are "stars" in their operations.

Several workers have expressed their belief that proper time-studies of the average worker would include the initial selection of men whose pay over a period of time had actually been average, and that a check on this should include a study of a particularly good worker and one whose record had been at the other extreme.

Case B. Differences in Machines Timed

In a hosiery company in which the basis of payment on the legging machines is by the number of dozen made, various workers object to the standard set, on the ground that the machines timed were newer than the ones used and that on the former, therefore, greater speed was to be expected. They assert that any rate adopted should not be on a mythical average machine or on the new machines, but that different machines should have different rates.

The engineers agree that when a machine is definitely a handicap to speed it should be taken into account in the rate. They maintain, however, that the "off condition" on many machines is the result of the lack of efficiency on the part of the operators rather than of the character of the equipment.

The workers counter by saying that decisions with regard to whether lower average production is due to the condition of the older equipment or to the inefficiency of workers cannot be decided impartially by any employer or his engineer.

Case C. Obtaining Fair Performance for Time Study

In a concern where piece work prevails in most jobs, the piece-rate is set by the time-study department after a detailed time- and motion-study. An allowed time is established for each operation from the time-study, and this is computed with the base-rate to give the piece-rate—usually expressed as so many dollars per 100 pieces.

The workers dislike the time-study process and do what they can to resist the time-study men. They lengthen the operations by working at a slower speed and making unnecessary motions. The time-study men are familiar with most of the tricks, but it makes the studies more complicated and liable to error. They must rate each man both on his efficiency and on intangibles in order to make the proper corrections. Sometimes they have to rate a man as working at such a low level as 25% or 30% efficiency.

An investigator reports what may be an extreme instance: "One clever operator kept talking to the time-study man about his hobby as he did his operation. The talking did not seem to interfere with the operator's speed. However, the time-study man discounted the study accordingly. The actual time of the time study totalled fourteen minutes. The time allowed by the time-study department was six minutes, and the time-study man feared that he had been a bit too drastic. But the operator confided in me, also, stating that he could easily do the operation in four minutes and maintain that speed."

The investigator raises the further question whether a fully scientific study is possible. He says: "While some job elements can be minutely measured, no means of measurement have yet been devised for other factors. Why be so scientific about the former when, for example, a 20% allowance has to be made for rest time because of these other factors?"

Case D. **Distrust of Time-Study Men**

In a metal plant there are many operations for which the time-studies and piece-rates are antiquated and out of line, and all the processes are being restudied. The workers mistrust the time-study men, on the ground that their purpose must naturally be to find ways of reducing rates, and that it would be foolish to think the plant would hire them for any other purpose. The workers have raised vigorous objection to the process of restudying rates and talk about a strike.

Questions:

1. What conditions of labor relations in general and the administration of wage systems in particular are necessary to assure labor's confidence in piece-rate methods?

2. If you were given responsibility for piece-rate administration in the four plants described, how would you deal with the difficulties experienced?

PROBLEM 13. FRICTION OVER PIECE-RATE GUARANTIES

Case A. Miscalculations in Piece-Rates

1. In the shearing shop of a plant producing rolled sheet steel it is the job of the workers to take the sheet steel as it comes from the rollers, unfold it and place it in the shearing machines, where it is cut to the proper sizes. In an endeavor to increase the output of their shearing shop, the officials of the rolling mill decided to put the work on an individual rate basis. Accordingly, on a certain date the company posted a new piece-rate schedule which it had carefully prepared.

Prior to this step the men in this department had been earning about $6 a day. To the astonishment of the officials, it was found that under the new system many men doubled their pay and some made as much as $15 to $18 a day. It is true that some of the men worked very hard to get these wages, but it had never been expected that the men would get such high wages for semi-skilled labor. Then, too, the workmen in the other departments began to complain, for they wanted similar opportunities.

2. A plant in which work is minutely subdivided has developed a wage system which involves, in addition to the piece-rate paid, a bonus after a certain standard is reached. At the time of installation the company announced that there would be no change in this plan for six months, and then only if justified. It had made close technical studies and did not anticipate any serious error. Two weeks after the announcement, however, it was discovered that the engineers had apparently overlooked certain possibilities in one process, involving only eight people out of the 4000 in the plant. These eight people, whose earnings

should have been about $20 a week, after holding back for a fortnight by making $30, decided to use their opportunities of earning the maximum. One girl made $100, and for two successive weeks every one of these girls has been making upwards of $80 per week.

A heated debate has been going on among the officials with regard to the effect on general morale and on piece-rate administration of permitting the eight girls to continue to earn their extreme wages for the remaining five months. One production executive says: "The evidence that the concern is 'a good sport' in taking this bitter pill when it has made a mistake will give the company a talking point when some employee wants the company to increase a piece-rate which he had already accepted." The plant committee on production, with six officials, is temporarily deadlocked over the question of what, from the long run standpoint, is the best decision for the company to take regarding this matter.

Case B. **Changes in Processes as Causes of Misunderstanding**

1. A shirt factory is installing what it calls a "line" plan of assigning work, under which the batches pass directly from one operator to another, instead of from operation to operation in bundles and trucks. The new system shortens time in process and eliminates the handling time required to go for a bundle, untie it, clip the piece-rate coupon, tie it again, and take the bundle back to the truck. This new plan means, therefore, that the worker will be able to do more pieces. The planning department states that the value of the new method, which it developed after some analysis, belongs to its credit, and it wants to readjust rates. The operators deny the justice of a cut in piece-rate. The issue is before the manager for decision.

2. A textile concern is trying constantly to discover new ways of laying out work, of simplifying processes, and of subdividing work. But because of the piece-rate method of payment the workers regard much of this as roundabout ways of cutting rates. They say that when an employee seems to be making more than the engineers expect, the pretext of simplifying or changing the operation masks the real purpose of setting a higher standard.

The engineer writes: "If every change introduced meant not lower costs but merely higher wages, there would be little incentive to management. Yet every change raises a hailstorm."

Case C. **Accumulated Small Changes in Methods**

In a concern making pen boxes the management had guaranteed its workers that it would never make a reduction in piece-rates as long as the same conditions and methods of work existed. No dramatic change had been introduced, but the concern, by studying the jobs continuously, had made numerous small changes, no one of which was important enough to warrant a reduction. The result was that after two years' experience the workers on several operations were earning from $10 to $15 more than the wage which the management had figured on paying. The management did not want to break its guarantee. At the same time it felt it was paying too much for these jobs and that it would be in danger of losing business if it figured its prices on such costs, or losing money if it did not reduce the rates.

Case D. **Effect of Changes in Personnel Standards**

In early 1929 a concern had made careful studies of the number of pieces per hour to be expected from each worker. It then fixed piece-rates and made a pledge to the workers never to reduce these rates.

But it had failed to realize that for rates to be fixed at a time of labor shortage, when a factory employs many workers whom it normally would reject, may mean that piece-rates set for the "average" worker are really what would be set for less than average workers at other times. The depression cut the company's business in half, yet its remaining workers were getting a high wage rate. In 1930, competition was hard to meet on this basis, and the company had to propose a general rate reduction of 20% to keep the full factory going.

The workers at once protested that the concern had promised not to use their efficiency records against them, and that it was violating its pledge and cutting the rates. The strong resentment shown disturbed the officers very much. They wondered just what form of guarantee they should have given which would have avoided this impairment of confidence in their integrity.

Questions:

1. *What general principles and methods of establishing piece-rates and of their presentation to workers would tend to prevent or minimize the friction indicated in these situations?*

2. *How should the issues be met which have already arisen in these cases?*

PROBLEM 14. EMPLOYEE DISCOVERIES AFFECTING PIECE-RATES

Case A. Rewards to Employee Inventors

In a metal products company a group bonus plan was instituted which left the initiative and responsibility for increased production up to the employees. Thus, if a group found that it could get along just as well with fewer numbers, those not needed would be transferred and those remaining would be able to get a larger bonus. Under this plan the standard time and rates were posted, and it was announced that "Standard Time will not be reduced for at least six months after being established, unless new equipment is installed or changes are made in product or general manufacturing methods."

In an inspection department the job of locating cracks or similar defects in valve stems had been done by inspecting the piece, but two employees found that by bouncing the valve stem on a steel block, the tone would denote any crack. Since this method reduced the time required to about one-half, and two workers could be transferred to other departments, the employees left could earn a bonus almost doubling their salary, making it way out of line. It was especially out of line because under this new method less than two weeks were necessary to train the employees to the required skill and speed, whereas formerly the operation required long training and experience.

The employees who first developed the plan felt that they deserved a reward. But one executive said that if the company did not change the rate for six months, the extra wage earned by the inventors would itself be a reward. The other policies considered were (1) a cut in the rate for all, with a special reward to the two inventors, and (2) no cut for anyone, with an additional reward or special payment as the reward to the inventors.

Case B. Share of Fellow Employees in Discoveries

In a clock factory a new method of individual piece-rate payment was adopted in order to secure higher output, coupled with a group bonus and other incentives which were intended to promote the cooperation of all elements affecting production. This incentive naturally led some of the cleverer workers to think of ways by which they could improve methods.

In one instance two men at a bench were doing an average of 90 points per hour, individually. They asked the management if they could try a new method they had conceived by which they could cooperate with each other on a joint amount of production. The result was that the two together produced 300 point-hours, or an average of 150 point-hours on the new scheme. Others at once copied the method, with refinements that made the wages of many workers 60% to 80% higher than anticipated.

Employees in other departments said that as the workers on that process who had copied this method had done nothing to deserve their extra wages, the increase should be reflected in general wages, or given as a general bonus, not handed to a few lucky ones.

Case C. Employee Short Cuts Undermining Piece-Rates

One of the operations in the manufacturing of switchboards, the binding together of a small bunch of wires with a piece of cord, is performed by girls who are paid on a piece-rate basis. The rate was set on the operation so that the girls could earn about $25 per week.

One clever girl, however, devised a means of binding and cutting the cable in such a way that her output was almost doubled, so that she could conveniently earn almost $45 per week. The other girls soon learned the trick, and the group managed to average about $40, instead of $25, as rated previously. Their wages were thus almost doubled through a chance occurrence.

This caused considerable friction in the plant. Many workers felt that they were being treated unfairly because they had been more exactly rated and could not develop a trick whereby they could earn much more.

The company's announced policy had been that rates once fixed would not be lowered, unless the whole process was changed or new machinery introduced. It continued paying the increased wage while considering the course to take.

Case D. **Animosity Created by an Employee's Invention**

An employee disclosed an invention to the management which resulted within two weeks in the discharge of twelve workers within his immediate department and the withholding of three opportunities for young men who had expected employment as apprentices in that department. All these became bitterly angry at the worker who had suggested the change. For months he saw the effect of his invention in the suffering of his neighbors. The wives of the displaced workers boycotted his wife. The children in the families of these displaced workers, hearing the talk about this inventor, made a butt of his two sons, so that he had to bring them personally to school, and his wife had to call for them every day.

The situation continued to be so uncomfortable that this worker decided, in spite of the depth of the depression and inability to obtain work, to leave the community. He said he would never give a suggestion of this kind again.

Questions:

1. What policies should be adopted in piece-rate plans regarding (a) the employees who discover methods permitting higher output and earnings; (b) the fellow-workers who copy these methods; (c) unanticipated drastic changes resulting through employee discoveries? Apply to Cases A, B, and C.

2. What may be done to reduce hostility by employees against fellow employees who discover short cuts? Apply to Case D.

PROBLEM 15. CONTROLLING THE PACE OF WORK

Case A. Difficulties in Retarding Workers

The officers of a plant manufacturing metal parts for automobiles have been very much disturbed by the charges made from time to time that the company overspeeds its men. A local labor sheet said of it recently: "If you want to see what tough work is go to the X plant and see how fast they have to keep moving to earn their pay. At the end of a day they are all washed out." Similar allegations have occasionally been heard in the comments of visitors who have been taken around the shop.

The president and the directors have been concerned about these charges. They state emphatically that they do not wish their employees to work at too hard a pace. They have investigated the conditions and say that they do not see what they can do about them. The situation according to the management is as follows:

Most of the operations in the plant involve repetitive labor and are paid for on a piece-rate basis. The output expected on a particular operation is analyzed carefully by time-study men, and the rate set is then specifically adjusted to make it possible to earn a good wage without overspeeding. But the workers cannot be kept down. If it is a low piece-rate, they have to work hard to make a decent wage. If, as the management believes in this case, it is a high piece-rate, they are lured by the possibility of abnormally high earnings. This pressure is the greater because the concern works five days a week of $7\frac{1}{2}$ hours each, or a maximum of $37\frac{1}{2}$ hours, and avoids overtime.

The management gives as an illustration a certain operation on which the rate set is such that a group called Class A, or the best workers, are expected to make about 95¢ an hour, and a group called B, or the mediocre workers, about 80¢ an hour. Both these rates are above what is paid for similar work in other plants. However, instead of adjusting their pace to such a wage the best workers put on extra pressure and actually have averaged about $1.15 per hour, while those in the mediocre group have made about 92¢ an hour.

Case B. **Employees Who Are Natural "Speed Artists"**

1. In the bindery of a press one of the operations consists of lining the covers of books. The bindery operates in rush periods and in slack spells, and it frequently happens that the liners have only a three-day week. When this occurs, all of the men work at maximum speed. One of these liners has such skill and speed that his full-time earnings average almost double the amount earned by the others.

The men are therefore demanding that the management limit this man's earnings in good times, and particularly when they are forced to go on short time, in order that the weekly wages of all might be approximately the same. The speedy worker says that he should not be penalized for greater efficiency.

2. In a plant manufacturing metal parts, piece-rate standards have been set which are considered by the management and workers to be fair to all concerned. The rates in force take into account the average ability of the workers, allowing some to earn a fair sum above the standard, but no worker except one makes much over 30% extra. This exception is a man who might be considered to be a star in his line. No matter what the standard is, he always makes 160% and sometimes more. In the present instance, he is doing 185% of standard, or almost the work of two average men. A complaint has arisen from the workers that he should be limited to 130% of standard.

Case C. **The Employee Who Overworks**

1. A boy who had completed his learning period in the winding department of a concern making small motors came to his

foreman and said that he thought that the rate set for the job would allow him to make high earnings, and he wanted to know if he would be permitted to work his hardest. He had personal reasons for wanting to earn twice as much as the job was supposed to yield. In two weeks he had worked himself into such a state that he had a breakdown and was taken to the hospital.

2. In an oil burner plant in which most of the employees are on piece work, a visitor who goes through cannot fail to notice the exceptional speed of one girl in particular, a packer of wicks, working in a corner of the room by herself, on a special job. Forty or fifty feet away one becomes conscious of this girl, working at so fast a pace that one wonders whether she is in a race with someone. Her earnings show that she packs an average of 1000 wicks per hour, or nearly twice as much as the company would expect from anyone else hired for the job. An official writes:

> She is an American born girl, of foreign extraction, twenty-six years old, and has been in the company's employ eight years and upon this same work most of the time. She is not a rugged, healthy type, but upon only one occasion has she been away from our employ on account of her health.
>
> She has been examined by our doctor, and it is his opinion that it is not so much the nature of the work upon which she is engaged as the fact that she is geared up by her nervous temperament to perform any work at the same speed. He recommended that she try to reduce her speed and take her work easier. We found, however, that she seemed unable to do so. She may wear herself out and impair her health much more quickly than most girls would upon this work, but we feel that it is a condition we cannot remedy.

Question:

Should the pace of work be controlled, and the amount of earnings limited, by action of the employer? If you favor such control, indicate the basic principles or methods which should apply to these instances. Whatever your answer may be to the question, indicate what action would be appropriate in each of the cases presented.

PROBLEM 16. ISSUE OF LOST TIME IN WAGE SYSTEMS

Case A. Machine Breakage Affecting Earnings

At certain times a hosiery mill operates on a double-shift basis. On the second or night shift no regular fixer is at the mill. In the event that the services of a fixer are needed, a telephone call brings in the day fixer. The knitters assert that time is lost to a knitter on the night shift "about once a week" because of lack of adequate fixing of minor repairs. The day shift also has some complaints on this score.

The union desires an arrangement for regular minimum pay during a break. The company representative contends that this would make men careless of machines and that some penalty should go with a break. The union agent says that such penalties, in the vast majority of cases, penalize efficient employees for conditions not under their control.

Case B. Waiting for Work

A shoe union asks that piece workers be paid for time at the employer's disposal when the employee is required to wait for work. Such enforced idleness has long been a grievance of piece workers, but the evil is particularly prevalent during slack times. In many a shoe factory the employees have stacks of magazines at their bench to read while waiting for batches of work.

The manufacturers voice strong objection to paying piece workers for waiting for work, on the ground that it is impossible to figure accurately this element of cost into the price of the shoes. The manufacturers also assert that if stoppages were paid at the usual hourly earnings there would be a tendency for piece workers to speed up, then help to produce stoppages for which they could be paid these high hourly rates while relaxing. The union replies that if compensation is paid for lost time, the employer will soon have enough information to figure in waiting time as a basis of future costs.

Case C. Early Morning Dismissals

Employees in a metal parts company are expected to report promptly at 7:30 A.M., every morning unless, when laid off, they are called back to work at some other hour. Sometimes they find that there is only an hour or two of work. They feel that it is up to the management to plan better and not call workers for incidental jobs. The union has submitted a proposal that this matter be covered in a clause in the new contract to read: "Employees called for work or expected to report, and reporting, shall receive not less than four hours' work or four hours' pay."

The employer says that some of this work is specialty business; that the workers should be glad to get the work when it is available; that they should cooperate in permitting flexibility of management; and that "too short periods of work occur only once in a while."

Case D. Rate on Work Temporarily Assigned

In order to avoid lost time when stoppages occur, a metal equipment concern assigns employees to other work temporarily. The question has arisen as to what shall be their earnings on this work. Some employees say that they should get at least the regular minimum hourly rate paid on their usual work, since during the short periods involved they cannot acquire enough skill to profit by the piece-rate established for the new operation on which they are temporarily employed.

The employer says that it is difficult to keep operations in balance and that the workers should cooperate by accepting the conditions involved in the attempt to maintain steady employment. The employees say that they do not want to go below their grades of work at any time, and that the acceptance of the minimum basic pay a grade involves, in fact, a sacrifice of extra earnings possible when fully engaged on their normal occupations. The employer states that the pay they get on temporary jobs is a learning rate to make them more versatile; the employees reply that versatility in any plant is an aid to management in stabilizing personnel requirements and is deserving of the basic rate payable to a worker on the job for which he was hired.

Question:

1. What principles should apply to time lost in incentive wage systems through machine breakage, waiting time, and temporary transfers to other work?

2. What ruling would you make in Case C if you were asked to arbitrate the issue?

PROBLEM 17. GROUP AND SUPERVISORY BONUSES

Case A. Negative Effects of Group Payment Plans

In former years a company with two plants had used individual piece-rates, set by detailed time-study. Because of the expense and trouble involved in keeping track of the earnings of each operator, and for other reasons, it was decided to change the method of payment in one plant to that of a group system. All of the operators doing the same operation on the same line were grouped together. Each one in the group received the same pay, which depended upon the total output of the group, regardless of individual differences within the group. It was recognized that the individual incentives in this plan were inferior to the individual piece-rate system, but the company believed that the savings in the cost of control more than offset this. For example, it required fifteen timekeepers fewer per thousand workers.

These groups showed certain unexpected reactions to the plan. They objected to the introduction of new workers since, in the particular system, it meant that the older workers would have to carry a new worker along until he acquired skill. Nevertheless, even when a new worker was forced on the group there appeared to be almost no cases of slow workers. Apparently the workers hated to see a man thrown out of work, and so protected him by covering up his deficiencies even though it meant harder work on their own part. Shielding the worker, however, remained a source of dissatisfaction to the faster and more experienced group.

In its Western plant the company then tried a combination of individual piece-rate coupled with a group bonus for exceeding a group quota. The total bonus was divided in accordance with piece-rate earnings. The result here was that the high producers found that some of the excess of quota they had produced was being shared with low individual producers. The groups thus tended to be carping in their criticism of older men and others whose piece-rate earnings were low, and to become ruthless in their attitude toward those who could not speed up.

Case B. Pressure on Workers Caused by Bonuses to Foremen

In a metal parts concern a new system has been introduced which is a cause of much resentment among those working under it. Each foreman starts operations at the beginning of the year with all machinery, tools, and supplies on hand, plus the goods and stock inventory, charged to him. As operations proceed, each new piece of machinery, tool or additional supply, even down to a new eraser, is charged against him, as are also repairs and scrap made.

These debits, plus the expenses of overhead groups, are matched against a certain plan of credits, consisting of his entire inventory plus the value of the output of his productive group. If the difference is more than the standard sum set and expected, the extra amount is divided half and half, between the corporation and the foreman, as an addition to his weekly salary. Each month the contract department issues a statement to the foreman to show him how his department stands.

The foreman, therefore, has a direct double incentive to increase his credits and decrease his debits. This has meant the speeding up of jobs by the foremen in an attempt to increase the output of piece workers, often resulting in more scrap and more breakage of tools and supplies. A worker states, "The foreman then hunts around to see where the trouble is, and when hunting trouble he usually finds some." This tends to make him gruff and surly and an atmosphere of hostility and tenseness pervades the department.

Certain foremen, in an attempt to keep down their debits, tend to be exacting as to the length of time a drill or a cutter or some other tool should be used, as sharpening or changing it will be charged against the foreman of the department to which it belongs. This often makes for harder work on the part of the worker, increases his fatigue and kindles grudges and hard feelings toward the boss. Some employees try to get along on what they have rather than face the possible frown of the foreman when he reluctantly gives in and permits an order for new equipment.

Questions:

1. What are the theoretical and practical advantages of group bonuses, and their disadvantages? Under what conditions are their advantages greatest? Under what conditions are their disadvantages greatest?

2. Is a plan by which a bonus is paid to a supervisor on the direct basis of the amount of work obtained from employees a justifiable method of payment? If so, how may such plans be made less oppressive? If not, what are alternative methods for attaining the advantages hoped for from foreman bonus plans?

PROBLEM 18. WAGE GRIEVANCES AND SALARY ADJUSTMENTS

Case A. Disparity of Salary Rates for Similar Jobs

In a bank which has grown in ten years from 1000 employees to over 2000, the salaries of different employees are considerably out of line with one another. Aside from the fact that employees were hired at different salaries during the periods of prosperity and depression which characterized the last decade, an employee's progress depended on whether his section head was solicitous in his behalf. Some supervisors were neglectful or hesitant in matters of obtaining money for salary increases. Also, the employee who asked for an increase each year and whose section head saw no reason for denying it, might have been raised several times, as compared with a more docile employee. The result is illustrated by the fact that in one large department three clerks doing similar work received $1320, $1800, and $1900 respectively.

A confusing element of the situation is that the differences in salary paid for the same job are obscured by a variety of titles for similar work. Thus an employee rated as a "stenographer" or "junior clerk" may actually be doing a higher grade of work at a lower salary than someone with a higher sounding title. The extreme example of such disparity in rates of pay, obscured by differences in title, is an instance in one department in which the salary for the same grade of work is almost twice that in another, the title of one of the two jobs being "statistical assistant" and of the other "clerk."

Case B. Wage Adjustments after a Business Depression

The improvement of business conditions for public utilities during 1935 presented problems of policy with regard to adjustment in wages for those whose earnings had been cut, or whose individual increases had been suspended during the years of depression. An official in such a company seeks advice as to what would seem to be the best thing to do in a situation described below:

> In January, 1931, the so-called merit raises were stopped due to general economic conditions. Later the base rates of everyone were reduced 10%. In January, 1935, 5% of this 10% was restored. As conditions continued to improve, there was in January, 1936, a demand on the part of the employees for some wage adjustment.
>
> We have three types of problems to consider. One group of employees had reached the maximum pay for their jobs prior to the stopping of merit raises. A second group of employees, who have never received a merit raise are still working at the initial rate; they are all doing different kinds of work and comparison is difficult, but they are in many cases underpaid. A third group of employees have developed different degrees of efficiency in performing similar or identical work but are out of step with one another because no merit raises have been given since 1931.
>
> The question now is, when, as, and if the management releases more money for payroll, how shall it be allocated? It is desirable that the 5% cut should be restored, but also that we shall catch up with the so-called merit raises. The sum of money necessary to make all these changes is relatively large, and it will not be possible to take care of the adjustments all at once time. I am endeavoring to build up a program which will distribute this money in the most acceptable manner, and I am faced with the problem of setting up a sequence in accordance with the right policies to follow.

Case C. **Policy concerning Individuals Found "Out-of-Line"**

In a concern in which a committee on job classification and salary standardization has been at work for several months on an intensive study of jobs and salary levels, a schedule has now been completed which represents the best thought of the committee and its experts, and has its unanimous approval. The salary schedule tentatively decided upon, as a result of appraisal of jobs, was put alongside the actual salary ranges, and glaring discrepancies were discovered.

Only 47% of the employees fell between the minimum and maximum of the ranges decided as belonging to their positions, and 15% were at the minimum for their jobs. Of the rest, 20% were below the minimum; 8% were at the maximum; 10% were above the maximum. The members of the management committee are debating what the proper course is concerning these three last groups.

Case D. Wage Increases Requested by Single Departments

1. In a spun silk concern complaints brought to the attention of the management revealed the fact that earnings were too low in the drawing room. The company voluntarily instituted in this department an increase in rates amounting to about 10%. There was an immediate and satisfactory increase in output.

However, the complaints concerning wages increased, for now the men in the sorting room, who had formerly received the same pay as the men in the drawing room, became discontented. The management believed that the increase in wages for those in the drawing room was justified because the work requires a somewhat higher class of labor than sorting. But it had not anticipated the stimulus this gave to complaints about pay and demands for increases in the other departments.

Case E. Justifying a Differential

An executive in a metal plant relates that the question was raised by the bench lathe operators as to why their wage rate was lower than that paid the engine lathe operators. He states that if the rate for a bench lathe operator were advanced to that of the engine lathe operator, it would not involve any very great sum for the particular men involved, but the general relationships would be destroyed. Unless there was some firm foundation for the change, there might result a generally disturbed condition because existing rates for these two occupations have been effective for a number of years. The concern therefore had to be particularly careful to avoid friction. He writes:

> I determined to make a thorough study of conditions so that a fair and intelligent decision might be reached. I found that there were at least fifteen different factors that had a bearing upon the relative value of one occupation to others in the group. Some of these factors were of greater importance than others and a given one applied in varying degrees to different lines of work. Being unwilling to be judge and jury in the matter, I called upon a group of executives who were familiar with the various job requirements to give their independent opinions as to the weights that should be assigned to each factor and the extent to which each factor applied to each of the occupations tested. The list of these factors had already been selected to include various types of work, as well as the two trades in question.
>
> These independent opinions when tabulated showed a remarkable agreement throughout the whole analysis, so that the average of opinions on a given item conveyed a very accurate idea of the relative importance of each point considered. By the simple process of multiplication of the weight of each factor by the figure indicating the extent to which it applied to the occupation being analyzed, and adding these products together, an index figure was established for that particular trade, its numerical rank with index figures for other occupations indicating its relative value. Having these index figures, it was a simple matter to convert them into wage rates by constructing a curve. The result of this analysis showed the two occupations in question, bench lathe operator and engine lathe operator, should receive the existing rates of pay.
>
> But because the reasons for the difference were convincing to me, they would not necessarily be regarded so by the workers. Those who questioned the present rates will think that the method used in studying the relative value of the jobs had been devised to accommodate the wishes of the company.

Questions:

1. Outline the type of investigation and the principles of classification which you believe would be required to initiate a more equitable salary schedule in Case A.

2. Upon what principles should the adjustment in Case B be handled?

3. Present the pros and cons of possible actions to be taken in Case C, defending the course you would follow.

4. What do Cases D and E point to as important general considerations in making wage adjustments?

5. Outline a method of approach which you would recommend to the executive in Case E in order for him to get the men to realize that the conclusions reached were the result of open-minded reconsideration of the facts, and if possible, to convince them of the validity of the relative difference in rates.

PROBLEM 19. MISUNDERSTANDINGS REGARDING ADVANCEMENT AND PROMOTION

Case A. Executives Who "Pass the Buck"

In a small electric manufacturing company the jobs are graded from 54¢ an hour for beginners to a top figure of $1.02. Salary increases are given workers either because of better service or longer service on the particular grade of work they are doing, or because of advance to a higher grade. When these salary increases and promotions are to be made, the foreman and superintendent who approve an increase or promotion must be willing to certify that the employee has done better work on his regular job, or is deserving of a better job.

Employees who have gone on for six months or a year without a raise in pay naturally feel that they are entitled to one; but their work may be mediocre, and they may not be entitled to a raise in the eyes of the foreman or the superintendent. These executives do not shoulder the burden of saying so, but make vague promises or indulge in conciliatory talk. In due time these employees become resentful. They spread their burden of complaint all over the plant, and, in particular, make demands upon their employee representatives to adjust their grievances.

There is an employee representation plan in effect which has been in operation two years. When a representative goes to see the foreman or the superintendent in behalf of a worker, he may be told in confidence, or at least given to understand, that the employees denied increases were considered unworthy of further advance in wages or position. When the representative goes back to the employee who made the complaint, he does not dare to tell him the truth, for the foreman or superintendent himself may have pretended to the worker that his work was good and would some time soon be rewarded by extra pay. If the representative does tell the employee the truth, he is assailed as having invented this as a reason for not doing anything, or as siding with the employers.

Case B. **Dissatisfaction with a Company's Promotion System**

In a manufacturing plant which has grown to 1500 workers, recommendations for increases in pay are in the hands of the foremen, each one making his recommendations whenever he sees the need. But as there are in some cases as many as 75 workers under one foreman, some workers feel that they are being overlooked in the crowd, and others that they are being discriminated against. Workers have become discouraged and dissatisfied because they were not rewarded when they believed that they were entitled to increases in pay or promotion.

The concern desires the foremen to retain their powers regarding advancement. It feels that they are in the best position to judge the merits of the workers and to penalize or reward them. It believes that as a permanent matter some system is necessary to control this situation and it is considering what this plan should be.

Case C. **Employees Who Have Reached Their Limit**

A clerical organization with several thousand employees is continually facing the problem of employees who do not seem to have the qualifications for advancement beyond their present posts, but who feel they are being mistreated.

A typical instance is that of an employee forty-three years of age, married, with a family, who is doing fairly simple bookkeeping work at $40 a week. He started with the firm twenty years ago, without previous experience. He is performing a routine task and he does his work in a parrot-like manner. The concern has grown rapidly, but his work has remained largely the same. The man himself is faithful and a hard worker, but he shows no originality and no apparent particular ability or executive qualities which would warrant his advancement to a more responsible job.

This employee does not see why he is not promoted rapidly to responsible work. He attributes his lack of advancement to mistreatment, and he has just voiced a bitter complaint to an executive, who is considering what to do about it, with fairness to all concerned.

Case D. **The Blind Alley Job**

In a small concern the advertising manager is an alert, energetic executive who likes to keep his finger on everything that is done. It is expected that in a few years he will resign. His assistant, twenty-eight years old, does well in his work because his personality harmonizes with that of the advertising manager. He does not, however, show the resourcefulness, originality, and executive ability which would give the company grounds for putting him in the advertising manager's place if the latter should leave.

The vice-president of the firm does not feel comfortable in this situation. He has no fault to find with the young man's work at present and no pressing occasion to raise the issue. He is asking himself whether he ought to do something, since the assistant may be led to stay on for years on a wrong assumption that he will graduate into his superior's job.

Case E. **The Time for Salary Increases Involved in Promotion**

John M. has been doing very well in his regular job. Two months ago he received a salary increase. Now the assistant supervisor has left. A conference has been held as to the man to be promoted to his place. All agree that M. is the logical choice.

The position of assistant supervisor involves a considerably higher salary than M. is now receiving. There is a division among the two chief executives as to whether or not the promotion should carry with it a raise in salary. One believes that M. should be given no increase, but an implicit understanding that if he makes good, an increase of some sort will be awarded him at the expiration of about six months; the other believes that he should be given an increase immediately upon promotion.

Questions:

1. Outline principles of general application which would reduce the malpractices described in Cases A and B and would tend to put matters of promotion and salary increases on a systematic and equitable basis.

2. Indicate briefly the specific, immediate course of action which should have been followed in Cases C and D, and the long-time policies which would tend to prevent their recurrence.

3. Which policy, in Case E, would you favor and why?

PART TWO: HOURS, WORKING CONDITIONS, AND LABOR REGULATIONS

I. Hours of Work and Leisure

II. Industrial Health and Safety

III. Protective Labor Regulation

PROBLEM 20. WORKING SCHEDULES AND WORKERS' EFFICIENCY

Case A. Physiological Aspects of Hours of Work

A metal products company has received an unusual petition from its workers. It employs over 500 persons, chiefly men, in repetitive machine and hand assembly work. About one-half of the employees are on an hourly basis of payment and the rest on piece work. For the past year the concern has given fairly steady work of forty-two hours a week. A press item recently announced that the management expected an increase in business shortly. This led, in a few days, to the presentation of a petition from employees asking for an increase in the number of hours worked to about fifty, so that they, instead of the outsiders to be imported into the town for the purpose, might make the extra money.

The situation that caused the request seems to be as follows: Several enterprises selling on the installment plan in the town in which the company is located had combined in exceptionally aggressive efforts to induce the employees to purchase new automobiles, radios, washing machines, and other objects requiring long time payments. The slogan had been, "Anticipate inflation." The employees soon found the burden heavy, and the extra earnings that eight hours a week or more would give them seemed a possible source of relief. A petition signed by 100 employees, claiming to represent the unanimous sentiment, suggested that whenever an employee left he should not be replaced but that the work to be done be given to the existing force in extra hours.

Before canvassing the situation further, the management is considering the request from the standpoint of how the longer work-week would affect the plant output, efficiency, and morale.

Case B. Alternative Plans of Sharing Employment

A concern employing skilled and semi-skilled labor in manufacturing tools and machines is faced with a curtailed demand for its product which seems destined to last for several months. Although it has already laid off some employees it has a force of workers still far in excess of its needs. Nevertheless, it is planning to keep these workers on the payroll on a part-time basis, rather than lay off some entirely. But it wishes to choose a plan of part-time work least harmful to its labor efficiency.

Forms of sharing which it is considering are: (1) three-day shifts for alternate groups of workers; (2) alternate days for such groups; (3) half days for all; and (4) alternate weeks for two groups.

Case C. Piece-Rate Employees Who Work Excessive Hours

In a small department of a concern five men had been employed on a certain operation when, through accident, three were lost to the firm. The remaining two, however, seemed to be able to do all the work that all five had done before. It was piece-rate work and the two earned extremely high wages but did their work well. When the management investigated the situation, it found that the men came to work earlier and left after hours. Both had lost weight. An additional worker was therefore employed over the protests of the ambitious men who had been enjoying these high wages.

To guard against similar situations the management announced that it was considering the adoption of a rule that special permission of the superintendent had to be secured for any work done before or after regular working hours. This was displeasing to many workers in the shop, as they had been coming early or staying late, either to cover up slowness or to make more money. These men asked that the rule should not be made and that things be left as before.

Questions:

1. Consider Case A purely from the standpoint of an efficient working schedule and not in its relation to the problem of reducing unemployment in the labor field as a whole.

If the concern were inclined to make, as an experiment, the change desired by the workers, what known principles and facts regarding fatigue and the maintenance of efficient working schedules should be considered as a basis for making the decisions? How should the change be applied, and what factors should be watched?

2. Rank the four alternatives mentioned in Case B in the order of the most desirable to the least desirable, indicating the chief considerations which led you to this conclusion.

3. Comment on the rule to be adopted in Case C.

PROBLEM 21. CHANGES IN HOURS AS A SOURCE OF FRICTION

Case A. An Increase of Hours Leading to a Strike

A motor company appointed a new manager for one of its four plants in order to reduce excessive costs in that division. He introduced economies in various operations but came to the conclusion that these were not enough and that labor costs were too high. He did not wish to reduce wages, as his predecessor had already done, but in the honest belief that he was doing the kindest thing to the men, he decided to add four hours to the working schedule immediately and thus to avoid competitive losses, announcing this in a short typewritten statement posted on the bulletin board.

His action had what to him were unexpected results. Union organizers in the neighborhood immediately joined issues on it. A strike broke out before the new schedule could be put into effect. Personal feelings evoked kept the excitement at fever pitch, and a few tactless blunders in handling the strike resulted in splitting the two sides hopelessly. The strike, eventually extended to the three other plants, lasted for more than eight months, cost the parent concern and the national union millions of dollars, ruined the manager's reputation, and caused a great deal of suffering to the communities in which the plants were located.

Case B. A Decrease of Hours Leading to a Strike

Some years ago a manufacturing company decided to reduce the hours of work from ten to nine a day. Before the measure was adopted, the employees had been working from 7 to 5:30 P.M., with a half hour for lunch. It was then becoming the practice in plants to reduce the working day by allowing the employees a greater portion of the evening free. The management took it for granted that its workers wanted fewer hours and so cut off the last hour. It felt sure that this step would meet with instant approval.

The new plan had been announced on the 25th to take effect on the first of the month. On the day of the announcement the entire plant went out on strike, the first in the factory's history. It was led by a few employees working in large departments. The objection raised did not seem to be to the one-hour reduction or any dispute in regard to how wages would be affected, but merely to the allocation of the working hours during the day. A tremendous debate had been in progress for a few days, and most employees, led by a few active workers, had the feeling that the plant should start work at 7:30 and stop at 5, rather than at 7 and end at 4:30, and they finally got worked up over it and into a mood for striking.

Question:

Analyze the human situation which makes such changes a source of possible friction with workers and outline the main procedures to be followed when alterations in terms or conditions of employment become necessary.

PROBLEM 22. CONTENTIONS REGARDING LEGAL REGULATION OF HOURS

Case A. Opposing Views Regarding Special Regulations for Women

The National Woman's Party is sponsoring an amendment to the United States Constitution which would not merely remove recognized legal disabilities of women, but would require all labor enactments to be upon a non-sex basis and thus prohibit protective legislation applying exclusively to women. The existing situation in the United States regarding labor laws for women varies from year to year, but a picture may be given by the status of such measures in 1935.

Women workers in manufacturing and mechanical industries and mercantile establishments were the groups most commonly covered by the law. Women in the professions, in agriculture, and in private domestic service have rarely been included. Only five states (Alabama, Florida, Indiana, Iowa, and West Virginia) had placed no limits on the daily or weekly hours that women might work. In eleven states the legal working day for women had been shortened to eight hours. In perhaps twenty states the legislation permitted ten to twelve hours in certain industries but did specify some limits short of these. Night work for women in one or more occupations was prohibited in sixteen states, the hours excluded being most commonly from 10 P.M. to 6:00 A.M.

The point of view of one of the ardent opponents of special regulation may be indicated by the following:

> The first effect of restrictive legislation for women will be the curtailment of the employment of women. When there is an ample supply of labor an employer is not going to bother with a class of

employees whose hours of work are regulated by law. There is no doubt whatever that so-called "protective" labor laws for women lower women's wages.

If that overworked plea of special "protective" legislation for "potential mothers" is brought forward, the reply is that if legislation is necessary for "potential mothers" it is just as necessary for "potential fathers." There is no objection to laws regulating hours of work when these laws apply to men as well as women.

At certain seasons of the year in certain industries and mercantile establishments overtime work is essential, and women might share in the extra pay without harm to themselves. While the regulation of hours for women employed in stores may not handicap the cash and bundle girls, the majority of whom are under twenty-one and therefore minors, it does handicap women in executive positions.

In 1919, when several so-called "protective" laws went into effect in New York State, women railroad workers, elevator operators, women working in the printing trades, in restaurants, in ice-cream parlors, candy stores, and drug stores were thrown out of work. As a result, these women were forced to seek employment in already overcrowded fields or to accept less desirable and lower-paid employment.

There are decided differences of opinion regarding the harmful effects of night work. If it is harmful for women, it is also harmful for men. To prohibit night work to preserve women's morality is absurd. Work and wages do not encourage immorality, but poverty and starvation do.

In the past women were economically weaker than men. Today they are emerging from many handicaps. If we fasten special labor laws upon them, we shall keep them in a state of economic weakness and make them lose all they have gained in the past twenty years.

The Equal Rights Amendment is opposed by the National Consumers' League, which in a recent statement says, in part:

The Equal Rights Amendment, if approved by Congress and ratified by three-fourths of the states, would add these words to the United States Constitution:

> Section 1. Men and women shall have equal rights throughout the United States and every place subject to its jurisdiction.
>
> Section 2. Congress shall have power to enforce this article by appropriate legislation.

> The proponents of the Equal Rights Amendment, who are for the most part women of the professional, business and leisure groups, want to remove discrimination against women, and they want to do it all with one stroke. In the attempt to abolish those civil and legal inequalities which constitute a real injustice to women, they would deliberately sweep away every hard-won piece of labor legislation which gives wage-earning women a fair chance in the industrial field. Evidence shows that such protective legislation has improved the status of working women and prevents their excessive exploitation.
>
> No member of the League needs to be told that women are peculiarly subject to exploitation in hours, wages, and general working conditions. With weaker bargaining power and less organization than men they are at the mercy of unscrupulous employers unless their rights are protected by law. We know too that women have a lower resistance to the strain and hazard of industry. Long hours at a noisy machine, ill-ventilated or unsanitary work rooms exact a greater toll from a woman's strength.
>
> Then why not make these laws apply to men as well, you may ask. The answer is this: While we believe that it is desirable eventually and as soon as practicable to secure for men as well as for women the benefits of labor legislation, we are not willing to destroy the benefits gained by one group merely because it has not yet been possible to attain them for all. In the opinion of the League that does not constitute equality. We have learned from forty years of experience that we must inch along in this push for better labor standards. Until the courts are willing to go farther we must be content to proceed slowly but surely.

This difference in attitude toward special regulation of working conditions of women has meant that many people who would favor the amendment, if it meant merely the removal of general legal disabilities, fear its potentialities, if strictly interpreted by the courts, as making impossible special regulations protecting women from exploitation. These opponents of the amendment would like to see it so expressed as not to leave that loophole for judicial interpretation, and thus to make the issue of protective legislation itself a matter for legislative power rather than absolute prohibition.

Case B. **Excessive Working Hours of Men**

Before the promulgation, in 1933 and 1934, of various emergency regulations supported by the sentiment at that time, male employees in many businesses worked excessive hours. For example, in some chain store organizations, particularly in chain groceries and in merchandise outlets selling products in the 25¢ to a dollar class, clerks worked up to eighty hours per week. This was due to the fact that these employees not only were present during the regular hours of the stores, which were often long, but had to stay after hours to put away the stock and prepare for the next day's business. Even Sunday work of this character was frequent.

The N.R.A. codes in 1933 and 1934 set a limit of forty-four hours for such clerks, but excluded supervisors, department heads, and executives from this protection, the dividing line being whether or not an employee was earning $35 a week. Various employees in the $28 or $30 a week class were, therefore, made "department heads" at the minimum of $35 a week, so that they might work unrestricted hours. When the N.R.A. lapsed, stores began gradually to increase their hours for clerks, and to reduce wages, so that in numerous instances the old conditions were soon approximated or actually reinstituted.

There are widespread complaints that working days are being required in many places which are excessive from any standpoint of health and citizenship. Transportation companies, restaurants, garages, factories of various sorts, and laggard businesses in all industries include some employees who work seven-day weeks, or seventy-, and even eighty-hour weeks, and similar stretches. These occupations or jobs are not subject to control of labor organizations because no union may exist or because there is evasion of arrangements made with unions. There has thus been resumption of effort to have these excessive hours barred by law, leading in time to more general regulation of hours.

Different methods for regulating hours of men are favored by various groups. Certain spokesmen for organized labor would like to see a flat limitation of hours by legislative fiat, as for example, to forty hours or less. Others would like to see hours fixed on an industrial basis, nationally and locally, through a modified N.R.A. procedure permitting trade agreements regarding hours of labor and other working conditions, but not permitting price fixing and other undesirable trade practices. Another group would like to see this done in a way similar to, or combined with, minimum wage commissions, acting whenever the existence of excessive hours is reported. Thus the procedure of regulation itself is a source of controversy. (The number of hours to be set as a standard is a separate topic, considered in a later problem.)

Questions:

1. Should women in industry be subject to protective legislation which does not apply to men? Give reasons for your answer. If you believe that separate laws setting standards for women are desirable, carefully indicate what principles and considerations should govern in order that such legislation shall be to their interest.

2. Is the proposed Equal Rights Amendment the way in which the issue between the two sides is to be decided? If, in your opinion, it is not, suggest an alternative wording.

3. Should the hours of work of men be restricted by law? If you believe not, indicate what other types of measures, if any, are needed to prevent excessive hours in the trades not affected by strong unions. If you believe regulation is necessary, indicate what basic social and industrial factors should be taken into account, and what legislative or administrative procedures should constitute the mode of regulation.

4. Compare the views at which you have arrived with (1) the legislation affecting hours of men which are in existence today in the nation and in your state; (2) the attitudes which have been taken toward legislation regarding hours of men by the courts; and (3) what, if anything, would be needed to make legal the plan of regulation you favor.

PROBLEM 23. MAJOR QUESTIONS REGARDING VACATIONS

Case A. Vacation with Pay vs. Increase in Wages

In 1933 a company which had been forced to the utmost economies because of the effect of the depression on its business was led to consider whether or not it should abolish its paid vacations and increase wages instead. The concern had always prided itself on its vacations. Two weeks with pay was the usual period granted to manual workers, and two or three weeks to clerical workers, depending on their absence and lateness records. The comptroller wrote:

> Since one 15% wage decrease has already been forced on us and a necessary one of 12% is in prospect, differences of opinion have arisen among the supervisors as to whether the decrease in pay should be less, with abolition of all paid vacations, or whether vacations should be continued and the full decrease made. The theory of those who wish to abolish the paid vacations is that wage cuts have already reached the point where many employees would probably prefer to earn all they can, and it is suggested that they would prefer to get more salary and forego a vacation. Under the proposed change, any employee who really wishes to take from two to four weeks at his own expense may receive leave of absence for this purpose.
>
> The management is unable to calculate the exact cost of the paid vacations because in some instances the work to be done during vacations is postponed and in others done by fellow workers, though this is only partly true of manual workers. The gross cost of paying approximately 400 of the latter for two weeks would, however, total for the summer about $16,000 or an average of $40, and for the clerical workers about $5000, or an average of $50. We could give this either in the form of a paid vacation or as an addition to wages.

Case B. **Manner of Deciding Vacation Issues**

A concern in the textile industry which pays competitive wages to its weavers, spinners, and other manual workers has not in the past given a vacation to such employees with less than two years' service. It is now contemplating introducing a vacation for all. This would cost $1.25 per week per worker—the wage increase it might otherwise be able to give. One supervisor, who favors a wage increase instead of a vacation, has suggested that the matter be submitted to a vote of the operatives, taken at a mass meeting or by ballot.

Instead of taking these days as a continuous vacation period, employees want numerous variations. A baseball enthusiast may want twenty afternoons. A camping enthusiast, in order to take long week-ends, may want ten Mondays, thus working ten weeks of four days a week. The manager questions the relative value of such periods as compared with a complete break of two weeks, and is loath to grant such requests, but the supervisor believes that the employees should make the decision.

The general manager opposes such a vote on the grounds that the great majority of employees would probably vote for the wage increase or for the option of days off, but that these are not in the best interests of the workers or of the plant. He believes that in many things of this kind the workers are likely to be short-sighted and that in the long run it will benefit the workers most to have the practice of an annual paid vacation, even though this amounts, in a given case, to a sort of deferred compulsory saving from wages.

Case C. **Justifiability of Differences in Vacation Privileges**

In a public utility which is now reconsidering its vacation policy, salaried workers have been given a day of vacation for each month in service up to the maximum of one month a year, but the wage earners, or so-called hourly rated employees, have always been treated differently. Until a few years ago, the idea had been prevalent among the executives that it was not good to give wage earners time off to waste, but nevertheless the company granted workers of

2 to 4 years' service	3 days' vacation
5 to 9 " "	4 " "
10 to 14 " "	1 week's "
15 or more years' "	2 weeks' "

A new group in the management is asking the question whether it is justifiable to make a distinction in vacations between hourly rated workers and clerical workers. The matter was precipitated by a request from the employees for equal vacations for all employees.

Those who believe that manual workers should be differently treated point out that only a small minority of concerns give vacations to them at all, or on the same basis as clerical workers; that when office workers are on vacations other workers will usually handle their duties so that no replacements are necessary, whereas paid vacations for hourly workers would in most cases mean double pay for the job; that clerical workers normally work overtime without extra pay, but that in the case of manual workers a higher rate is payable for such overtime, adding this extra expense.

The new management group is therefore frankly puzzled about what to do and submits the following issues: (1) "Should the employees' request, regardless of conditions, be considered by us as a major obligation? (2) Are shorter vacations justified for hourly rated employees?"

Questions:

1. Consider the alternative policies proposed in Case A, indicating which you believe more desirable and why.

2. With which of the two policies considered in Case B do you agree, and why?

3. Draft a reply to the management in Case C.

PROBLEM 24. PROVISIONS AGAINST THE "THREAT OF LEISURE"

Case A. Company Supervision over Leisure Time

1. A concern in Boston which grants a vacation to its employees finds that many seem unable to use the two weeks satisfactorily. One group shows a lack of judgment in the selection of places to go, so that individuals come back with disappointment and lowered morale. In other cases family obligations prevent the employees from using this time in the most desirable way. A frequent evil is the imposition by parents who do not permit children money for such vacations. The company is planning to take up such cases with parents and relatives so that their workers will not be exploited.

The company also complains that while a vacation is designed to help employees to recuperate their powers, the actual activities of many leave them exhausted, and they come back to work in a bad physical condition. One of the common difficulties is that of employees who drive too far in their cars. A few extreme cases are known of those who went clear to the Coast and back, during a two-weeks' vacation, driving night and day. Some of the girls who go on cruises dance until dawn every night and come back to their jobs to catch up on their sleep.

Many of the vacations turn out not to be vacations at all. Married men may take their families camping and, being inexperienced in the art, may work harder and rest much less than they would on the job. Others may not go away. They may build a house or paint it during this "vacation," working night and day.

The concern is giving thought to the question of how they may curb, forbid, or discourage harmful use of vacations.

2. A factory reports many instances of week-ends used in ways which impair workers' health. Some take long automobile trips, driving all day on Saturday, perhaps all of Sunday, and part of the night to be back on time. They are described as being "wrecks" on their return. Others engage in hard physical sports, such as football and boxing, coming back to the plant with bruises and aches. Still others expose themselves to excessive sunburn, coming to work in a condition which impairs their efficiency for days and sometimes longer.

3. An insurance company finds that there are a certain number of its employees who are taking full night courses in law, accounting, and other subjects. This means that they have to use the time between work and school for study, as well as nights and week-ends. Such employees are over-worked, more liable to error, and generally less able to devote their thoughts to their work. The company is therefore planning to make a rule that no worker may engage in such activity without applying to the personnel director or the superintendent of his department for authorization.

Case B. **Community Provision for Leisure Time**

Have we reached a point where there is an undesirable excess of leisure? Many manual and clerical employees are finding that by working a mere thirty-six hours, or even less, per week, only a small fraction of their time is occupied in earning a living. Their spare time may not be needed for home or family duties. Many people are living in apartments; families are smaller; schools are more accessible; and much of the work of the house is eased by the availability of mechanical contrivances and prepared foods.

People who are released from responsibilities and who do not have enough work to occupy them are often bored, restless, and disillusioned about life, asserting that they will "go mad" if they do not have something to do. Much has been said in the past concerning the strain of work, but comparatively little concerning it as a boon. Life is full of strains, and many a busy person finds at least temporary relief from other problems in the absorption which gainful work and other responsibilities require. Work has a psychic value as a distraction and temporary respite from personal worries and problems. Its daily grind is, in many cases, a most helpful employment of energies and interests which otherwise might have difficulty in finding an outlet and might generate serious personal maladjustments.

A practical program, planned to meet this social need, and conceived on a community and national basis, has been urged.

Questions:

1. What would a company be justified in doing to reduce the unfavorable effects reported in the instances related in Case A?

2. Make at least an informal survey, to whatever extent possible, of what working people of your acquaintance or community, whose working schedules are admittedly inadequate to absorb their full energies and interests, do in their spare time, what opportunities they complain of as lacking, and what they might like to do. In a comprehensive analysis indicate what is needed in present-day society to put these energies to constructive use.

3. With this as a basis, outline a practical program which will indicate the relative responsibilities and activities which local, state, and national agencies might undertake in order to reduce the negative aspects of leisure and to encourage the best use of the opportunities afforded.

PROBLEM 25. EMPLOYEE COOPERATION IN HEALTH AND SAFETY

Although safety regulations in industrial plants are of the utmost importance to the workers, it is often difficult to obtain adequate observance of safety practices and safety regulations. The manager of an industrial corporation voices a typical complaint in stating:

> A large proportion of our accidents are not mechanical but personal. We believe that 80% of them are attributable not to mechanical failure, but to personal carelessness or human failure, ranging from failure to report slight accidents to the first-aid station to complete lack of cooperation, if not recklessness, which so many employees exhibit.
>
> A corporation selling safety equipment has pointed out the relative ease of preventing accidents due to mechanical difficulties as compared with the difficulty of preventing those due to carelessness and to psychological factors. I certainly believe in making operations foolproof, but the personal factor always looms large.

The types of human problems arising in various plants are illustrated by the following cases.

Case A. Disregard of Nose Guards

The atmosphere in a granite plant is generally heavily charged with granite dust, arising from the stone while it is being worked. The dust inhaled by the cutter tends to cause an abrasion of the lung tissues, which furnishes excellent soil for the development of what is known in the trade as stonecutter's consumption.

The company has provided certain nose guards which would practically prevent the inhalation of the dust. Naturally, there is some disadvantage in wearing these, and from time to time they need to be cleaned. As compared with the minor annoyances involved they would be a very distinct aid to the employees' health. But the cutters are negligent in the use of these nose guards and they resent any regulations to force them to do so. They say their health is their own lookout.

Case B. **Failure to Use Goggles**

Among the published safety rules in a wire plant one is that in certain operations, as in the handling of scrap, goggles must be worn by the worker, for there is great danger that wire may spring up anywhere, with the resulting loss of an eye.

The workers do not like to use the goggles because these occasionally steam up, interfere with the speed of work and, in general, are a disadvantage except in those rare moments when an eye injury might be averted. The workers are continually taking the goggles off. The company is considering a safety regulation that any employee caught not wearing goggles, especially one who has already been caught once before, will be summarily dismissed.

Case C. **Removal of Safety Equipment on Machines**

Several times a year a state safety inspector visits a certain metal plant. The news of his presence travels fast and is the signal for all the workmen to drag out safety devices for use only while the inspector walks up and down the aisles. He makes pleasant comments on how much is being done to guarantee the safety of the workingman. The moment he leaves the factory, however, the men revert to their own unsafe methods, "rushing" in order to make up the time they lost while using the safety devices.

In putting into effect a new safety program, the company provided a hospital in the factories, with nurses always in attendance, and a doctor always somewhere in the plant. Immediate reporting of accidents was requested as a safety rule.

But the cooperation in this was not satisfactory. Cuts and bruises were often neglected until they became dangerously infected. A man would limp around with a sprained ankle rather than see the nurse and have it treated. Some of the men were afraid to report accidents for fear that they might be laid off as a result of the accident and might not receive their full pay.

Case D. Older Workers vs. Newer Workers in Accidents

Two different plants in the same industry, in comparing accident records recently, had the peculiar experience of finding contrasting results with regard to the groups of employees having most accidents. The management of one of these plants states that the older workers are the most frequent violators of safety rules; in the other the management finds that it is the new worker who most frequently gets hurt.

In the first plant a sample group of sixty-eight accidents over a period of one year were recently taken as the basis for a study. It was found that about 70% occurred to men with over five years' service, and that in 90% of the cases, in the manager's opinion, the injured man himself was to blame. He states that the new worker is taught the right method, is a little fearful and uses care and caution, but that the older worker begins to feel, after going along without an accident for a number of years, that he is immune from injury and danger.

In the second plant, the experience is almost exactly opposite, for the largest number of accidents occur in the case of the newer employees and comparatively few among the older and more experienced ones. This is held to be the normal situation in accident frequency. As the manager explains it, aside from awkwardness and ignorance causing accidents among new employees, the more reckless older employee has probably eliminated himself from industry by unintended suicide or self-imposed disability. The two managers, after a discussion, have come to the conclusion that both these groups present serious safety problems, and they are considering what special methods are needed to obtain cooperation in each case.

Case E. **Friction over New Safety Equipment**

An explosion was caused in a mine by the ignition of a gas pocket, killing fifty men. The mine companies felt that one of the reasons for this and similar explosions was the use of the open carbide lamp, and decided to make universal the closed, safety carbide lamp, which had now been invented. They were met, however, with determined opposition from the workers.

The mine companies then secured the introduction of a bill in the state legislature making the safety lamp compulsory. This move was vigorously opposed by the miners' union, whose members had been killed in the last explosion. The bill was defeated. Many impartial persons made statements disapproving of the miners' stand.

The arguments of the miners were that the operators would rely on the assumed freedom from danger and would be lax in their inspection of the coal chambers. They feared that the operator would think the danger of ignition was small because of the new safety lamp, and might allow big gas pockets to accumulate, so that when an explosion did occur it would be more serious than when he had to keep watching the mines for gas pockets.

Case F. **Management Policy Following an Accident**

A state safety official observes that what a foreman or supervisor says to a worker at the time of an accident, or at various stages of his recovery, may have serious consequences for the person involved. While legal provisions protecting the worker may be in force, if they are inadequate the management should be prepared to know what it is able and willing to do to help the employee in medical aid, financial assistance, and later readjustment, and thus to relieve his mind of worry to the greatest extent possible. The official points out, however, that some expressions may be unwise. Where an accident is a permanent injury, involving readjustment for life, it is necessary for the injured to be put in the frame of mind to face that fact courageously rather than expect the company or society to support him.

A case the official cites as an example is the following: A man working in the yard of an industrial plant cuts his hand in some way with his own shovel. A tendon is affected. It appears to be a serious injury and, for all one knows, the employee may lose part of his hand. The shock of the accident may affect the foreman or supervisor just as well as the employee, and he may make statements which will give the employee the feeling that the burden of rehabilitation is on the company, not on himself. As a matter of fact, as often happens in these cases, three months later the wound is almost healed, and the doctor is of the opinion that with adequate exercise the employee will in time resume work. The safety expert writes:

> If the employee's morale is not impaired the chances are good, but if he has learnt to baby himself, he may go from bad to worse and end up as one of the unemployables dependent on relief. Even if the accident incapacitates one for life on his regular job, it may still be true, actually, that a man forced to change his occupation gets to earn much more in the new field. Several instances of this are of men formerly doing manual work at low pay who, in this way, became company salesmen or life insurance salesmen and materially improved their position.

The letter continued with the statement that it is recognized that the foreman or supervisor must know his man in order to know what it is wise to say to a particular worker, but that, nevertheless, general principles should be formulated as guidance. In a safety booklet the official is preparing for managers and foremen, he is attempting such a formulation and has asked for suggestions.

Questions:

1. Analyze in organized fashion the chief factors which tend to explain why workers may not use safety equipment or observe safety regulations, and then outline the principal methods which might aid in inculcating the habit of cooperation. Indicate, incidentally, the conditions under which penalties should be imposed on workers for non-compliance.

2. What are the points of particular emphasis or especially appropriate procedures in applying these principles to Cases A–D?

3. Should the industry, in Case E, have tried to have the law passed? If not, in what way should it have proceeded?

4. What action would you take, if you were the manager, when a serious accident was first reported to you? Indicate what you would say, or avoid saying, to the employee in order to avoid creating a misconception in his mind or impairing his morale.

PROBLEM 26. FINANCIAL RESPONSIBILITY FOR ACCIDENTS

Case A. Employers' Liability vs. Workmen's Compensation

A small construction company has twelve employees. Eleven of the workers are covered by the workmen's compensation act of the state, but one, to be called A., in charge of a big, electrically-driven splitting saw, is not so covered, as he elected to be under the employers' liability provisions. This alternative was included in the workmen's compensation law merely to minimize opposition to its passage and to assure its legality. The employee had a notion that he could do better in case of a real accident by suing the employer under employers' liability, and since he was a good workman, the employer hired him in spite of his refusal to abide by the prevailing plan.

One day one of the other employees, B., a teamster, in loading his team, found that he needed several boards of a width that was not in stock. He thereupon took some boards of wider widths into the shop where the electrically-driven splitting saw was. A. happened to be absent, so the teamster proceeded to split the boards by himself. While doing so he caught his thumb on the board. Before he could withdraw his hand, his thumb was cut off. He could not return to work for five weeks.

In the meantime A. came into the yard from another part of the plant and found the teamster's truck in the way. To move it, he pulled the horse and, in walking backwards, fell over a hydrant and cracked his skull. He was incapacitated for almost eight months.

From these peculiar misfortunes a tangled situation now resulted with regard to the payment of damages. The concern itself refused to compensate A., on the ground that the accident occurred when he was doing something which, the concern stated, was no business of his. On the other hand, the insurance company with which the company had insured the other eleven men refused to pay workmen's compensation for the accident to the teamster, on the ground that the man had been insured as a teamster and not as a man to run machinery.

Case B. Interpretations of Workmen's Compensation Laws

The illustrative cases which follow are those in which the right of the injured workers to awards of workmen's compensation were vigorously contested by employers, or by insurance companies for the employers, before administrative boards and in the courts.

Accident Occurring during Conversation with Fellow Employee: Jim Murray was employed as a forger's helper on a hammer. One morning, just after the power had been turned on and all the hammers were in motion, Jim began to perform his usual functions of cleaning the hammer's steel rolls. A fellow workman passed by and greeted him in passing. Jim paused to throw a "good morning" over his shoulder. During this fractional interval of inattention the waste became entangled in the rolls and dragged Jim with it, pulling Jim's arm through up to the shoulder before being stopped. Several bones were broken, and the arm was rendered practically useless. The insurance carrier alleged that the accident occurred because of the worker's lack of attention to duty.

Crossing Room to Ask for Chew of Tobacco: The work of a young man in a clothing mill involved carrying spools into its card room. Having deposited the spools at the usual place upon one such occasion, he did not return directly to his own room, but instead crossed the card room, a distance of about fifty feet, to ask one of its workers for a chew of tobacco. Failing to obtain the article, he looked out of the window a moment and turned to go. In turning, his foot slipped on the oily floor and his hand went into a moving machine. The insurance carrier asserted that this accident did not occur in the course of or because of the young man's employment.

Traveling Salesman Shot by Hitchhiker: A man who had been employed by a printing company as a traveling salesman for a period of fifteen years had the duty of calling on various customers within a certain district, using his own automobile. One day, when traveling with samples, on business, he permitted a hitchhiker to ride in the car with him. He was held up, shot, and later died from the injuries. His widow brought suit to recover compensation.

The employer contended that the deceased had brought the injuries upon himself by inviting the stranger to ride with him. Counsel for the widow contended that one who was required to travel in an automobile on business to sell goods was in no wise different from one who might be inside of a store and held up. He stated that the incidental charitable act of inviting a hitchhiker to ride was not of importance in the case, especially since there was no evidence of instructions from his employer forbidding such a practice.

Assault upon Employee Walking along Street: An employee was on his way at six P.M. from his employer's factory to get his car from a garage, to proceed thence to a tailor shop connected with the factory to see how its work stood and to bring back work that it might supply, if any, to the factory. Two men attacked him, knocked him unconscious, and ran away. There was no evidence whatever as to who the assailants were or why they attacked him. The insurance company contended that the injury was not in connection with employment. The worker's attorney maintained that it was part of the man's duty to visit the tailor shop, that in so doing he was an outside employee subject to street risks.

Accident during Lunch Period: Three linemen were drilling a rock anchorage for a telegraph pole alongside a railroad. The locality had steep embankments and the nearby brush contained poison ivy, hence in choosing a place to eat their lunch, they sat on the track near a curve. A train was coming down the main stretch, and so they failed to hear or see another train suddenly coming around the curve. Two of them escaped, but the train hit the third man, killing him instantly. The employer contended that recklessness in choosing this dangerous place for his lunch took the deceased out of the classification of being injured during his employment.

Death Caused by Windstorm: A violent July whirlwind struck a sawmill located on a slope at the edge of some woods and tore part of the roof off. A falling rafter killed the fireman of the mill as he was fleeing from the building. The insurance company which had the employer's account contended that the accident was "an act of God," the fireman being exposed to no more danger from storm than other persons in the United States.

Questions:

1. What are the probable chances of recovery of damages by each of the men in Case A, under (1) existing laws and interpretations, in general, and (2) the laws and precedents in your state?

2. In states having modern workmen's compensation laws, what general principles of law and reasoning by administrative agencies and the courts are likely to be the basis of the decisions on such issues as those presented in Case B? In stating your opinion indicate whether your ruling would agree with the probable decision, and why.

PROBLEM 27. FINANCIAL RESPONSIBILITY FOR OCCUPATIONAL ILLNESSES

The extent to which diseases stated by the worker to be caused by occupational conditions should be included in the coverage of workmen's compensation laws is an issue being contested in legislatures throughout the country.

Occupational illnesses may be classified into three groups. The first would include certain diseases rarely contracted by persons not engaged in or connected with certain industrial processes. Such are anthrax, incurred by those handling wool, hair, hides or skins; lead, zinc, and mercury poisoning, incurred largely in handling preparations or compounds of these substances; "the bends," a condition suffered by compressed air workers; and illnesses arising in connection with the handling or breathing of phosphorus, arsenic, benzol, carbon disulphide, vitrous fumes, formaldehyde, radium, carbon monoxide, and other harmful substances.

A second group of diseases consists of those to which people as a whole are subject but which, nevertheless, are more frequently found among those in certain occupations. Examples are tuberculosis, pneumonia, and similar illnesses, which may in fact have been brought on by the conditions in a given occupation, but which cannot be proved to have been so caused in individual cases.

A third group of disputed diseases are those in which the worker had an actual or potential condition which was aggravated by some circumstance of his occupation. An issue is then fought over the question as to whether the condition was so much aggravated or accelerated as to deserve compensation. An example might be a glass worker who at the age of sixty develops a cataract in one eye. The insurance carrier might argue that the loss of vision was an inherited personal defect or due to old age, while the worker might say that the condition had been greatly accelerated by the nature of his occupation. This type of issue presents a difficult kind of case for the courts.

The laws of the various states differ widely in the number of diseases specified as being compensable, and there is constant contention over whether this or that disease should be included in the list. A medical officer complains:

When a worker in one corner of the factory gets lead poisoning he has all of his hospital bills and compensation paid, and when a man in the same factory in another corner gets silicosis and is equally disabled, perhaps more so because he is not going to get over it, he is told by the industrial commission, "We cannot do anything for you because it is not on the schedule."

The secretary of an association promoting labor legislation urges a wide "all-inclusive" coverage, as compared with the "specific schedule" method which covers only a limited list of occupational diseases. He says:

The vast majority of workmen's compensation laws in America do not provide compensation for disability or death due to occupational disease. Experience indicates that occupational disease cases represent but a small percentage of the total number of cases compensated under the law. Thus, in one year studied, in Wisconsin, where the all-inclusive method has been in successful operation for years, less than 2% of the 20,473 compensable injuries and about 2% of the cost were due to occupational disease.

Expediency as well as justice calls for this plan of broad coverage. It offers—in the absence of comprehensive workmen's health insurance laws—the most effective aid to prevention of industrial sickness. It provides the means by which the constantly increasing number of disease danger-points in modern industry may be uncovered. And it then provides the incentive for prevention. Because the coverage of the "all-inclusive" type of law is broad, cases due to new diseases can be met promptly, the victims compensated, and all the preventive value of workmen's compensation brought to bear immediately to assist in safety work.

The secretary of an agency of private accident insurance companies, in contrast with the authority just cited, urges narrow coverage. He writes:

> Some of our American compensation laws provide for compensation for every "injury" resulting from the employment—including diseases (generally or indefinitely)—either by express words to that effect or implicitly by omitting the requirement that the injury must be "by accident." And there is now a strong tendency throughout this country to liberalize the compensation laws in that direction. Where such tendency prevails it means that the commissioners who hear claims and decide questions of fact can hold industry responsible for any and every impairment of health in any way or degree contributed to by the patient's going to work.
>
> True the commissioners may not go to an extreme at first in the application of this rule. They may start hesitatingly. But from such a start, the tendency will be to progress, applying the rule ever more and more liberally, giving claimants ever more and more the benefit of every doubt (and nearly everything is doubtful in the case of an illness of gradual growth or contraction), until they wind up by holding employers liable as general insurers of the health of their employees without any responsibility therefor on the part of the employees themselves.
>
> The remedy, in my opinion, is: Compensation to be payable only for injuries by accident arising out of and in the course of employment, and for specific trade diseases contracted in the course of the employment. No compensation to be payable for: (1) Ordinary diseases, common to the public (including outbreaks of disease brought on by merely normal work), without accident; (2) the results of pre-existing diseases and infirmities aggravated or accelerated by accident, except to the extent that only the aggravation or the acceleration shall be compensated for; (3) the results of neglect or mistreatment of injuries by the injured person.

Question:

Evaluate the industrial and social effects of the alternatives presented and indicate, with supporting reasoning, the course which appears desirable.

PROBLEM 28. NATURE OF AN ACCIDENT PREVENTION PROGRAM

Case A. Description of a Negligent American Factory

The plant as here described by a student who has worked in it for two years is engaged in the manufacture and machining of drop forged parts. Part of its products consist of automobile parts, manufactured on order in accordance with specifications, the rest of a staple line of wrenches, hammers, and tools made for stock. The drop forge shop itself requires an all-steel construction with sliding metal walls, steel pillars, and a sheet metal roof. The drop hammers require a firm cement base set some thirty feet into the earth. Each hammer has an oil burning furnace near it, in which the metal bars are heated red-hot previous to the actual forging.

Noise and vibration are, of course, continuous elements in this department. A man who stays in the drop forging work very long becomes deaf to noises of a certain type after a period of years. Conversation is very nearly impossible in the forge shop. A particular tone of voice will not carry even when one is shouting into another's ear.

In the press room the majority of the accidents in the industry occur. A huge drive shaft runs down through the center of the room with belts dropping obliquely from it along its entire length. These belts connect with the drive wheels of the presses, the wheels being about five feet in diameter and about five feet above the floor. There is thus a veritable tent of flying belts, all uncovered, in the press room.

The nature of the work itself carries added dangers. It is here that the forgings are pressed and punched from the "flange" or surplus stock. Of the fifty pressmen employed in this department, not one who has worked there more than five years can show two hands having ten fingers. One young worker related: "I had been employed in the department only three months when one of the pressmen lost four fingers: the press head had come down while he was engaged in setting up the press. The foreman came to me and offered me the job as press operator instead of the job as helper on which I was engaged. I was supposed to have had no experience in operating a press at that time, for the helpers are forbidden to operate under any conditions. Thus, with no instructions and with only what knowledge I had picked up through observation and a little 'secret' practice, I undertook the new job and operated a press until my transfer to another department."

The press room is especially crowded for floor space, and a man operating a press sits with his back not too far away from the spinning drive wheel and belt of the press behind him. If this belt slips the wheel—an incident which happens quite often in the course of a single day—the operator is apt to experience a very vigorous pat on the back by the swirling belt before the power is finally shut off. The sound, too, of the half hundred presses working at the same time causes a noise quite too much for the human voice to overcome in its natural expression.

Being so crowded for space, it is difficult for the stockmen who bring in the material from the forge shop to the press room in wheelbarrows to find ample space for depositing the stock. The floor of the press room is composed of sheet metal, for much of the stock is brought in while it is still very hot. This material is dumped on the floor previous to the pressing operations. The spaces between the presses are such that a wheeler often jars the press operator as he brushes by him to unload his stock. The danger of such a situation is that the operator is obliged to keep his hands under the head of the press while operating it and the jar may throw his hands further than he intended.

An electric bulb just under the plunger of the press furnishes a yellow glow for the pressman to work by. This is continually spattered by oil, for much oil is used to maintain the proper temperature while the dies continually cut the cold forgings. Iron dust, noise, and grease are continuous annoyances in this department. The inattention to safety is illustrated by the following:

An old hammer had been dismantled and was being repaired. A few days later the news spread rapidly around the factory that one of the wheels of number 40 hammer (the one in question) had become loosened and had fallen from its pinion. It rolled behind one of the wheelbarrow men, hit him and broke both of his legs as it rolled on. A few men who saw the accident could not shout a warning because the incessant noise of the hammers made a verbal warning impossible.

The chief contributory cause of this accident seemed to lie in the deficiency of the hammer. Most of the hammers are quite old and badly in need of repair. Very often a hammer has been seen to "skid" when it was supposed to be "hung up" at the top of its stroke. The forgers, striving to gain their day's pay, are, however, partly at fault, for they know better than anyone else the condition of their own hammers. It often happens, however, that a forger, realizing that a hammer is defective, after he has reported the situation to the repair department, will continue to use this hammer in its poor condition until the millwrights get time to repair the defective machine. But the repair department always operates to capacity, and it may be many days before a millwright becomes available for that particular job, dangerous as it is.

Case B. **Lax Accident Prevention in Soviet Russia**

An industrial engineer who has been employed both in this country and abroad, and who is an expert in problems of accident prevention, believes that in the better American plants methods of minimizing accidents are far ahead of any plant in

Russia, and that in the average American plant much more attention is given to the problem, resulting in a better record, than in the average Russian plant. One reason he supplies is that financial compensation for accidents is here borne directly by the employer and reduces his profits, while accidents paid for in Russia are chargeable to the general public treasury. He says: "I have seen the same contrast of interest in safety among government departments in this country, which, on the whole, are not as safe as those with similar kinds of work in the more progressive private plants."

This engineer then supported his statements by excerpts from an authoritative report on labor conditions in Russia, "Labour Protection and Rationalization," published a few years ago in Russia itself by an official agency and reprinted by the International Labor Office. This study deals with the failure of the government system for the enforcement of safety laws and the protection of the wage-earner's life and health, and says in part:

> So long ago as 7 January, 1926, a circular of the Supreme Economic Council sounded a note of alarm on the subject of the considerable increase in accidents. . . .
>
> The Labour Section of Leningrad noted an increase in accidents from 4,000 to 10,000 in the year, and pointed out that they "were due in the majority of cases to inadequate lighting and the fact that (as a result of the introduction of piece work) the workers endeavoured to earn as much as possible." The circular mentioned above observes that the "technique of accident prevention is inseparable from general measures for preventing too rapid exhaustion of the workers." A Conference convened by the Central Council of Trade Unions pointed out that "among the causes of the increase in the number of accidents were the abuse of overtime, the absence of pauses for meals, and the failure to observe the rule of forty-two hours' rest. . . ."
>
> Explosions have become more numerous in the mines. The cause is always the same. Comrade M. Ostrovsky justly remarks that "a number of explosions and industrial disasters are the direct

consequence of the small amount of attention given to questions of workers' protection. . . ."

The explanation of the causes of accidents which attributes them to the carelessness of the workers is often too easy, and in many cases entirely inaccurate. Carelessness on the part of the worker is certainly common, but it is desirable to learn precisely why the worker is sometimes careless. Such carelessness shows itself regularly at certain moments. One arrives at the conclusion that the carelessness of the worker is due to causes independent of himself—for example, worn out tools, bad lighting, and fatigue. . . .

What is still more abnormal, however, is the fact that the workers themselves and their organization apparently remain passive in face of this intolerable position in regard to workers' protection. It is stated that the trade unions in Siberia adopt a purely formal attitude towards the protection of the workers. An enquiry by the Joint Trade Union Council of Moscow also showed that the trade unions paid little attention to questions of workers' protection.

It may be admitted that the picture is not equally sombre everywhere, but generally speaking, the situation is sufficiently alarming. Too little attention is given to the protection of the workers.

The conclusion to which the engineer desires to call attention is: "Accident prevention is largely a matter of proper organization and rounded and efficient technique. Good intentions alone, or fallacious assumptions that work being done by a government agency or by a non-capitalistic industry, or even by a philanthropic institution will, of course, be safe, are dangerous generalizations rooted in ignorance of what is needed to keep the accident rate down. The intelligent companies which are using their ingenuity in this regard achieve results once regarded as miraculous. In safety matters 95% of the noncapitalist plants, of whatever sort and wherever located, have more to learn from the technique of these concerns than can be learnt in return."

Case C. **Greater Accident Hazards of Small Plants**

A safety engineer who has analyzed safety records points out that the small contractors in building, construction, mining, and other employments of this sort, and the small establishments in general as compared with the large ones, provide the chief resistance in the reduction of accidents. He states that large industrial establishments have the lowest frequency of accidents, in spite of better reporting, and also the lowest rates for the severity of accidents. The evidence he submits is the fact that the frequency rate (number of lost-time accidents per million man-hours of exposure) of small plants is 50% greater, and in severity (number of days lost through injuries per thousand man-hours of exposure) their rate is also somewhat greater. In comparison, also, with a so-called middle sized group of establishments, the large plants show a much lower frequency rate and a markedly lower severity rate.

The engineer concludes: "The screws should be put on the small sized plant to harass it into observing safety rules. Some of these concerns may, of course, be unable to survive. From my point of view that's all to the good."

Questions:

1. Itemize and classify the sources of danger and evidences of neglect indicated in Cases A and B, as well as others which you may know about or which occur to you.

2. Evaluate the industrial engineer's contentions regarding the technical rather than the economic nature of a safety program, by constructing a topical outline of the major approaches to accident prevention, in terms of equipment, organization, and other procedures found effective in outstanding concerns as reported in the literature of safety work. Then indicate in what essentials, if any, such an outline would differ in emphasis as between a privately owned plant, a government plant, and a Soviet plant.

3. How would you deal with the problem presented in Case C?

PROBLEM 29. INTERSTATE COMPETITION IN LABOR LEGISLATION

Case A. State Subsidies as Lures to Factories

In the New York *Herald Tribune* of September 21, 1936, Miss Dorothy Thompson, a columnist, makes the following statements concerning Southern competition with Northern plants:

> The Mississippi Legislature is considering the enactment of a program which is called "A Plan to Balance Industry and Agriculture," and which was presented to that body last Monday by Governor White. The Governor's speech, reported in *The Commercial Appeal* of Memphis, contains some statements very significant for the industrial states of the more prosperous North and East.
>
> He said: "Industry in the North and East is now in an unsettled condition. There is need for the type of labor we have to offer here. Many outstanding plants are looking for new locations. . . . Many factors are beckoning these industries to locate in the South."
>
> The type of labor which Mississippi has to offer is not distinguished by any special skills. It is cheap labor, simply that and nothing more. The Governor's proposals represent an organized attempt, through legislative action, to lure capitalists from the North to the South under the promise of cheap labor plus state governmental assistance.
>
> The new legislation proposes a wholesale growth of such industries, under direct state government planning. Furthermore, there is already evidence that the idea will not be confined to Mississippi.
>
> The immediate cause of these measures is the desperate poverty of the state which is taking them. For Mississippi is 83% agricultural, largely planted to cotton, a crop which is in a declining condition for reasons which are both domestic and international.

The first result of such a program, if it goes through, is that these factories will undersell all the rest of the country. A warm climate, which means a low cost of living, plus low wages, plus free rent and no taxes, will be an irresistible combination. Non-Southern manufacturers will have to lower their wages, go out of business, or move South. "Moving day has arrived," said Governor White. This obviously means a tremendous dislocation of labor and industry all over the United States, and that will inevitably mean labor disturbances in the form of strikes and labor pressure on the Federal government.

Manufacturers in this country are complaining that they can not compete with Japan because of her government subsidized industries plus low-cost labor. They will soon be faced with precisely the same condition in the United States, with no Department of State to complain to. It looks as though we needed a national economic conference fully as much as an international one.

Case B. Request for Relief from State Legislation

At a conference on the economic conditions of New York State, the following contentions were made by a spokesman for employers:

The laws relating to workmen's compensation insurance in New York mean a serious loss to industry. New York State concerns cannot compete with those outside the state whose compensation rates are half of the local rates. A few years ago I made an analysis of comparative costs. The cost of workmen's compensation per $100 of plant payroll in Connecticut was only 54¢, in Chicago 59¢ and in New York $1.35. Taxes laid on a New York plant were $3.92 per $100 but only $1.63 for a similar plant in Illinois. Therefore no further liberalization of workmen's compensation and no further social legislation should be passed by this state until the others catch up or something uniform is done about it.

New York is virtually bereft of the textile industry, which has gone South. No industry can compete with the same industry in another state if the latter is permitted to operate one hour more a day. There has to be an equality of laws in the states if some are not to have advantages denied others.

Case C. **A Suggested Basis for State Legislation**

A manufacturer who opposes certain types of legislation passed upon by any one state, although in favor of furthering the aims of such legislation, expresses the following views regarding the proper policy:

> If innovation in social legislation is to be introduced state by state, any one state must proceed by exceedingly small steps. If not, that particular state simply creates for itself, first, intermittent employment, and soon thereafter, the closing of plants. We have, in that respect, the example of Massachusetts from 1922 to 1929 in the cotton textile industry. The example of Massachusetts, far from causing other Southern states to follow, was held up in the South as an example to be avoided, because of the resulting unemployment. Those who ran mills in Massachusetts would have been well advised to close them down in 1923, and to move the machinery elsewhere. A very few did so, and prospered.
>
> This naturally brings up the question of how innovation in social legislation may be accomplished. I know that it will be pointed out that workmen's compensation and other desirable laws exist in a large part of the country only because some states pioneered, gave an impulse to the movement, and thereby made passage possible in some competing states. But this has been a costly process to individual states. I favor a different procedure for the future.
>
> Massachusetts should have passed a 48-hour law to be effective when the bulk of its competing states, at the most eleven or twelve in number, passed similar legislation. This would have stood out as an example and a beacon-light which would rapidly have been followed by a number of other states. It would have been the easiest way out for the politicians in other states to have met demands for a 48-hour law by passing the legislation similar to Massachusetts. The average politician would have considered that this avoided the issue, because it would not have been effective until all the competing states had joined. Soon the issue would have narrowed down to two or three states, and the opponents of the legislation would have had little or no ground to stand

on. This country must move forward, but by considerably larger areas than single states, or even such a section as New England.

Case D. **Possibilities and Limitations of Interstate Compacts**

Compacts between states have been in existence for many years on such matters as boundaries, interstate bridges, and waterways. The application of the compact to labor legislation has come into prominence within the past few years as one way of obtaining greater uniformity in labor legislation, the first of such agreements being the Minimum Wage Compact, signed on May 29, 1934, in Concord, New Hampshire, by representatives of the governors of seven northeastern states. Many people now favor this form of advancing labor legislation.

Others, however, view compacts as unworkable forms of agreement which really do not force any competing state to enter into them and do not bind those states which are signatories to abide by the terms adopted. They say that regional groups of states may agree among themselves and yet be unable to pull into the compact those states which are really important from a competitive standpoint to such an arrangement, for these may have to give up one of their chief competitive advantages by submitting to the higher standards of the other states. It is also pointed out that if a real compact were made it would, in fact, become a national regulation of all states involved, and that therefore initial plans for definite action of a Federal sort would be preferable.

Questions:

1. What, if anything, may be done to induce states to desist from competing on the basis criticized in Case A?

2. Evaluate the methods proposed in Cases B, C, and D for dealing with the problem of maintaining and raising labor standards in a progressive state and for advancing them in the country at large.

PROBLEM 30. FEDERAL VS. STATE ACTION IN LABOR LEGISLATION

Case A. Differences among States in Accident Protection

Workmen's compensation acts of one kind or another to indemnify workers for accidents occurring in connection with their occupation may be found in practically every state, but there is a wide divergence in their terms. The injured worker is usually given a portion of his salary, from one-half to two-thirds, for the time during which compensation is payable. In several states the maximum payable is $12 a week; in New York, California, and a few other jurisdictions it is around $25 a week. In the case of permanent partial disability, the loss of a leg is valued at 50 weeks in one state, 175 weeks in a second, and 381 weeks in a third.

The schedules of the various states are full of such irrationalities. The situation may be illustrated by the facts given in the following excerpts from a recent article on the subject, although the details change from time to time.

> In the first place, millions of workers still stand outside of the pale of legal relief. Exemptions are made for certain industries. There is no protection for men in cotton-ginning in Texas, in logging in Maine, in distilling in Kentucky. Office workers are unprotected in twelve states. In more than half the states relief is denied to workers in shops employing less than a stipulated number; in Georgia the minimum is ten, in Alabama sixteen.
>
> The man who drives a truck may fall off his seat into a pool of water, contract pneumonia, and die, and his family will receive compensation without question. But let him work all day in the rain, contract pneumonia, and die, and there is no recompense. Only five states (and the Federal government where it has jurisdiction) require without reservation compensation for occupational

diseases. Six other states go less than half-way by establishing official lists of certain illnesses caused by specific substances and declaring that these, and these alone, must be compensated for—a compromise resulting in both bizarre and tragic miscarriages of justice. All other states refuse compensation for disease, mainly through fear of imposing too heavy a burden upon industry.

Minors and learners who are permanently maimed, either partially or totally, are in particularly distressing situations in many states. Twenty-seven states award compensation to minors which is based merely on their actual wages when injured, regardless of the fact that they had not yet reached their full development and that the injury means they will never reach it.

The monetary value placed upon a man's life by the different states varies widely. South Dakota places the amount as low as $3,000. Just over the line, however, North Dakota grants $15,000 to the family deprived of its breadwinner.

Other critics have stressed the important differences among the states in administrative procedures in handling workmen's compensation cases. Most states have adopted the commission form of administration but some still retain what is known as court administration. One authoritative comment states:

> Experience has shown that courts are not properly equipped to render the type of service needed for workmen's compensation administration. Judges have many duties beside looking after the needs of injured workers or their families. They tend to confine themselves to the small percentage of contested cases which are brought before them, and to pay little or no attention to settlements made between the injured worker and his employer or the insurance company, giving the chance to the latter to settle on a payment which is far below what the worker should get. Courts are particularly unfit for the type of administrative work involved in the promotion of accident prevention or in the rehabilitation of injured workers.
>
> Compensation commissions, on the other hand, have a better opportunity to study the problems of compensation administration and in more detail than is possible under court procedure.

Injured workers cannot afford the delay, the expense, the waste of time, or the uncertainty involved in court trials.

But merely because a state has a commission procedure does not guarantee an effective system of adjustment of workmen's compensation claims. In some states the procedure is cumbersome, slow, and burdened with red tape. This difference is due largely to the provisions of the workmen's compensation law which relate to appeals. Where appeals from the decision of the commission to the courts are allowed on questions of fact as well as of law, the procedure before the commission becomes necessarily complicated. Frequently, elaborate and costly records must be compiled in the event of an appeal to the courts. This procedure makes the administration resemble the court method which workmen's compensation legislation was intended to replace.

Aside from these problems there is the question of whether the workmen's compensation commission is staffed by people who are incompetent because appointed for their political usefulness instead of on merit. The absence of civil service procedure in the vast majority of the states thus affects the actual benefits received by citizens in different states even though the laws may have similar terms.

Case B. Federal Regulation of Child Labor?

A joint resolution proposing a child labor amendment to the United States Constitution was approved by Congress in 1924. A vigorous controversy at once began over the desirability of this amendment, and ratification proceeded so slowly as to discourage, in retrospect, many who desire social change through this method. The text of the amendment reads:

> Section 1. The Congress shall have power to limit, regulate and prohibit the labor of persons under eighteen years of age.
>
> Section 2. The power of the several States is unimpaired by this article except that the operation of State laws shall be sus-

pended to the extent necessary to give effect to legislation enacted by the Congress.

Before Congress submitted the Amendment it had made two attempts to regulate child labor nationally, but each had, in turn, been declared unconstitutional by the Supreme Court. Both laws set fourteen as the minimum age for employment in factories, mills, canneries, and workshops, with an 8-hour day, 48-hour and 6-day week, and prohibition of night work for children between fourteen and sixteen; and sixteen as the minimum age for children in mines and quarries.

Another temporary national regulation of child labor was achieved under the National Recovery Administration. The National Child Labor Committee reports:

> Under the N. R. A. codes, sixteen years was set as the minimum age for industrial employment; in certain dangerous occupations the limit was eighteen. As a result, workers under sixteen virtually disappeared from industry and commerce. When the codes were declared invalid in May 1935, the trend was reversed. During the last seven months of 1935 the number of children under sixteen leaving school for work in areas reporting to the Children's Bureau was 55% above the total for the twelve months of 1934.

The opponents of the amendment found a champion in Nicholas Murray Butler, President of Columbia University, who, in a letter to the New York *Times*, stated:

> The proposed child labor amendment . . . would attack our government at its foundation by once more enormously extending the Federal police power to the invasion and destruction of the historic rights of our state and local governments as well as those of the family. . . .
>
> The Congress might then send Federal agents and inspectors into every home, every family, every school and every church in the land to see what anyone under eighteen years of age was doing and whether he was doing anything which the Congress, under authority of the amendment, had either limited, regulated or prohibited. Nothing more indefensible or inexcusable than this amendment has been brought forward at any time in our nation's history.

The point of view of other people with regard to the child labor amendment is not so much an opposition to this one measure as a desire to keep the Federal government from extending its sphere of influence over local conditions. The fear is expressed that the next step will be Federal regulation of the hours of work of women and then perhaps of men, and that then our government will become too centralized for safety regarding political stability or for administration efficiency.

An answer to President Butler's criticism, by two legal authorities, stated in part:

> Under the Constitution, a state, while it can regulate its own child labor, cannot prevent the importation into and sale in the state of the product of child labor in other states, no matter how lax or non-existent the state child labor law of the second state may be. Unless Congress has that power, we are in this country in an extraordinary and lamentable position. The people in each state and the nation are powerless to remedy a condition which places the people of all the states which desire to restrict child labor effectively in such a position that they can do so only at the cost of submitting their manufacturers and other employers of labor to ruinous competition.

Miss Frances Perkins, Secretary of Labor, in another defense of the amendment, wrote:

> This proposal contains no prohibition or regulation of the employment of children in the amendment itself. It merely gives to Congress authority to legislate in this field, and any law passed can be changed by a simple majority in any session of Congress. If the Eighteenth Amendment (Prohibition) had been worded as an enabling act like the child labor amendment, its repeal would not have been necessary when the opinion of the country changed.
>
> Only places where children are, to use the Census language, "gainfully employed"—in other words, employed at wages for profit, are affected. The amendment gives Congress power only over the labor of children for hire, and nothing else. Therefore Congress would have absolutely no power to send inspectors into families, schools or churches any more than it has now.

> Every state today prohibits the employment of children below a certain minimum age, and regulates in some way the work of minors after they reach that age. Some of these state regulations apply to minors eighteen years of age, and a few to twenty-one when the employment presents special physical or moral hazards. It is necessary that Congress be given power to regulate up to eighteen years of age at least, in order to regulate, if necessary, employment in such occupations.

The issue took a different turn early in 1937, following the Supreme Court decision upholding the Ashurst-Sumners Act, which made it illegal to import convict-made goods into a state having a law against their sale. Many people came forward with the plan that instead of the amendment, Congress should pass a law similar to the Ashurst-Sumners Act, and the individual states should then pass laws banning such goods.

This proposal was strongly opposed by the National Child Labor Committee. It pointed out that such legislation would protect only children employed in the productive industries, and do nothing for those in laundries, hotels, restaurants, and the like; that the legislation would have to be adopted in every state, and the process of pushing it through would be long and difficult; that enforcement of such legislation would require that goods be labeled, which would not be so easy to require and supervise as the labeling of prison-made goods, since prisons are definite and limited places known to the law; and that even if this could be done, the differences in standards established by the states would present another tangle of difficulties.

Questions:

1. To what extent, if any, and for what reasons, is the retention of differences among the states in labor legislation affecting children, or in terms of workmen's compensation and accident regulation, desirable or necessary?

2. If it were desirable to have minimum standards for workmen's compensation laws, through Federal action, what possible forms of Federal legislation might be considered to put such minimum standards into effect without a constitutional amendment?

3. Is the procedure of an amendment the remedy in the establishment of minimum national standards for minors? Support your answer with adequate reasoning, giving full attention to the objection raised by some publicists who feel that the tendency toward a concentration of power in the Federal government is dangerous to our ultimate political stability.

4. Should the extension, if any, of the power of the Federal government in controlling labor conditions be effected by a series of separate amendments as needed, or be obtained by a cover-all amendment giving wide and practically unlimited powers in the field of labor legislation? Explain fully the basis for your judgment.

forms of Federal legislation might be considered to put such minimum standards into effect without a constitutional amendment?

3\. *Is the procedure of an amendment the remedy in the establishment of minimum judicial standards for workers? Support your answer with adequate reasoning, giving full attention to the objection raised by some publicists who feel that the tendency toward a concentration of power in the Federal government is dangerous to our ultimate political stability.*

4\. *Should the extension, if any, of the power of the Federal government in controlling labor conditions be effected by a series of separate amendments as needed, or be obtained by a more all-amendment giving wide and practically unlimited powers in the field of labor legislation? Explain fully the basis for your judgment.*

PART THREE: OLD AGE, INSECURITY, AND UNEMPLOYMENT

I. The Older Worker

II. Technological Change

III. Industrial Practices Affecting Employment

IV. Public Provisions for the Unemployed

PROBLEM 31. THE MIDDLE-AGED WORKER BARRED FROM EMPLOYMENT

1. An interrogation of witnesses in hearings held by the United States Senate Committee on Education and Labor some years ago brought out points of view and practices illustrated by the following testimony:

Mr. L. (a railroad official).—We decline to give employment to a man when he is aged.

Senator C.—What age?

Mr. L.—Forty years of age.

Senator C.—What are we going to do with the men who are past forty? What is the country or what is society going to do with the men who are past forty?

Mr. L.—I can tell you what we do with them; we keep them in the service.

Senator C.—Then what is this committee going to recommend to Congress to be done with the man past fifty, who is healthy, who is able-bodied, but who cannot get employment because industry will not take him?

Mr. L.—I think that the question is not, can he not get employment, but the question is why has he not got employment.

Senator C.—There are 250,000 more employees in the bituminous mines than are needed. Some of those employees are undoubtedly able-bodied men who have been diligent and capable, but who are fifty years or over. Suppose one of the men applied to you, with a perfect record back of him of decency and of employment, out of work because of the conditions in that industry. What would you say to him?

Mr. L.—We would have to say, "We have not got a job for you today."

Mr. N. (a steel executive).—We are building up older employees from the standpoint of age and service in our plant. In order to protect them and not to bring them into competition from the outside with men who have had no previous connection with the company, we must have some limit at which we will avoid bringing into competition with our permanent employees people from the outside.

Various surveys have brought out that the small and isolated concern may be haphazard in its selection policies, but the majority of the medium-sized and larger concerns, and those with employment departments, have definite policies prohibiting the employment of applicants who are beyond a certain age. Some state and local governments in their civil service regulations, and departments of the Federal government, have similar restrictions, though these governmental requirements may bar workers who are fifty years of age or fifty-five instead of at earlier ages.

2. An officer of a national organization conducting an employment exchange for women states that the barring of older people from work is more frequent and serious in their case than in that of men. She asserts that women of thirty-five years of age are often rejected on this score and, indeed, are told that that is the reason. She relates instances of extremely capable women in the late thirties with first-rate experience and reputations who were rejected by banks, advertising companies, and others. This, she asserts, is true almost as much of women who are well groomed, who do not show their age, who have not been long out of a job, or who perhaps may even be in one at the time they desire a change. She states that many private employment agencies refuse to accept applications for positions from women who are thirty-five years old or over, and if they do accept them, favor the younger women because the chances of placement are so much better.

Question:

What would you recommend to the Committee as possible measures for dealing with the problem of middle-aged workers (forty-five to fifty-five years old) who find it difficult to obtain employment because of age rules?

PROBLEM 32. RETAINING THE MIDDLE-AGED WORKER IN EMPLOYMENT

The worker who is definitely aged in years may be covered by pension schemes, but those of pre-pension age are not so covered, and they desire to continue at work, both for their own sake and because of their financial needs. The kinds of problems which some older workers present to their organizations are illustrated by the following cases.

Case A. Impaired Physical Ability

A worker forty-seven years old has been employed in coal mines since the age of thirteen. He has never had any other occupation, as there is no other industry in the neighborhood. Until recently he worked as regularly as the industry permitted, but has begun to suffer from rheumatism, which he believes he contracted from the dampness in the mines.

He has been going down to the pits, though not regularly, often staying down less than the hours underground required by the union agreement with the operators. In this way the miner has made enough to maintain himself and his wife, for miners are paid on the tonnage basis.

The company says that the more men it uses underground, the more expensive it is to conduct operations. It desires to eliminate this man and several others of like sort from its employ, on the ground that it is not getting as high an output from them as it considers necessary to justify the investment.

This has created a good deal of bitterness among the miners, who say that the industry owes the man a living and should support him in his declining years. They say that no matter if the cost is high, the mine should at least allow him to earn what he can. The company answers that coal is sold on a competitive basis, that working with a picked crew is the practical way of doing business, and that rheumatism is not of industrial origin.

Case B. **Inability to Measure Up to Competitive Pace**

In a Western manufacturing concern a good deal of emphasis had, until about four years ago, been placed upon length of service. Since then this policy has begun to be viewed in a new light. Previously the protected position of the concern had permitted "easy going" methods. Under the stimulus of competition during recent years, however, a good deal of attention has been devoted to increasing the efficiency of the plant, and an intensive drive has been made for a higher individual output. The expected output per employee has been greatly increased. Every operation that could be put on a piece-work basis has been changed to that form of payment; detailed records of the individual efficiency of the employees have been established; and in some few operations the work has been regulated by movable conveyors.

The resulting pace of the shop is one that is not considered as being too hard on the young and vigorous men. But it is a standard that the men of forty-eight and fifty are finding difficult to meet. They may have been with the firm twenty years or more, but in some cases have reached the same stage in their business careers that a baseball star reaches at the age of forty. They are by comparison much less productive than the younger men, and their piece-rate earnings also tend to be much less. The foremen know which of the men have made for a high average efficiency and which have reduced that efficiency. Every time that a foreman shows up unfavorably with regard to costs, he knows which workers are contributing to this record and tends to try to ease them out.

The atmosphere of the shop has therefore become rather trying on the older men. Some of them have seen the handwriting on the wall and have quit. Since this is equivalent to the discharge of the older, loyal men, the company wants to meet the situation by reviewing its policies and revising its procedures in order for its practices to square with those policies. It does not want its older men to be earning half the wages of its younger workers, and it does not wish to penalize the foremen by double costs for their older workers, even if this were a desirable solution. It does not wish to pay a worker twice as much as the next for doing half the amount of work, and it questions the justice of demoting men to jobs which involve paying them half of what they have been earning on the occupations on which they had long been engaged.

A committee of the management is deliberating on the subject and desires a fair solution.

Case C. **Inadaptability for Other Work**

1. A paper manufacturer established an employment guarantee plan, aimed to promote length of service on the part of the employees. The understanding was that should a slack period occur, workers with less than five years of service would be laid off first, thus maintaining the guarantee.

A difficulty which arose almost immediately after the expiration of the five-year period perplexed the officials. The company had had a loft department for the drying of paper, but at that time it had begun constructing an air dryer. When this was completely installed, the loft could be dispensed with entirely. But the loft department had employed about ten workers, several of whom were older men to whom the guarantee of full-time earnings had been made and who had in some cases been with the concern ten or fifteen years. Seven of these men had been hired especially for loft work, which is not difficult work, but is of a specialized nature. The company writes:

> The men are not called upon to do any heavy lifting, the paper being hung on poles in the loft only a few sheets at a time. We have, therefore, always used in the loft types of men who could not be

placed on other work about the mill. Our sweeping crews and forces for other light work of that low-paid nature are now fully manned. There is nothing that we can think of about the mill on which we could successfully use these particular men from the loft. Most of our work is hard physical labor and they simply are not physically able to step into the other work. Nor are they the type of men who might be mentally capable of grasping more technical work, such as in our repair department. Should we keep these men when we could put younger and more adaptable men into future vacancies?

2. A construction company finds itself burdened with the problem of the older workers whose most productive periods have passed. It is handicapped in its treatment of the older worker problem by its size. Large construction firms often can take care of older men because of their greater range of jobs. Positions like that of watchman, timekeeper, and elevator starter on the material hoists are easier for older men to handle and are essential to the functioning of the plant. But this company, with its twenty-five employees, only infrequently has jobs like this for its older men. Only twice in the last five years has the company been in such a position, as for instance, on a large department store job. In that exigency the organization had to be expanded to cover several hundred employees, and could assign various easy jobs to the shop veterans.

Case D. **Set or Narrow Points of View of Middle-Aged**

A financial company has tried to build up a corps of workers and executives with long service records. Prizes, medals, bonuses, and other rewards were given those who stayed five years or more, and special honors were accorded to the men who passed the twenty-year mark. Now the company has a substantial proportion of section heads, superintendents, and minor heads of departments who have been twenty years or more with the firm.

A critic of the plan asserts that in the main this large group of men with long service is not at all an asset to the firm, but a heavy liability. He says that the company has a large proportion of minor supervisory executives who have been with the firm for a long period without growing, who stand in the way of progress, who are narrow-minded, suspicious, unprogressive, and inflexible. He complains that having for years seen the jobs under them done in a routine way, no matter how much better a new plan of doing the work may be, they can see only objections. Their attitude towards their employees is lacking in real leadership, yet having themselves been brought up under a system of autocratic domination, they are not open to suggestions for improving the manner of handling their own subordinates. They may oppose granting privileges to employees merely because they themselves never had them.

This critic would like to see those of the older men who are too set in their ideas gradually weeded out, and younger men put in their places. He has expressed his views privately to some of the other executives. Most say that this would be no long run solution of the concern's difficulties or of the general problem, unless, perhaps, in the exceptional case.

Case E. Personality Difficulties

A publishing house employs a woman of fifty who has been working with the firm for twenty-one years. In efficiency, according to her supervisor, she "isn't worth half her salary," but she is very much dissatisfied with what she calls the unfair treatment the firm has been giving her, and has been complaining to one person or another periodically, repeating her story at great length. Everybody dislikes her. Besides the irritation she causes, the supervisor feels that probably she is complaining to her fellow workers, and thus has a bad influence on general morale and on the attitude of the younger employees toward the firm.

The supervisor does not know exactly what to do in her case, and in that of several others, since their long service entitles them to special consideration. Moreover, the concern probably should have handled the matter years ago. The question which it now propounds is, "What should, or what *can*, we do about situations like these when they arise?"

Questions:

1. What, in physiological terms, does middle-age obsolescence represent, and to what extent may such physical impairment be delayed through industrial health work or other company activities?

2. In what other ways may management anticipate the other types of difficulties shown as arising in connection with older workers and thus correct these faults earlier in their careers? Present your answer in a comprehensive analytic outline containing both general principles and concrete applications.

3. What can or should a concern or industry do with regard to retention of job and payment status when all its efforts have been without avail and an employee, at the age of forty-five or fifty, has become a distinctly subnormal worker whose output is perhaps 50% of what is to be obtained from a younger worker, or when the middle-aged employee presents personality difficulties? Indicate what the companies might do in each of the cases cited.

PROBLEM 33. METHOD OF PRESENTING A TECHNOLOGICAL CHANGE TO WORKERS

NOTE: The hope that the economic system may permit much better conditions of work and a much higher standard of living for the workers, at the same time that it amply supports a wider scope of activities and services to be provided by government, depends upon the ability of industry to improve its technical efficiency so greatly as to yield a vastly larger production per worker. Such changes, however, are not merely technical in nature, but involve also the ability to overcome successfully the human resistance which may be encountered in their installation. The problem of introducing the "stretch-out" in textile mills provides an excellent illustrative application. The report which follows is from a case study made by the Yale Institute of Human Relations.

A mill engaged in cotton spinning and weaving has for several decades been located in a company-owned village in an isolated rural section of the South. This village has less than 2000 people in all, of whom about 800 are employed by the mill. The workers are all of Anglo-Saxon stock, of rural origin, and with an industrial background limited to the Southern cotton textile industry. About 60% of the workers are employed on skilled and semi-skilled jobs and 40% on unskilled jobs. Working conditions in the mill are relatively good. Worker-management relations are on an informal basis, the major point of contact between the individual worker and the management being with the overseer.

The problem of competition for business has become especially serious and the need for reduction in costs is seen as imperative. A radical change of method of operating has begun to be considered, with a view to increasing the effectiveness of the workers, since labor costs especially are high.

In investigating the possible means of reducing operating costs, the management employed a consulting engineer who has recommended the introduction of the multiple loom system as an effective means of reducing labor costs and generally increasing the efficiency of the workers. The consulting engineer and his staff, cooperating with the mill operating executives, are to be placed in charge of the introduction of the system.

A "stretchout" or "labor extension" is therefore to be attempted in the weaving department of this mill, based upon a scientific introduction of the multiple loom system, a method of increasing the number of looms operated per weaver, and a general improvement in raw materials, conditioning, mechanical operation, and operating efficiency.

This engineer, who is a "human" type of manager, realizes that a major change in working arrangements is not likely to be successful if introduced by mere executive fiat. He feels that every step required to make the change successful has to be analyzed and every difficulty anticipated, since the division of weaving labor is a comparatively new development in cotton mill operation. Accordingly he has made a careful analysis of the prevailing conditions of operation in the mill.

As a result, preparations for the introduction of the multiple loom system will probably require the following to be done: machinery throughout the mill to be inspected, repaired, and adjusted; the installation of some new machinery and some revisions of layout; installation of a new humidifying system; improvements in the mixing and conditioning of raw cotton; general cleaning of workrooms; improvement of the system of artificial illumination; and the conduct of tests to determine the exact operating efficiency of the looms, as revealed by end breakage and loom stoppage.

At this time the weavers are operating from 15 to 30 looms each, and averaging about 24 looms. They perform both the skilled and unskilled tasks incidental to weaving and follow no specific working methods or routine for patrolling their looms.

Some 80 weavers are employed, and they, with the assistance of six smash hands and two pick out hands, operate the 1940 looms comprising the weaving equipment of the mill.

Each weaver is obliged to attend from 17.1 loom stops to 47.4 loom stops per hour on sets of from 14 to 20 looms, depending upon the kind of cloth woven and the width of the loom operated. Based upon the type of cloth woven, the width loom operated, and improved loom and general operating efficiency, the consulting engineers estimate that the weavers, assisted by battery hands and cloth doffers, following a given loom patrol and performing only the skilled tasks, can reasonably be expected to attend to 36 loom stops per hour. The number of looms per weaver may on this basis be increased, reducing the number of weavers from 80 to 26, increasing the average number of looms operated from 24 to 70 per weaver, and reassigning some 35 weavers to perform the unskilled tasks of battery filling, loom cleaning, and cloth doffing.

The general manager and his assistant personally checked the finding of the consulting engineer to be sure the particular conditions of the plant had been fully considered. Also, personal checks of experimental runs with larger sets of looms convinced them that some 70 to 90 looms could be operated by a weaver with the assistance of a battery hand, loom cleaner, and cloth doffer, without creating an excessive job burden. It is felt that while the number of looms per weaver is much greater, the actual amount of work required of the weaver is not greatly increased.

The weaving overseer and other operating executives concerned have been informed of the proposed extension by the management and the consulting engineer. The necessity for cost reduction, the nature, purpose, and advantages of the system have been carefully explained to them and now the cooperation of the operatives themselves has to be obtained, largely in their own interest.

Questions:

1. Indicate in as full detail as you can, and in carefully planned sequence, the steps which the manager might now take in order to obtain at least the acquiescence of the workers in the change, if not a certain degree of interest and satisfaction in it. In this procedure take into account the psychological problems involved, the attitude to be taken by the management and the extent of the information to be given to those concerned.

2. What precautions should the management take in operating the new plan during the first few months, or year?

3. The managers feel that these technological changes, when once put into effect and accepted, will reveal possibilities of reorganization and further change imposing no extra hardships on the worker, but having elements of danger because of the natural misunderstandings or resentments that such changes introduce. Indicate what the management might do to prepare for the additional future developments or extensions expected in this connection two or three years hence.

PROBLEM 34. DISPLACEMENTS THROUGH TECHNOLOGICAL CHANGES

Case A. Effect of New Methods on Amount of Labor

The management of a concern engaged in finishing raw cotton cloth has desired to cut costs without purchasing new machinery. It recently employed an engineer who, with a number of assistants, introduced an excellent task and bonus system of wage payment.

Without any changes in machinery or equipment but with incidental changes in method, the new plan will enable the concern to cut down its number of employees in two years from 1100 to about 850. In the immediate situation, the most striking case is in a department where seventy-five older women were formerly employed to run machines, wrap, sort, and pack, but where now only twenty-five girls will be needed to do the same amount of work. The concern must decide what to do about this situation in the present instance, and in the two years ahead, about those in excess.

Case B. Effect of Plant Specialization on Personnel

A company manufacturing chains employed about 650 people for several years in a plant located in a Connecticut town. The company then purchased two other concerns, one located in Pennsylvania and the other in Michigan. The management now finds that it can move all the general chain business to its Michigan plant, most of its tire production to Pennsylvania, do away with some of the labor force, and avoid much duplication and expense. Among the advantages of the change seen are the ability to cut the freight rates on raw materials shipped, the smaller overhead involved, the lower taxes of the

Pennsylvania factory, and the lower costs of electric light and power and coal in the other plants.

The change is thus desirable on almost every ground of efficient production, but disastrous to the workers in the Connecticut plant, where only a hundred workers at most might be retained for special work.

Case C. Substitution of Machine for Skilled Hand Labor

1. One of the most important processes in a concern manufacturing shoes is known as lasting. A new machine released by a shoe machinery company automatically pulls the sides of the shoe in process over the last and fastens the lining to the leather with small wire staples. These staples are left in the finished shoe so that no tacks need to be pulled from the sides of the shoe. As a result the man operating this machine can do the work of eight or ten hand side lasters, and the number of tack pullers required is also reduced.

Side lasters are skilled men. Most of them have devoted their whole working days to that one job in the shoe industry. The superintendent of this plant states, "If I have to discharge these men, neither they nor I have any idea where they might be able to secure work. There are no other jobs where we can place one of them. It is safe to say that the shoe industry has closed its doors to them. Moreover, similar changes in other operations are coming within the next ten years. Operations which are now done by machines but which are not automatic will soon become so, and welters, stitchers, edge-trimmers, and others will necessarily be displaced. I am at my wit's ends trying to figure out how to handle this proposition."

2. In the knife assembly department of a well-known company making silver plated tableware, there were employed approximately forty to fifty men engaged in soldering by hand the hollow handles of the knives to the knife blades with the use of a blow torch. This was a skilled trade, learned after

years of apprenticeship, and the men were earning between $50 and $60 per week. A device has recently been invented for automatically soldering the knife handles by electricity, making it possible, it is stated, to replace these men by fifteen unskilled operatives, either women or untrained men.

Case D. Effect of Major Technical Advances

A concern which manufactures all the electricity for a mid-Western city has had to establish various new stations to meet the growing demand. Each new station has been a technical improvement on former ones, both as to methods of manufacture and efficiency of operation, making it possible to produce electricity at cheaper cost with fewer men. These men, however, have had to be more skilled and to have better training than the men who were employed in running the first station.

The city has become stabilized, and the company can discontinue an obsolete station with its high costs of operation and produce the needed electricity in the other four stations. The obsolete plant employs over a hundred faithful workers, some of whose service records are longer than twenty-five years. The company is not going to build another plant in the city, as all the sites suitable for such a generating station are too costly. If it does build one, the number of workers required will be small, as the automatic principle will be applied throughout. The plant superintendent asserts that the next plant built will be practically a building and machinery, with automatic controls from a central station.

Questions:

1. What company policies and practices might reduce the extent or effect of technological installations in displacing those actually employed at the time the changes are introduced?

2. What general industrial or governmental policies and measures must be adopted to meet the social problems which technological displacements create?

PROBLEM 35. THE PLACE OF REGULARIZATION IN AN EMPLOYMENT PROGRAM

In the discussion of programs for reducing the instability of employment, there is one group of advocates who, though agreeing on the need for a rounded program, emphasize the widespread opportunity for business to study its operations and provide more regular work. They point out the neglect of the problem in various industries and urge a program of "regularization." This may be briefly illustrated by the following distribution, production, and labor policies:

1. Market analyses in order to provide more accurate estimates of the demand for the ensuing six months or year and thereby supply a better basis for planning and budgeting of production and operations.
2. Diversifying the output with side lines, fillers, and new products that fit into seasonal or predictable slack periods.
3. Simplifying and standardizing products so as to permit production for stock.
4. Educating the consumer to buy seasonal products more regularly, through price reductions and various sales efforts.
5. Research to eliminate the weather factors and other obstacles in the case of those kinds of products which, by change of processes or equipment, may be made at seasons when they are not now produced.
6. Careful anticipation of the effects of technological changes so that they will cause a minimum of displacement.
7. Training for versatility so that workers may be transferred around to different jobs and thus kept on the payroll.
8. Organization of the labor market in such a way as to reduce the excess reserve of labor associated with various types of concerns and industries.

In special industries the approach through regularization is applied with different emphasis. The following are illustrations:

> In building and construction, better planning of building operations so that the shell of a building may be ready in early winter and the work continued indoors, and also special arrangements for the kinds of winter work now considered feasible.
>
> In the longshore industry, which is notoriously irregular, the hiring of labor, to the degree possible, through central exchanges which distribute the workers in accordance with the requirements of the docks as a whole, rather than having each steamship company build up its own labor reserve and thus create a highly excessive labor surplus.
>
> In bituminous coal mining a variety of measures, involving a fundamental reorganization of industry so that the better mines, strategically placed, would serve the country rather than employ an excess capacity and a widely distributed and intermittently employed group of workers.

This program, however, is subjected to criticism that regularization will increase unemployment rather than decrease it, and that it is merely one more type of technological change. As one writer puts it:

> In a hypothetical plant let us assume that 200 men worked full time for nine months and 100 men worked full time during the remaining three months. If employment could be regularized there would be full-time employment for 175 men. But 25 workers would be out of a job as far as this company is concerned. That this result has actually been effected is well known on the inside. Managers have told their stories of this accomplishment with pride, which is well justified from the standpoint of company economy. But we must face the fact that unemployment is increased in the process.
>
> It is difficult to escape the logic that the specific result in each case of stabilization, whether of seasonal fluctuations or of cyclical trends, is the doing of the same or a larger amount of work with fewer men. Part-time employees are turned into full-time em-

ployees after stabilization—that is, after some of them have been taken off the payroll.

The issue of regularization thus suggests the possible contention that it would be better for most industries to remain chaotic, planless, and inefficient in their handling of labor, because more people are employed thereby. But this, according to those who feel that regularization has a very definite place in stabilized employment, only perpetuates the irregularity of employment. The alternatives seem, therefore, to involve a dilemma.

A leading exponent of regularization writes:

> It is true that as individual plants become better organized, a smaller labor supply is required for the same amount of work. Therefore if regularization plans were installed suddenly, they would bring great harm. The change should be made in a painless manner by relying on normal labor turnover as far as possible, so that the workers actually in employment need not be affected at all, but only outsiders who might wish to enter it.
>
> The reduction in the number of workers necessary for a given output is not necessarily a disadvantage. Over long periods of time the labor supply will adjust itself to economic development. It should mean lower costs for the products affected, lower prices, and where the demand for the goods is elastic, the demand in time for a larger volume of goods. This will require the employment of some or all of those laid off. In any event when the same amount of production is done by a smaller number of people, we would not be the losers financially or economically even if we supported those without jobs by some form of insurance. Or, if planned, the country could use the excess of labor in flood control or other large projects.

The possible extent of regularization, as well as its desirability, has long been a source of contention in relation to the subject of unemployment insurance. At one time regularization was urged as a substitute for such insurance. In recent years it has been an issue in determining the form of unemployment insurance to be operated by the states.

One group of advocates believe that a great deal of progress may be made in the reduction of irregularity of employment if enough pressure is put upon management to do so, and with this in mind they favor a differentiation in tax rates levied on employers for insurance, in accordance with the results that concerns obtain in minimizing lay-offs. A tax which recognizes the principle of "merit rating," it is argued, offers an incentive to management to regularize employment.

Those in the opposing camp take the view that what an employer or an industry can do to reduce instability of employment is negligible or unimportant, and therefore they do not favor any difference of employers' unemployment insurance tax rates. The question from a standpoint of unemployment insurance (a separate subject) is therefore dependent upon the issue whether regularization is both feasible and desirable in a program for dealing with unemployment.

Question:

Evaluate the contentions of the two sides, preparing a reasoned view of the place that regularization should play in a program of unemployment prevention and employment stabilization.

PROBLEM 36. EFFICACY OF SPREADING WORK BY SHORTENING HOURS OR OVERSTAFFING

Case A. Economics of the 30-Hour Week

In various quarters there is a demand for a 30-hour week as a means of taking up the slack in employment. The reduction may not prove adequate in some industries. There might therefore be a demand for a 20-hour week. Shall hours of work then be cut until workers are practically all absorbed? If not, on what principle shall such cuts be limited?

The question of wage rates to be paid in connection with these changes are important considerations. Shall the hourly wages be kept the same, with the result that workers will earn a lower total weekly wage because of this sharing? Shall the rates be increased to offset, partly or wholly, the reduction in the number of hours of employment permitted? Shall the rates be cut somewhat so as to make possible the employment of more people even if excessive, as in the instances cited in Case B below? Each of these possibilities should produce different effects, perhaps interfering with the economic efficacy of the plan. These possible results need to be evaluated from a broad industrial and economic standpoint in determining the policy to be followed.

The question of shifts needs also to be considered. Should shifts be left single, or increased to two or more shifts per day as, for example, two 6-hour shifts? To use costly machinery inadequately or for too short a shift will increase costs of production, while to use two or more shifts may, under certain circumstances, require a total larger production. Several shifts may thus cause over-production or reduce the market for machinery and equipment.

Case B. **Reducing Unemployment through Overstaffing**

Where only one shift is normal to an employment, there arises a question of overstaffing. Some years ago an article on France illustrated the possibility of a condition of this sort. It stated:

> There is one cardinal weakness in the economic life of contemporary France which never fails to provoke wonder in the bosom of a stranger. It is that in so many industrial and commercial concerns and certainly throughout the whole of the bureaucracy, two and often three individuals are performing what should be the labor of a single one.
>
> Take, to begin with, the case of the banks. They are notoriously overstaffed, as compared with English or American banks. Not long ago there was a strike of bank clerks. Twenty thousand of them, dissatisfied with their pay, walked out one fine morning. What happened? The managers merely readjusted, revised, and in some cases suppressed, the work of their respective offices, and, with only a third of the staff remaining, the business of the banks went on as before.
>
> Have you ever tried to buy a postage stamp at a French post-office, to have a parcel weighed, to have a letter registered? Across the counter there are twenty employees—heaps of printed forms are dealt out and afterward checked sedulously, as though for printers' errors. If more than two stamps are purchased recourse is had to a pencil and abstruse ciphering. All stamps are affixed not by the sender but by the clerk. To cover a bulky package with five-centime stamps affords rare scope for the decorative faculties.
>
> In the Paris underground system the excessive amount of controls and surveillance makes the life of the traveler a burden. It is not the checking but the constant counter-checking, super-checking, over-checking that seem so fantastic.
>
> "We are obliged to take these precautions," one official confided to me. He pointed out that without this system of surveillance 700 inspectors would be out of a job, which was undeniably true.

This suggests that by employing fewer people French industry could increase wages, or to put it another way, that at present it is maintaining more employment by paying lower wages. This policy has been suggested in one form or another in this country.

A dispatch of December 28, 1936, sent by Harold Denny to the New York *Times*, states that much of Soviet industry is overstaffed and that if excessive personnel were laid off, a large number of workers would be without jobs. He writes:

> Soviet industrial executives calculate that the original cost of articles is multiplied from two to four times by top-heavy office staffs. Instances were reported where a piece of machinery costing 100 rubles to make was loaded with an additional 300 rubles of paperwork.

The correspondent states that a visitor to almost any Soviet office is impressed by the battalions of clerks, doing work that a small fraction of their numbers do in any American office. It is common, for example, for a factory to make out several hundred complicated order cards for the manufacture of one part, whereas in America two small cards suffice. He states:

> Thus the Kalinin plant employs 1,700 workers, whereas an American plant of similar size employs only 600 or 700. The Commissar for Heavy Industries found only 30 per cent of the Kalinin plant's personnel engaged in actual production. The rest were office employes. In an American factory, he reminded the executives, 75 per cent of the personnel is engaged in actual production.

The *Times* editorially suggests it may be that this explains why we are so often told that "there is no unemployment in Russia," and suggests:

> If we wished to establish a similar state of affairs here, we could study the Russian paper work system. As there are now about 44,000,000 persons employed here, we should need to put only 20 per cent additional to making out more order cards, and so take care of our entire 8,500,000 jobless—and still, apparently, be much below the Russian percentage of paper workers.

Questions:

1. Appraise the economic and social effects of shortening hours of work as a means of providing employment and maintaining prosperity. In your answer consider the various conditions of application regarding shifts and relative wage rates.

2. Assume that Congress is forced by popular pressure to pass a 30-hour law. Draft its terms in a way which will be the most likely to achieve some of its intended purposes and do the least harm.

3. Discuss the pros and cons of overstaffing as a means of reducing unemployment.

PROBLEM 37. APPLICATION OF EQUAL DISTRIBUTION OF WORK

Case A. Procedure in Permanent Reduction of Force

A shoe company asserted in 1932 that its business was permanently reduced. It submitted to an arbitrator figures showing that if the plant worked according to its proposed schedule of forty hours a week with a reduced crew, operating costs would amount to between $15,000 and $20,000 less than if the plant operated on about the same schedule for twenty hours a week with the full crew. The company did not, however, emphasize the decreased operating costs as much as it did the heightened morale which it would expect to result if a smaller crew were doing a full week's work at a full week's pay. The company produces high-grade shoes, and its theory was that improved morale would reflect itself in the quality of workmanship.

The position of the union was that unemployment among shoe workers in the area was already very serious; that many of the employees had been with the company for many years; that despite the pessimistic outlook of the management, these workers looked forward to improved conditions and desired to hold fast to their present tenure, insecure though it seemed; that the workers would, under the existing conditions, find it impossible to secure places elsewhere and consequently would be compelled to join many of their brother craftsmen on the relief rolls.

A proposal from a neutral source was to the effect that if there was enough production to give the full crew twenty hours of work a week, the pay would still be higher than the relief rates, and therefore all should share. The proposal stipulated that if the retention of the full crew resulted in less than an average of twenty hours of work a week in a particular month, the company might be permitted to reduce the crew only to the extent necessary to give the remaining employees twenty hours of work a week.

Case B. Allocation among Plants of a Company

A Chicago men's clothing firm operating a coat shop on the northwest side expanded by opening up a new shop, #2, on the west side. The firm later came to the conclusion that the expansion of its business had been due to abnormal buying, that to have opened it was an error, and that henceforth one shop would fully meet its needs. It therefore decided to dismiss the 90 men in shop #2 and so informed the union, expressing the intention of filling vacancies in the other shop from these workers. The issue has now come before arbitrators.

The union contends that all of the workers in shop #2 must share equally in the firm's work, be that much or little. The firm objects on the ground that to keep shop #2 open would require two sets of foremen, examiners, etc., and that these, with rent, light, and heat, would entail a disastrous increase in overhead amounting to several hundred dollars per week. It contends further that because of the small amount of work in the two shops, it would involve other problems, such as a larger turnover of labor and a deteriorated quality of product.

The union counters by the assertion that the purpose of the union and of the rule has been to develop some degree of responsibility for all union workers brought into the trade by a firm so long as the firm continues to manufacture clothing, and that the extra cost, though regrettable, is no reason for shifting the burden to those laid off.

Case C. Allocation among Types of Work

In a shoe concern there is a clause of the collective agreement with the union which reads as follows: "The manufacturer agrees that there shall be no laying off of members of the crew during slack periods, and during such periods work shall be distributed as equally as possible among the crew."

The company has been segregating certain fancy stitching, known as gimp stitching, by having this work done mainly by a specialized group of operatives. This style of stitching has grown popular. Single-needle fancy stitchers in the company's employ now have little work. The union requests that the gimp stitching be equally divided among all fancy stitchers, including the single-needle stitchers, instead of being divided among the smaller specialized group.

The employer maintains that as a matter of factory operation increased efficiency and increased earning power of operatives are possible through specialization. He asserts that the phrase in the agreement "as equally as possible among the crew" means a reasonable division of work, and that no measure of equal division of work is "possible" which is not reasonable with due consideration for successful and economical operation. He further contends that what the equal division clause means by a "crew" is that work shall be divided among those who perform a kind of work markedly different from other work in degree or kind of skill required, or in method by which performed, or in equipment used. Gimp stitching is held to be such a different kind of work and hence suitable to performance by a crew distinct from those doing general fancy stitching.

The union asserts that the basic purpose of this rule was to provide work for everybody and that equal lay-off may be less efficient than choosing the star workers for full-time employment, but that such hardships are definitely intended for the larger social purpose of keeping the working force from starvation.

Case D. **Right of Company to Dovetail Workers**

A men's clothing company, engaged in special order work, finds that the present volume and the immediate future demands of its business do not justify the employment of its full number of cutters on full time. In the meantime it wishes to make an arrangement for the temporary transfer of certain of its cutters, whose skill in special order work it does not wish to lose, to another firm with the understanding that they will be returned on request. The cutters themselves expressed a willingness to be transferred.

The union maintains that this would favor a special group of cutters and that in all cases transfer of union workers must be through the union. It says that under another arrangement the available work would not be properly spread among the membership of the union as a whole, a purpose which the organization is expected to effect.

Question:

Formulate the general principles for putting into effect a policy of equal division of work, giving supporting reasons, and apply these to each case as though you were the arbitrator.

PROBLEM 38. POLICIES IN LAYING OFF AND IN REHIRING

Case A. General Principles in Lay-offs

The business depression, in 1930, brought the subject of reduction in force sharply to the attention of a concern which had had nine years of steady growth. The officers were admittedly quite unprepared, from the point of view of personnel management, for the drastic reduction which finally became necessary.

At first operations were reduced to a more or less hand-to-mouth basis, depending on the number of orders received each week. The working week was reduced to a $3\frac{1}{2}$-day basis, the schedule being announced to the employees about a week in advance. When this required further reduction, the company decided it had to cut some of its people off the payroll rather than that all should have insufficient work.

As there had been no definite policy for lay-offs established, and as the executives were too heavily burdened with other trying conditions to consider the formulation of a satisfactory lay-off policy, the problems were at first handled individually in each case. This led to inconsistencies in principle and treatment regarding the length of notice, the basis of selection for lay-off, and similar matters. The executives soon became aware that the conditions were not satisfactory and decided that a careful consideration of policy in dealing with lay-offs was necessary.

Case B. Rehiring Practice Alleged to Favor Spendthrifts

Mackenzie is a thrifty Scotch metal worker whose desire to provide for his future and for the education of his children has been so strong that over a period of fourteen years he has rarely permitted himself such incidental luxuries as "movies" or tobacco. At the beginning of the depression he was known to have cleared a mortgage on his modest house, and he was known also to have about $4000 in the savings bank.

John Flanagan, in almost similar circumstances, had accumulated almost nothing and had paid off only a small part of his mortgage when a serious curtailment in the business of the metal company forced a lay-off of these two men and several others. In a few months Flanagan was in the deepest distress while Mackenzie was drawing on his savings even though living more frugally.

When business picked up for this company, early in 1935, they could take on only a few of the metal workers doing the job upon which both Mackenzie and Flanagan had been engaged. The question which arose was which of the men should be taken back. Because it was known that Mackenzie had savings while Flanagan was in debt, the latter was given the job.

Within the committee of supervisors arranging for the rehiring of men on the preferred list there was considerable dissension as to the justice or merit of this policy. One of the supervisors said that in rehiring Flanagan the company was taking it out on Mackenzie for his past sacrifice of comforts, and thus penalizing thrift. Another supervisor said that the primary consideration in rehiring should be need, and that the action taken was the right one.

Case C. Penalization of Employees Who Found or Accepted Temporary Work

When a paper company laid off a large part of its force, many of the men who had special skill in certain of the processes involved were urged to seek odd jobs in other concerns. They were told, however, that they would be on the preferred list when business picked up.

Many of the men who had worked for the paper company had long periods of service and wanted to continue working in that organization as soon as conditions permitted. Immediately after the lay-off some workers began to "rustle around" to see what they could find. A few were able to obtain jobs, but most of them had to accept lower wages. In some instances the men did not hesitate to take menial jobs, but on the supposition that it was a temporary matter. Other men were either less able, less active, or less fortunate, and stayed unemployed or went on relief.

When the company was able to resume rehiring, a peculiar situation arose. The employment manager would look over the names of those who had been on the rehiring list, and wherever it was known that certain men had jobs elsewhere, he would hold their reemployment in abeyance and offer the jobs to those who were unemployed or on relief. Criticism was made of this by some supervisors on the ground that this was favoring the "stay-at-homes" and penalizing the better, more industrious and more conscientious worker for having taken a job.

The employment manager defended his practices on the ground that many of the workers would resent the idea of a man being given a job who already had one; that in some cases the job which would be offered might suddenly terminate or might last only two or three months and the worker attracted away from the other job might then feel a sense of real grievance; and that it would be harder for employees out of work to get jobs if it was known that as soon as business picked up in the concerns from which they had come, they would be called back by those concerns.

The company has rehired some people without clearly deciding what principle should be used as a guide, and it is at sea as to what would be the desirable policy and procedure.

Case D. Do Men with Large Families Deserve Precedence?

A company of 1000 employees has reached the point where it must lay off part of its force. One of the issues arising is whether to favor the men with large families over those with few dependents.

A case in point is the issue in Department G between two men of equal efficiency, each earning about $24 a week when on regular time. Tony S., thirty-four years old, has six children; John W., thirty-five, has two. The oldest of Tony's children, a girl, only sixteen, is shortly to go to work; it has been the hope of John W. that both his boys would go to high school and perhaps college. The decision of the company, if carried out, would leave Tony on the job, although he has in John's opinion been improvident in having so large a family. He has asked the company not to favor Tony, and says that if one of the two must be laid off, a fair decision would be at the least to let the two flip a coin. But the management wishes to make the decision on principle, and is reconsidering the case.

Question:

Assume that a concern of 2000 employees in or near your home town had to make a lay-off of about 500, but with a possible prospect of rehiring 200 during the year. Outline the policies which you think should apply (1) in selecting those for lay-off, and (2) in rehiring. Include comment on the validity of the methods used in the cases presented.

PROBLEM 39. PRESSURE FOR DISMISSAL OF MARRIED WOMEN

A strong feeling has developed among unmarried girls and some men, in a plant hit by the depression, that married women whose husbands are at work should be the first to be laid off. As a result there is discussion about several people, particularly Mrs. Smith.

Mr. Smith and his wife are both employed by the same concern. Mr. Smith has a manual job which pays him about $20 a week. Mrs. Smith, who works in the costing department, had left work for a few years after marriage and then came back at the age of twenty-nine. She has been at work for five years. She earns $32 a week. On the basis of the combined earnings they purchased a home some years ago. Mrs. Smith has a woman come in by the day who does most of the housework, gives the children their lunch when they come from school and takes care of them until Mrs. Smith gets home.

Mrs. Smith, and others who support her views, state that it would be a great injustice to her to be laid off merely because she is married; that in her case it would not decrease unemployment because the maid would lose her job; that it would involve a radical adjustment to try to live on her husband's wages, and that it would nullify the value of all her efforts to do good work, to build up a home, and to arrive at a fair standard of living.

Some of the workers say, "Then let Mr. Smith be laid off and Mrs. Smith continue working." Mr. Smith says that if it ever comes to pass that he has to live at his wife's expense, he will leave home and "go on the bum" first. He says he is entitled to his job with the same priority and preference as anyone else, as he has been working at the plant since he was a boy.

Mrs. Smith says that if she were laid off for a few months it would be bad enough, but that it would be longer than that and perhaps forever, since the same reason used in discharge would be even more potent when she desired reemployment. She would, at that time, be out of experience and her requests for reinstatement would receive less consideration.

The local secretary of the Women's Trade Union League, having heard of the plan to have all married women laid off in this concern, gave out a statement to the local paper stating that the idea was just another of the injustices heaped upon women; that when they get a little bit more than the average in position or pay, one reason or another is found to lower their status and undermine their independence, and that matters of sex and marital relations should not be a primary factor in matters of promotion or lay-off. She says that such a movement would be a blow to women's independence and progress.

The concern must, however, lay off about one-fifth of its workers. It wants to decide this issue in fairness to all concerned.

Question:

What should be the general policy of companies with regard to this question in its selection of those to be laid off?

PROBLEM 40. POLICIES AFFECTING APPLICANTS FOR WORK

An electric light and power company in an Eastern city has about 3000 people in its employ, about half of whom are women. It has chosen its personnel carefully. Nearly every year a normal labor turnover and other reasons make it necessary to hire perhaps 400 workers. Nevertheless 20,000 persons applied at its offices for work.

The employment manager of this company states that a rough classification of these people who come to the office would be somewhat as follows. Perhaps one-third of the applicants are obviously of the type that the company feels it would not be justified in considering at all. They fail to make even the preliminary impression which would make it worthwhile to go far into their qualifications. They may be illiterates, "floaters," or have undesirable personal characteristics. They may show definite physical defects or give other indications that they would be unable to pass the concern's physical examination. The manager says: "We retain those who become physically impaired while with us, but we won't go out of our way to hire them." Some applicants are clearly in their age of senescence; others are minors under sixteen who are under the age requirements of this company.

Another third are people of the type whom a person of experience would intuitively reject for the organization. Some give evidence of low-grade personality, ability, or judgment. Often such applicants are entirely well-mannered, well-meaning citizens, but they are of low industrial quality, and many of them have never held a job anywhere for long. They are not geographical floaters, but they drift from job to job for reasons of temperamental or personal instability. Some are women over forty-five or men over fifty whom the concern does not employ, but who may try to pass for much younger.

In the third group of potential candidates, the major portion consists largely of employees who do not have the actual requirements established for positions in this concern. Some may have insufficient education, in view of the fact that the company greatly prefers persons of high school education or the equivalent. Some are beginners applying for types of work for which they are inexperienced. As there are only a limited number of positions available for people who are seeking their first job or applying for entry into certain of the special occupations of the industry, few can be offered an opportunity. Some of the applicants are married women with husbands at work. While it is the company's policy not to discharge any married women already employed, it does not hire them unless they are entirely dependent upon their own earnings.

The result is that out of about 20,000 applicants, no more than perhaps 2000 or 2500 are possibilities for employment because potentially good for one job or another in the concern, and of these perhaps 400 would be hired.

If one multiplies the yearly number of applicants, 20,000, by ten, as representing the total number of candidates who will apply to the concern in the next decade, it may be said that out of 200,000 applications for employment in the next ten years, 196,000 will be turned away and perhaps 4000 hired. This is not an abnormal instance. In greater or less degree business concerns throughout the country are faced with a similar situation.

Questions:

1. What policies and practices should the company follow in dealing with the various types of applicants?

2. What measures of a social nature are necessary to aid those applicants who find it difficult to obtain employment?

PROBLEM 41. AGENDA FOR CONFERENCE ON NATIONAL UNEMPLOYMENT INSURANCE

Early in 1934 a small group was called together privately for a preliminary consideration of a possible Federal law providing unemployment insurance. The purpose of this conference was to explore the general ideas of the group regarding the type of plan which they favored at that time, and to lay out fields of further study and inquiry which would permit of a more mature judgment on the whole matter.

In connection with this conference an outline was prepared of a few of the major questions to be considered. The chief items in the agenda dealt with certain issues regarded as fundamental, and were as follows:

1. *A national or a Federal-state system?*

Should the plan proposed be a strictly national measure, such as the British unemployment insurance scheme, or should it be a Federal-state measure providing different spheres of responsibility and activity for the Federal and the state governments? What are the main advantages of each form and its disadvantages? If a Federal-state measure, what should be the relative functions and powers of the two jurisdictions?

2. *Tax-offset or grant-in-aid?*

If a Federal-state system were desired, should the participation of the states be secured through a Federal tax on industries within the state, to be rebated or waived if the states lay an equivalent tax for unemployment insurance purposes, or should the Federal government collect the tax and then make grants-in-aid of lump sums to states which pass approved laws? What are the advantages and disadvantages of each of these methods?

3. *Employer tax alone, or employee contribution as well?*

Should the taxes levied include a tax on the wages of the workers, so as to put part of the load directly on them, or should it be non-contributory?

4. *Self-sustaining or assistance from general taxation?*

Should the employer tax or the joint taxes of employers and workers be put at a level which will completely meet the costs of unemployment insurance, or should there be a contribution from general taxation in order to broaden the incidence of the burden?

5. *Methods of handling surplus reserves of funds?*

If a Federal-state system of insurance is adopted, shall each of the states be (a) permitted to invest its own reserves as it sees fit, (b) be required to invest them in ways stipulated by a Federal agency, or (c) made to deposit them with a central Federal agency which will invest the funds in accordance with its own judgment? If the latter is decided upon, in what manner shall these reserves be handled by the Federal government?

6. *Degree of enforced standardization of the state plans?*

If a Federal-state system of insurance is desired, to what degree should national standards be imposed as a basis for receipt of tax-offset or grants-in-aid? Indicate, in principle, the extent of diversity to be permitted with regard to:

a. *Coverage* under the state acts (those who are to be included within the protection of unemployment insurance).

b. *Rates of contributions* from employers or workers.

c. *Benefits*, with special reference to possibilities that these may be so low as to fail to be of real assistance in avoiding destitution, or so liberal as to bankrupt the funds and make them unavailable for those who do not apply for benefits in the first few years of the plan.

d. *Eligibility* for benefits, from the standpoint of conditions and requisites imposed upon the workers which might lead to industrial strife or public dissension.

e. *Administration*, with reference to whether (a) enough funds are appropriated to make possible an efficient operation of the plans, and (b) enough care is taken, through appropriate measures, to assure impartial administration of insurance operations.

Questions:

1. Attempt to formulate a preliminary memorandum regarding the points in the agenda, listing the pros and cons but arriving at a tentative judgment in each case as to which course or alternative seems, on balance, to be desirable.

2. Compare your tentative views with the actual framework and terms of the Social Security Act passed in August, 1935.

3. Compare the general terms of the state laws approved by the Board with the tentative conclusions arrived at in answer to item 6, and indicate needed revisions, if any, in the Federal standards which the Act contained regarding such approvals.

PROBLEM 42. ISSUES IN DRAFTING A STATE PLAN OF UNEMPLOYMENT INSURANCE

Case A. Exemption of Employers Who "Guarantee" Employment

Several large and well-known concerns have petitioned a state unemployment insurance commission that they are willing to undertake a guarantee of employment to their workers for a definite period during each year, and that the state plan should exempt such employers from taxation required by the unemployment insurance measure. They call attention to the fact that in the first state act passed, that of Wisconsin, the employer who guaranteed forty-two weeks' work each year, at a stated rate of pay, could contract out of the plan.

Their proposal is that the law shall exempt plans of guaranteed employment in the case of concerns guaranteeing 55% of the employee's regular wage for fifty-two weeks a year. It is stipulated that financial guarantees shall be given by such concerns and that "guaranteed employment plans are to be permitted only when the guarantee applies to all employees of any company, plant or separate department (properly defined) of such company." These employers urge that such exemption will encourage the provision of steady employment to a larger proportion of the state's industrial population.

The exclusion of such concerns is entirely opposed by two members of the commission, who assert that it would undermine the insurance plan. One member has prepared a memorandum containing the following paragraphs.

> The concern which will undertake to guarantee employment is pretty certain to be either one which is favored by circumstances, such as a public utility, and which already may be working regu-

larly, or a concern which achieves the ability to guarantee employment by competitive methods at the expense of other concerns.

Obviously, if a concern introduces some invention or change of method which gives it an edge over competitors, or if it fills in during its slack season by producing work at cost, the regularity which it achieves for its employees is at the expense of irregularity for the rest of the industry. For that reason it should be contributing to the damage by paying its share to the unemployment insurance scheme created in order to aid in taking care of unemployment in the state as a whole.

Case B. Individual Company Reserves vs. Pooled Funds

In a state in which unemployment insurance legislation is being considered the members are at a deadlock over its basic principle. The efforts of two member employers have been directed towards having it provide what is known as individual company reserves, such as are provided by the Wisconsin law. Two other members desire instead a "pooled" plan, such as that adopted by New York.

The proposal in the present case is that every establishment in the state covered by the law is to be required to set up individual unemployment funds. From this fund a scale of unemployment compensation payments will be payable to the employees of that establishment. If the establishment's fund accumulates, in spite of benefit payments to workers, to a surplus amounting to 7½% of the annual payroll, the employer's contribution will be reduced, and there will be a progressive reduction in tax until the company's reserve amounts to 10% of the payroll, at which time the employer will be permitted to cease making further payments into the fund. All of these individual company funds will be held by a central state fund, but each company's reserve will remain the property of that particular employer, subject only to the liability for payment of unemployment benefits.

The advantage of this plan, it is urged, would be that of giving a very great incentive to each establishment to regularize its employment as far as possible, because such an achievement would enable an employer to pay a lower rate, or nothing at all, in employment taxation. The vice-president of a large manufacturing company argues this point before the commission as follows:

> The treasurer of a company, the guardian of the exchequer, has a keen eye for any cash outlay which can be avoided; thus, when the treasurer realizes that the cash leak of contributions to the reserve can be reduced or stopped by regularization of employment in his company's manufacturing department, he will be very insistent in his demands that the sales and manufacturing departments cooperate in stopping the leak. If an employer is able to regularize his employment 100%, he is then giving steady employment and has made effective the primary purpose of the law. Besides, it will pay a concern to finance such efforts.

The opponents of the individual company reserve principle quote among other authorities a report issued in 1934 by the New Hampshire Commission on Unemployment Reserves, in which it called attention to unemployment as a common risk and rejected the principle of individual company reserves. Its reasons included the following:

> The Wisconsin plan establishes thousands of individual company reserves, ranging from that of the small establishment with as few as ten employees to that of the plant with thousands on its payroll. It is like having fire insurance consisting of each household's own savings, or life insurance giving only what a person had himself contributed. The benefits available to an employee depend entirely on what has been accumulated as a reserve in the particular establishment with which he has been employed. If his firm has had bad luck the unemployment reserve available for his protection will also be in bad shape, thus intensifying the worker's misfortune.
>
> The risks of business are so great that a concern which feels itself extremely strong now may, a few years later, find itself in a serious condition. At that time it may not be able to take care of its employees within the terms of the established benefit scale. It would need some support from the premiums contributed by

other concerns participating in a plan having the insurance basis of at least a partial pooling of contributions.

The experience of Great Britain is enlightening on this point. When the insurance law was originally projected, the industries which, surprisingly, had a particularly low percentage of unemployment were coal mining, with 1.5%, textiles with 3% and boots and shoes with 3%. These industries wished to be excluded from the general unemployment act, and there was serious question as to whether their superior position from the standpoint of unemployment did not merit special schemes contracting them out of the general scheme. Yet these industries in a few years became among the most depressed of British trades and have ever since been a heavy drain on the unemployment funds.

Case C. Proposals regarding Pooling of Contributions

A commission which is studying the problem of unemployment insurance is considering the following two alternatives, (1) complete pooling of contributions, and (2) partial pooling. Under the complete pooling plan each employer would pay 3% of his payroll to a state fund from which employees entitled to benefits would receive unemployment compensation. Under the partial pooling plan the employers would merely begin by paying 3%, but after several years had elapsed, would be given a "merit rating" which would permit them to pay 2½%, 2%, 1½%, or even a minimum of 1%.

To institute this "merit rating" would require that a ledger account be kept for each employer, to show how much of his contributions had been used for payment of benefits to his employees, and how much remained as a surplus to his credit. The tax rate the employer would pay would then be based on the relation between this surplus and his annual payroll. If this surplus amounted to 15% of his payroll, he would pay only 1%, instead of 3% to the state fund; if it amounted to 12% or more, but less than 15%, he would pay 2½%. On this sliding scale, if his surplus was less than 8% of his payroll he would, however, pay the full 3%. No employer would pay less than 1%—the partial pooling feature.

A calculation made by the opponents of partial pooling shows that the lower rates some employers would pay, because of merit rating, would probably reduce the average contributions from employers to about 2%, instead of 3% as under complete pooling, and thus reduce the funds available for the payment of unemployment compensation. To overcome this loss, one group urges that "the range of contributions to be levied on employers should be increased to 4% or 5%, so that the *total* amount received from employers would *average* 3%." Some of the advocates of merit rating have not, however, accepted this proposal for fear it might involve too high a tax on employers.

Another group represented at the hearings opposed the principle of merit rating entirely, stating that no employer could do anything about unemployment. The opposite side has retorted by a long report on the possibilities of regularization. It sees advantages in a lessened tax in providing a direct incentive to employers to stabilize their operations.

Questions:

1. In the light of the discussions in the three cases, decide the features of a model state plan with regard to the points under consideration, and explain fully why you are opposed to the alternatives rejected.

2. In which respects does the unemployment compensation law established by your home state, or another with which you are familiar, and that of an adjoining state of either of these, differ with or conform to the standards you have favored? Comment on the reasons and advisability of such differences in the illustrative plans you have chosen.

PART FOUR: THE PERSONAL ENVIRONMENT

I. Supervision and Discipline

Problem 43. Relation of Employee Efficiency to the Capacity of Supervisors
44. Complaints regarding Actions of Minor Executives
45. Handling of Disciplinary Problems
46. The Place of "Paternalism" in Industry

See also:
Problem 24, Case A. Company Supervision over Leisure Time
Problem 25, Case F. Management Policy Following an Accident
Problem 31. Retaining the Middle-Aged Worker in Employment

II. Fellow Workers

Problem 47. Friction among Fellow Workers

See also:
Problem 54. Majority vs. Proportional Rule
Problem 60. Jurisdictional Claims and Disputes
Problem 62. The Closed Shop and the Check-off

III. Suggestions and Grievances

Problem 48. Eliciting Suggestions from Employees
49. Discovering and Adjusting Grievances

See also:
Problem 50. Membership and Business of Employee Representation Plans
Problem 63. Employee Discharges under Union Agreements

PART FOUR: THE PERSONAL ENVIRONMENT

I. Supervision and Discipline

Problem 43. Relation of Employee Efficiency to the Capacity of Supervisors
44. Complaints regarding Actions of Minor Executives
45. Handling of Disciplinary Problems
46. The Place of "Paternalism" in Industry

See also:
Problem 27, Case 4. Company Supervision over Leisure Time
Problem 37, Case 1. Management Policy Following an Accident
Problem 41. Retaining the Middle-Aged Worker in Employment

II. Fellow Workers

Problem 47. Friction among Fellow Workers

See also:
Problem [illegible]. [illegible] "Promotional Rate"
Problem 60. Jurisdictional Union Disputes
Problem 62. The Office Force and the Union

III. Suggestions and Grievances

Problem 48. Eliciting Suggestions from Employees
49. Discovering and Adjusting Grievances

See also:
Problem [illegible]. Membership and Functions of Employee Representation Plans
Problem [illegible]. Adjusting Grievances under Union Agreements

PROBLEM 43. RELATION OF EMPLOYEE EFFICIENCY TO THE CAPACITY OF SUPERVISORS

The home office of an insurance company employs several thousand clerical workers. Of these, approximately 1000, divided into twenty-two sections doing identical work, perform the routine of issuing policies, taking care of lapses, revising old policies, and providing for transfers of policies. Practically all of these 1000 employees are girls.

In 1933, this whole group had been under the uniform, consistent management of a high-grade executive for almost two decades. The informant asserts that every detail of the work had been completely studied to reduce unnecessary routine. Conditions had, so far as possible, been standardized, and production standards had been set. A continuous interest had been maintained in possibilities of improvement. The result was that the management had come to believe, apparently with good reason, that further gains in these twenty-two sections were to be sought, not in further systemization from the top, but in certain intangible personnel factors.

Early that year a new plan providing for group incentives to the twenty-two sections was inaugurated. Briefly, the plan was as follows: First, costs of the various sections for the previous twelve months were carefully computed. Each section was then offered a group bonus of 50% of the savings it could effect over the cost of that year as a base. All members of a section, including the supervisor, were to share in these savings monthly on the simple basis of salaries. Individual salary increases were to be given as heretofore, in accordance with established company policies, and were to be unrelated to and unaffected by the group bonus offer. Therefore employees had nothing to lose by the new plan, but could gain an additional increase in salary commensurate with their group showing. There was no competitive feature among the sections, the "bogey" being each section's own record for 1932.

At the end of 1933 every section had made some improvement. But there was a large spread in the results. The lowest saving was 2%, the highest 12%, and several were around a modal point of 8%. When these results were published, the unfavorable comparison for many sections naturally raised the question of whether a more uniform high improvement could be obtained. It caused much discussion.

Some supervisors whose sections had shown small reductions in costs took the position that they already had such a near-perfect condition of morale and efficiency that very slight improvement could be expected at best, and that therefore the higher bonus earned by some other departments was an unjust reward for past inefficiency. Another group of supervisors explained the disparity by pointing to differences in working conditions, or to an inherently poorer grade of employees. A supervisor would say: "Oh, yes, if I had Section X and its group I could have made just as good a showing or better. But Supervisor X should try a hand with the green hands and numbskulls in my department and we'd see how much of a bonus there would be!"

To meet these criticisms the general management of this division, early in 1934, shifted practically all the section heads to different sections, with the general aim of putting those who had been in charge of above-the-average bonus groups into those of less-than-the-average sections. The hope was to obtain a first demonstration as to whether differences in results were related primarily to differences in management or to differences in conditions. At the beginning of 1935 the range of progress was again compared.

In this second comparison the lowest saving was 6%, the highest 18%. The general plane of comparison had been raised. But the striking fact was that, in progress made, the order of the supervisors remained practically the same. The previous leaders were still the leaders; the laggards were still the laggards. Changes in relative order were limited to three cases of supervisors who had moved a step or two.

Allegations of supervisors not near the top continued as before, however, with assertions that the changes made had benefited some supervisors and handicapped others. The old complaint recurred, "If supervisor Y had my section, . . ." Hence, early in 1935 the management met the situation a third time by shifting, by lot, twenty of the twenty-two supervisors. Although they were thus reassigned by chance, the listing at the end of the year showed the surprising result that in progress made the same general order of supervisors again prevailed.

Further analysis revealed certain other significant facts. Thus, a weighted record of errors applied to 1935 and 1936 earning records showed perfect correlation between the standing of the accuracy record of the work under a supervisor and the standing on the earning record. This suggested that better quality as well as greater quantity was being obtained from the supervisors and groups earning the highest bonuses.

The records of these three years are now regarded by certain executives of the company as proof that the differences in the costs—and therefore in the efficiency—of these sections constitute differences in the level of executive leadership of the supervisors. The question therefore before them is how this conclusion may be used for the practical purposes of the concern.

Questions:

1. What characteristics of an employer or supervising executive play a significant part in the degree of cooperation and efficiency obtainable from workers? Illustrate by examples drawn if possible from personal experience or observation.

2. How may a concern faced with the situation here revealed put the knowledge gained to practical use in improving the supervision of the working groups?

PROBLEM 44. COMPLAINTS REGARDING ACTIONS OF MINOR EXECUTIVES

Case A. A Mean and Temperamental Section Head

One of the men working in the filing room of a clerical concern went into the assistant secretary's office in a mood of defiant exasperation to complain about the chief of his department. He said that his section head was always grouchy; that he issued contradictory orders; that he would tell his subordinates how to handle certain papers and later, when some issue arose that showed the papers had been handled wrongly or might have been handled differently, denied that he had authorized such procedure; that he was so difficult to deal with that it was impossible to cooperate with him; and that he would "bawl out" his subordinates even when they had acted in accordance with his instructions. The employee stated further that he was speaking for the other twelve men in the department as well as himself, and felt that something should be done about the situation.

Case B. Prejudices and Favoritism Shown by Foremen

1. In a mid-West flour company the majority of the foremen are native-born Americans, while most of the workers are foreign born. The former have developed an attitude that "this country should be kept for Americans," and they show this by limiting the foreign-born workers to lower positions. While a worker who is American born, Irish, or Canadian, is treated on a man-to-man basis, foreign-born workers of other lands may be shown disdain and made to feel inferior.

This attitude has made it harder for a Swedish worker, for example, to obtain promotion than for one who is American born. One complains that while he has been in the plant for fifteen years, a youngster with less than five years' experience has just been recommended for promotion. He asserts that unless a Swedish worker is especially good the American foreman will not recommend him for promotion.

While there is some question as to how much these grievances are justified, the fact remains that various workers at the plant are resentful of the company because of the impressions created by the foremen.

2. The boss weaver in a mill does all the hiring, discharging, and laying off in his department. Such lay-offs come usually during the sample season, which occurs twice a year and at which time only a few weavers are kept to run off the samples. The workers say (in private) that extreme favoritism is shown; that often the boss weaver keeps his friends and relatives at work and lays off men who have served the company longer. The management hears few of these complaints. Workers say that there are so many other weavers out of jobs and looking for work all the time that if they acted in a way which put them "in wrong" with the boss, they might not be taken back when work was available.

Case C. Wrong Handling of the Inefficient Worker

1. A girl employee was transferred from her regular operation to a new one which consisted of cutting two crosswise slits on the top of a very small round nut of about a quarter of an inch circumference. After a day the girl became adept at the job and was able to produce about 350 pieces an hour and after another day at the job, 400. But the required amount asked by her gang boss was 500, and she reported that she could not reach this requirement. The boss insisted that she could raise her production if she wanted to, and that she was holding back purposely because she wanted her old job back. Her name was reported to the foreman as being one of those who refused

to meet production requirements. The foreman called her down and told her what he thought of her.

The girl, being of a nervous nature, became upset and was unable to do anything for the rest of the day. After this occurrence her production decreased in quality and quantity. The other girls in the department spoke of her as an example of "what thanks the company gives to a good worker."

2. In a lens factory an employee of long service, Polish, forty years of age, an expert in his semi-skilled work, had an altercation with his foreman. It arose when the night shift was discontinued and he was transferred to the day shift to give him employment. It was a combination job, comprising two kinds of operations, grinding and polishing, with not enough of either task to occupy full time.

This man worked hard all day for several days, went home exhausted, and was so upset that he could not sleep. His quality was poor, although he is an expert at either operation. His wages went down. His foreman, himself unable to avoid criticism, called this man a rough epithet. The man's pride was touched, but he controlled himself and said, "Mister, I have a family, but I will never take that from you again."

He then reported his inability to do this work to the foreman's superintendent, said the foreman was hard to deal with, and asked a transfer, in the presence of his foreman. No satisfactory decision was given, because the department had been curtailing and other jobs were not available. He then told both men he was going to take the matter up with the personnel director. The foreman asked him not to. A few days later he did report the story to the personnel director, in tears as he did so, and begged a transfer, when in fact there was at the time no chance for a transfer.

Case D. **Foreman's Complaint of Impaired Authority**

In the tailor shop of a department store there is an Italian tailor who had trouble with his foreman, and quit. But he was such an unusually good worker that the factory manager brought him back to work. He had supposed that all the trouble would be over, but very soon Tony began to have arguments with his foreman again.

The workers soon learned the Italian's story, whereupon the manager went up in their esteem and the foreman lost prestige. The foreman wants to get Tony dismissed in order to show the men that it does not pay in the long run to flout his authority. He asks, "How can I keep discipline, maintain production, and preserve order if the manager gets tender-hearted and will not back me up?"

Questions:

1. What can be done to improve the capacities of minor executives and petty bosses in leadership and human relations with subordinates? Make a topical outline of the suggested program.

2. What should be done by the higher officials in cases when the issues put directly up to them may require ruling against a lower executive? Apply your answer to Case B.

3. What method or machinery for registering grievances against immediate superiors might be established which would effectively give managements a realization of conditions to be corrected? Illustrate by application to some of the cases presented.

PROBLEM 45. HANDLING OF DISCIPLINARY PROBLEMS

Case A. Carelessness and Costly Mistakes

1. A Polish worker in a metal plant has used the wrong size of iron wire in making up an order. There is no question as to who made the error. The work in the machine as well as the order tag were both evidence of it. His excuse is that he made a mistake in reading the gauge. But the result is that he has made a product for which there is no order or sale, and at the same time a customer has been put to great inconvenience.

He has been with the concern for nineteen years. He is forty-four years old, and has four children. His employment record is good, except that he occasionally gets careless and his poor work at those times has sometimes been costly. A year ago he had been reported for a similar difficulty over poor work.

2. Splicing cables in telephone company work is not a difficult or complex job, but occasionally faulty splices, called "splits" are made. The men are fined for this. Some workmen make almost no splits; others make them more frequently. A spokesman for a group which had made several splits pointed out that the orange and red wires looked somewhat alike in the dark of the manholes and that the error might be caused by a hurry job due to an emergency.

Case B. Inattention to Duty

Four workers employed at the end section of a large steel plant are caught playing cards during working hours. They had been known as good workers, and such a practice in the plant had not been observed within the three years that the present foreman had been in charge. This is distinctly against rules.

In another section a man is found sleeping on the job. This is his third offense for this. He has been with the firm a year and a half, and his work and record otherwise have been good.

Case C. **Employees Who Drink**

1. A worker who is a narrow gauge engineer in a metal plant comes to work one morning drunk. It is his first offense.

2. A power engineer was reported to be drinking during working hours. He has been with the concern seven years. He has a family to support. The superintendent reprimanded him, but made a note of it and two or three times within that month went by the boiler room with the secret intention of checking on this man's habits. To his surprise this last visit coincided exactly with the time when the man was taking a swig.

Case D. **Dishonesty and Questionable Practices**

1. An old and presumably loyal worker is seen secreting a small electric motor worth $22 under his coat. This is telephoned to the doorman, who stops him and, after an altercation, forces the man to admit he was taking it out. He gives a lame excuse, but it is obvious that he was stealing it.

2. In the press room of a factory a schedule of piece-work prices was posted two years ago. The management has suddenly discovered that the men have not been basing their time sheets on the rate schedule. Nearly every job has of late been listed on their sheets as one or two cents higher than the rates on the posted schedule.

The men maintain that verbal changes had been reported to them in regard to the rates. It appears that whenever a pressman changed his dies for a new operation, he would inquire of his neighbor what the rate was on the particular job. In this way a common scale had developed among the workers quite different from the authentic one of the management. The time sheets of the men had been looked over daily by the foreman of the department and then were turned in to the cost accounting and payroll divisions. Apparently this foreman aided the men by making his examination casual. For a year this error passed by unnoticed, when suddenly the management called to the workers' attention the fact that they had been paid for work on a false basis.

Case E. **Excessive Tardiness**

In an office which has grown to 350 employees, there are perhaps thirty employees daily who arrive too late in the morning to start work promptly at 9 A.M. A check-up made on different days showed that of those involved in tardiness about half arrived after 8:55 and before 9, requiring usually ten minutes or so to get adjusted, and that the rest arrived after 9 A.M.

The manager first notified the various section heads that this should be stopped. But each section head acted in accordance with his own ideas and practices, so that in some departments there was considerable severity and in others there were incidents impairing morale.

The company is now interested in establishing company-wide policies and methods which will maintain discipline without creating resentment.

Question:

In each case indicate what would seem the appropriate action to be taken, explaining the assumptions and principles upon which it is based.

PROBLEM 46. THE PLACE OF "PATERNALISM" IN INDUSTRY

Case A. "Intrusion" in Medical Matters

1. A company with many foreign-born employees has found that ill-health has been a persistent factor in the amount of absence, in listless work, and in labor turnover. Considerable attention has been given to matters of health in the plant, but much of this has been nullified by the home environment and traditions of the employees.

Two extreme examples are the following. Margaret L., one of the younger girls doing a skilled operation, had a slight attack of throat trouble and fever. The doctor advised a gargle and some medicine, and sent her home. When she had not returned after several days, an inquiry was made through fellow workers, and it was found that her mother, an illiterate Hungarian woman, had not allowed her to use the doctor's medicines. For her fever, she gave her some kerosene to drink, and for her throat she tied a herring around her neck. Because of this foolishness Margaret became worse and lost ten days from work instead of one or two.

The second instance is that of John T., a Bohemian boy who gashed his arm. On investigation it was found that his mother had insisted on her own pet remedy, a mixture of wet bread and onion and soap, to be applied to the fresh wound. It became infected, and this home treatment nearly cost John his arm.

The manager and the company doctor cite these cases to illustrate the range of misconception of health problems. They believe that the concern cannot secure maximum efficiency unless it counteracts the home environment of its own employees. They urge, among other steps, the employment of a nurse for home visiting work to teach new habits of living. The legal adviser of the company, who is also a large stockholder, is doubtful as to the wisdom of this step. He has heard a good deal of criticism of "welfare work" as being an unwarranted interference with the private life of the employee and as an autocratic intrusion into the home. His objections are temporarily holding up the plan.

2. A financial institution has newly established the practice that, when an employee has been out ill for two weeks or more, a physical examination is given before he is allowed to go back to work. It was intended chiefly to avoid epidemics of communicable diseases. But such examinations have exposed the need for dental work and for treatment for other easily remediable defects, and revealed heart trouble, progressive diabetes conditions, and similar serious ailments. The advice then given by physicians is often disregarded, whereas more drastic action would force the workers to consider measures that would prolong their lives. The company is considering how much authoritative pressure, even though disguised and sugar-coated, it should permit its medical director, who has raised the question. One executive is opposed to action which reaches beyond mere advice.

Case B. **Participation in Contributory Insurance**

A factory has established a contributory group insurance plan and is anxious to interest its employees in it. The plan is so liberal that it may be termed a gilt-edged proposition. It is also free from any "strings." It makes it possible for people to get insurance without a physical examination. The company has issued a brief leaflet clearly explaining the terms, but the response has been slight. The plan has been carefully prepared from an actuarial standpoint, and while the company pays a large part of the premium, the calculations have been based on having a very high proportion of the eligible employees participate in the scheme. If they should not do so, the plan would have to be changed. Without such a plan the concern would later be faced with the destitution of the families of employees who had not been wise enough to join the plan adopted in their interest.

Present indications are that if nothing more is done than the issuance of the explanatory leaflet, only a small proportion of those eligible will accept the provisions of the plan. This is because the younger men and women do not customarily give much thought to their future. They are more likely to be reluctant to make the present expenditures than to foresee the future need.

Case C. **Supervision over Personal Finances**

1. From time to time employees of a textile company get themselves involved in installment expenditures that seem burdensome and unwise. The company is made a party to it by the fact that if the employee is unable to meet his payments, an assignment of salary is sometimes forced by the creditor.

The kind of situation to be dealt with is illustrated by that of Jones, an employee, who on $22 a week is supporting a wife and three children. He has been induced to buy a second-hand car costing in all $400, on the installment plan, under a scheme of financing that would involve a regular deduction from his salary in behalf of the automobile agency.

There is a possibility that there might be a wage reduction in the plant which would reduce the employee's income. Aside from this, his supervisor and the employment manager feel that the employee is making a mistake in taking on the obligation. Jones, however, has been quite elated over the idea of having the car and has talked about it to all his friends. He will hate to back down after all this publicity. If the company does not sign the authorization, he is of course free to go to a small loan agency.

2. A concern has been maintaining a group insurance plan,

to which the employees also contribute, which gives the relatives of employees from $500 to $2500 on the death of the worker. One unlooked for result has been that various "funeral parlors" exploit the relatives during their extreme grief by inducing them to have elaborate funerals, or to buy expensive caskets, and thus to dissipate a disproportionate share of the funds which would otherwise go to the support of the dependents. The officials are considering what steps the company would be justified in taking to minimize such expenditures.

Case D. Outside Worries of the Employee

A gas company put in as its local branch manager in a suburban office, at a salary of $2500, a young man whose wife's tastes tend toward extravagance. The result is that he is always owing a large number of the merchants in town more money than he can pay. For the manager himself to have unpaid bills puts him at somewhat of a disadvantage in settling accounts of unpaid bills which local merchants owe to the company. The question before the concern is how far it is justified in reviewing the ways of living of this employee and advising him in family budget management.

Questions:

1. Present the pros and cons of having industry engage in the types of activities here considered.

2. What action should be taken in each of the concrete instances described? Suggest procedures by which the company involved would be least open to the charge of paternalism if it does decide to act in these cases.

PROBLEM 47. FRICTION AMONG FELLOW WORKERS

Case A. Office Workers vs. Factory Workers

The manager of a concern having about 200 office workers and about 900 factory employees has observed a certain aloofness in the relationship of the two groups. The employees in the office seem to regard themselves as a different class. They do not "mix" with the others in the factory, and they make the factory workers feel inferior. This is true not only of the girls but also of many of the men. It is noticeable particularly in the dining room and recreation hall, during lunch hour, when as a whole, office employees seem always to be in the company of one another, and the factory workers are likewise by themselves. The exclusiveness of the office employees arouses resentment among the factory employees and creates a poor plant morale.

Case B. Prejudice of Workers against Foreign Born

On a terminal grain elevator there are sixteen foreign-born workers and some thirty-five native-born. The foreign-born are all Lithuanians, who are either recent immigrants or still accustomed to speak among themselves in a foreign language and observe foreign ways. It happens that they are doing work which involves getting into the actual car of grain and guiding the automatic grain shovels which clean out the cars. The work is dusty and tends to make the men hot and dirty.

The company recently provided a welfare room in which the men eat the noon-day meals. It soon found out, however, that the two groups tended to form in opposite corners of the room, and, as a result, a latent feeling of animosity has exhibited itself. The native employees do not like the ways of the Lithuanians and complain of the smell of garlic, which is asserted to be a favorite seasoning used in their food. The foreign employees on their part speak their own language and always seem to separate themselves from the others.

One solution suggested is the installation of another welfare room. The chief problem here is how to do this without acknowledging that there really is any friction between the groups and that the management is trying to stop it. If the foreign employees really believe there is hard feeling against them, the act of putting them in a separate welfare room would probably intensify it.

Case C. **Prejudice on Racial Grounds**

A factory in southern Pennsylvania, with an office staff of eighty people, has always used white workers but has come to the conclusion that Negroes available in the community and elsewhere should be given an opportunity in the plant.

This conclusion has been reached several times before, but the factory was troubled with regard to possible friction arising from the following sources:

1. Resentment of the white employees against the company for introducing colored help.
2. Hostility of the white workers against the colored workers, showing itself in boycotts and non-cooperation.
3. Trouble that might arise from objections of white workers against the use of the same washroom facilities and lunchroom.
4. The probable prejudice of the clerical and technical workers in the laboratory against having Negro typists, stenographers, cost clerks, or technicians, leading to the loss of such white employees.
5. The complexity of the situation which may arise when some Negro may show unusual merit, making him eligible for appointment to a supervisory position over white employees who are adverse to working under him.

Nevertheless, the concern has decided to go ahead, if it can, with this plan of introducing Negroes into the plant. It wants to work out a careful procedure so that the friction will be at a minimum.

Case D. **Labor Union Contract Involving Discharge of Negro Craftsmen**

Various surveys have shown that Negroes are barred nationally from a few unions through written rule or well established practice, while in many other cases where unions have no national policies of this sort, a bar is put up by the local rule or practice of the local union. That such discrimination is not limited to any part of the country may be illustrated by the following complaint which appeared in the newspapers on October 18, 1936.

An electrical equipment company in New York had been employing twenty-five Negro electrical workers, for periods ranging up to ten years. In May, 1936, the company was forced to accept a closed shop contract with the local branch of the International Brotherhood of Electrical Workers, a union chartered by the A.F. of L. Under the contract the employer could hire only union members. He stated that he was anxious to continue the employment of the Negro workers, but he could not do so unless they were permitted to become members of the union. Since, however, they did not have union cards, he was forced to dismiss them all.

These Negroes charged that the reason for their inability to obtain union membership was the refusal of the union to admit one of their race. Furthermore, they asserted when they tried to make the best of it and sought employment in other plants, they had found that, in the process of unionization, these plants had been forced to drop them because they did not have union cards. They stated that while they were native Americans many of the white men who had replaced them were either foreign-born or aliens.

A few of these Negroes have employed an attorney to see what legal remedies are available. The executive director of the New York Urban League, an organization interested in the welfare of Negroes in the city, is considering the question as to whether they should start a legal action to compel the union to enroll the Negro employees whom the electrical equipment corporation was forced to let out when it signed the union contract.

See also:

Problem 62, Case H. A Tacit Closed Shop Affecting Negroes

Questions:

1. What are the general policies applicable to Cases A and B and the additional special measures to be attempted in each?

2. Outline in detail a plan and procedure likely to obtain the maximum acquiescence of the white workers in the change to be instituted in Case C.

3. If Negroes in Case D were in fact unable to obtain employment because of a closed shop contract with a union which did not admit workers of their race, what possible remedies could be effected through legal or other action taken in their behalf?

PROBLEM 48. ELICITING SUGGESTIONS FROM EMPLOYEES

Case A. A Written Suggestion System

A concern manufacturing stationery and paper novelties desires to install a suggestion system enabling its 800 employees to submit ideas of value to the business. It previously had a suggestion system in force which consisted of three big boxes in prominent places in the factory, signs that suggestions might be deposited, and the posting of notices on the bulletin board giving five prizes a month, ranging from $5 to $25. The plan had a little vogue at first, but soon fell into disuse.

A new manager desires that suggestions from employees be forthcoming more frequently and continuously. On investigating the difficulties in the way of the use of the suggestion system, he finds that one of the most general obstacles is the resentment of foremen and section heads when an employee suggests a desirable improvement which should have been thought of by the foremen themselves. Another obstacle found is the fact that many employees who have good ideas may not be able to express themselves clearly and do not have the facilities for submitting charts, graphs, or blueprints. One supervisor stated that he fears that a suggestion system may give occasion for friction arising because employees may have an exaggerated or distorted picture of the usefulness of their suggestions, and when these are not adopted, may feel that the firm is backward, unappreciative, or unfair.

Case B. Soliciting Oral Suggestions

A laundry has been taken over by three new owners. Seventy people are employed, the large majority being women.

The management desires to find out from the workers more efficient ways of doing work, and whether these workers are in any way dissatisfied with the way they are being treated.

In accordance with a plan adopted, each worker has been called into the office alone and quizzed by the managers and the owners of the plant. This has been done at those times when the management found itself free. The interview was conducted along informal lines. The worker was informed of the purpose of the questioning and was asked to be frank and specific in his replies. The management asked questions relating to scheduling, routing, quality of the work, difficulties that were had with the machines or equipment, such as the irons, criticisms of the raw materials used, such as starch, soap, or bluing, and whether or not the workers had difficulty in doing clothes made up of different kinds of goods.

During these interviews most workers seemed bashful and reticent in answering the questions. They replied as briefly as they could, and by "yes" or "no." The management found they could not make the workers talk on any trouble being experienced in their work. Most of the workers said that they hadn't thought of any trouble that they had in the plant. As a whole, according to the management, the procedure was a failure from the standpoint of eliciting worth-while aid from the employees. The owners are not discouraged, however, as they believe that the fault is probably their own.

Questions:

1. Outline the human and organizational factors explaining the difficulties encountered in obtaining suggestions from employees by the methods used in these cases.

2. Present the essentials of a plan for obtaining suggestions which should be successful in most concerns, with special attention to phases of its administration which are important in its success.

PROBLEM 49. DISCOVERING AND ADJUSTING GRIEVANCES

Case A. Effectiveness of Manager's Open-Door Policy

1. The New York office of a surety company of 140 clerical workers is under the charge of a treasurer who is general office manager. He states that the door of his office is open to any employee who has a grievance. He offers as proof of the fine treatment afforded that not more than one or two employees ever complain to him in a year. He is certain that his concern has good morale and he regards the open door policy as successful.

2. The executives of a manufacturing company employing 420 people state that they have always encouraged open discussion of grievances by their employees, on the theory that there will be practically no labor friction as long as everything is open and aboveboard. The company finds, however, that the men do not avail themselves of this privilege as fully as they should. In some cases, more frequently among the foreign born, men leave without giving the concern an opportunity for such discussion or without even giving a reason. A worker sometimes suddenly throws down his tools and quits, for no cause whatsoever as far as the superintendent or the foreman knows. He regards the open-door policy as unsuccessful.

Case B. Functions of an Employment Manager

A food products company which had a great deal of friction with employees finally found the solution, it is stated, in the appointment of one of its chemists as employment manager. The latter has given up chemical work and has developed the confidence of the workers to the point that anyone entering his office, which is conveniently located and always open, may feel sure of friendly reception and fair advice. If the employee's cause seems right to the employment manager, the latter will "go to the mat" for him even to the point of taking his defense against other executives, and it is also stated that if the employee is wrong, the discussion can be frank with no after effect or prejudice. A visitor to the office gets the impression that employees feel at ease with the employment manager and that they are inclined to bring their grievances to him.

Case C. An Open Survey of Employees' Views

An electric company appointed five interviewers from the supervisory group to approach employees and ask them to express their comments relative to the things they like and the things they dislike in their working environment. Women were selected to interview women and men to interview men. The interviewers were instructed not to interview employees whom they knew, since acquaintanceship might influence the comments. The whole procedure was aboveboard, and the employee was given absolute freedom to express himself frankly.

If the employee's place of work afforded a chance for confidential conversation, the interviewer talked with him there; if not, they moved to an appropriate location. The interviewer explained the program to the employee in some detail and asked him if he cared to express his views. As the latter talked, the interviewer made rather complete notes or took his comments verbatim, depending upon the speed with which the employee formulated and expressed his thoughts. If the employee evidenced a willingness to talk, but was at a loss for something to say, the interviewer encouraged him with questions. The employee was assured that his name would not appear in any record of the interview, and that it would be summarized along with other reports for general company use.

Case D. Secret "Information Representatives"

1. The management of a textile company has a system in operation designed to keep it constantly informed on how the

workers feel about conditions in the plant. The company has "information representatives" recruited from among the workmen, who have been in the plant for some time. They are located conveniently throughout the company and, for a secret addition to their pay, obtain information that is desired concerning the reactions of the 1800 male employees. These agents associate with the workers, whose grievances, thus freely expressed and secretly communicated, give the concern suggestions for improving conditions and removing cause for complaint.

2. A concern is considering the employment of men from an agency, called the Smith Industrial Service, to keep it informed of chronic troublemakers and radical agitators. The men hired are private detectives who apply for work to the personnel department in the same manner as other employees. They associate with the other workers and often go to their parties. The management is kept in touch with labor conditions. This, the Smith Service says, allows the company to correct unsatisfactory conditions before they cause much trouble.

Questions:

1. Analyze the possibilities and the limitations of obtaining knowledge of the grievances and desires of employees through each of the methods indicated, pointing out the special difficulties or dangers which these may involve.

2. Propose principles and methods for adjusting grievances which would appear to have few, if any, of the defects noted above, and indicate with some detail how your suggestions would be applied.

PART FIVE: GROUP RELATIONS, UNIONS, AND LABOR LAW

I. Employee Representation and Company Unions

II. Establishment of Relations with Unions

III. Unfair Tactics in Organization Campaigns

IV. Structure of Unions

V. Phases of Operation of Collective Contracts

(Continued on next page)

PROBLEM 50. MEMBERSHIP AND BUSINESS OF EMPLOYEE REPRESENTATION PLANS

Case A. Who Should Participate in Voting

Should executives be included in an employee representation plan? An industrial relations manager of a public utility asks for guidance concerning a decision which the concern needs to make. He states:

Two years ago when the employee representation plan was written, it was prepared in two sections, the first being a constitution prepared by the employees themselves. Under Article V., "Qualification of Voter" the plan states that any regular employee of the company shall be entitled to vote.

In the agreement between the company and the employee council in which a special committee of the management shared, it was stipulated among other things that there should be "regular joint monthly conferences of the Employee Council Conference Committee and not more than an equal number of appointed management representatives for the presentation, discussion, and settlement of matters coming within the scope of the employee representation plan." It was also stipulated that "there should be regular joint conferences of the departmental councils with the respective department heads."

We made a point of not interfering with the plan as prepared by the employees themselves. When the final copy of this plan was presented to us we objected to Article V. It was not changed and therefore we privately informed those individuals whom we considered to be management that we did not believe they should participate in the employee representation plan. Most of us thought that to keep the two sides apart was to emphasize class conflict, but we felt that if we did have management in the voting it would give a basis for saying it wasn't an employee plan.

It is now time for another election and the election committee of the council has distributed ballots to everyone in the company, except the President, with the information that they may vote and nominate any regular employee, except the President, to the council. Should we again refuse to participate? What do you believe we should do under the circumstances?

Case B. A Joint Council Which Is Seeking Business

A textile concern of 2000 employees, chiefly women, encouraged the formation of an employee council to discuss with the management various matters of joint interest. There had never been any form of representation in the plant before, or any known interest in a union. The employer's reason for attempting an employees' council in this case, was, in the main, to supply a form of communication which would provide some substitute for collective bargaining.

Meetings of the council have been held from time to time at which various matters of interest to all concerned were discussed. Among these are the following: payment by cash instead of by check; reestablishment of an employees' savings association which had previously lapsed; decision whether the hours of work were to be from 8 to 4:30 with a half-hour lunch period, or 8 to 5 with an hour; handling of the Community Fund drive; provision for better lighting, resulting in the putting of individual lights on many of the machines; and minor matters of safety and sanitation and convenience.

The employment manager now states: "We seem to have arrived at a point where there is not much to discuss. This worries me, for an organization must be active or all interest dies. I asked our time-study man to talk at a meeting at which I knew there was not much business to come up, and explain what that department is working on. We have been discussing the matter among ourselves, considering subjects we could profitably take up with them. I wonder what we ought to do now."

Case C. A Representation Plan Which "Didn't Register"

A concern making small electrical specialties employs about 1500 men and women. Relationships with workers seemed cordial but, in accordance with what it regarded as the trend of the times, the company organized an employee representation plan. The management never had any serious intention, however, of bargaining with the employee committee concerning hours and wages. It made a show of presenting such issues to the employee representatives, and was able with a little manoeuvering to get its decisions accepted by the workers.

This lasted for over a year and a half. The company was quite satisfied with the plan until, at the beginning of the seasonal production in 1937, a wage issue precipitated a strike which threatened to stop production in mid-season. The company sensed the situation quickly, however, and in two days made terms, thus relegating the affair to a merely temporary misunderstanding. The manager writes frankly:

> As I now look back on what happened, I can see that while we could talk the representatives into accepting anything we really wanted, they could not get the workers to accept it. The plan didn't register, in fact, it seemed a demonstration of the futility of employee representation and possibly was itself a source of discontent. I am convinced that wages and hours must be dealt with through the employee plan if it is to satisfy the workers.

Questions:

1. What should the concern in Case A decide about the basis of membership in its plan of employee representation?

2. Reply to the employment manager in Case B, diagnosing possible causes of the situation he describes and offering suggestions of subjects and procedure which you regard as within the scope of an employee representation plan.

3. What counsel might be given to the manager of the plant in Case C?

PROBLEM 51. DEGREE TO WHICH EMPLOYER MAY FAVOR COMPANY UNIONS

Union officials have asserted it to be unfair for the employer to show interest in competing organizations which may exist in a plant, or to engage in various activities which seem to show definite preference for a company union against an outside union. The following cases illustrate the nature of controversies which have come before government authorities.

Case A. Profit Sharing and Benefit Plans Dependent upon Non-Union Representation Plan

1. A union attempted to organize a collective bargaining plan in a large soap company. When the situation developed, the employer assembled the employees and pointed out to them that the company's various forms of employee benefits, such as its profit-sharing plan, its guarantee of continuous employment, accident and sickness compensation, as well as its conference committee plan, were all essential parts of a unified system of industrial relations, no part of which could be abandoned without discontinuing other parts; and that the entire system was predicated upon definite policies of, and had to be administered by, the company.

The union charges that this is intimidation, and desires a government board to order the employer to notify its employees that participation, either in the company union or in the labor union, is not a term or condition of their employment or of the continuance by the company of any of its various plans for their benefit.

2. A union was formed in a dry goods company. Within a few days, however, the insurance department of the company

announced that the group insurance for terms of one year, which the company had formerly taken for its employees, paying half the premium cost, would be available after the next renewal date a month later, through "an organization now being formed to be known as the E. & W. Employee and Management League." The chairman of the board of directors wrote the employees "personally," pointing out the features of the plan and expressing the hope that "we may see enrolled on the membership list . . . the name of every employee in our organization."

All the expenses of the League are defrayed by the company. Membership is open "to all employees and officers of the company who shall elect to accept the benefits and duties of a member." Continued membership in the League is subject to the condition that it be used "as the sole and only means of representation in effecting collective bargaining."

Case B. **Employer's Contributions to Services or Expenses of Non-Union Organizations**

1. A bronze company has an employee association which is presumably an independent organization of the employees opposed to the labor union group in the plant. Recently the association held a picnic for its members, which was paid for by the company, along with the cost of the printer's notice regarding it. The labor union demands that such favoritism shall cease and has applied to a government board that an order be given to the company prohibiting such subsidies in the future.

2. The forty-eight employees of a committee of a large plant meet regularly for an hour or two every two weeks. During such time all the representatives get regular pay for the full time of the meeting. The union demands that either their representatives be given similar amounts of time at company pay or that the company desist from paying the employees of the other plan for the time they spend in meetings.

Case C. **Employer's Assistance to Non-Union Employee Representatives**

In a company in which the employees have, by free election, indicated a large majority in favor of the employee representation plan as compared with the union, the employer has observed that many of the workers, being unused to self-organization, are not getting the maximum value of their representation plan. With this in mind, the employment manager has advised the persons chosen, aiding them in making up a manual for representatives and showing them how to handle their jobs to the best interest of their constituents. For instance, this manual indicates what is the desirable procedure in case some constituent complains of an unjust act by a foreman. In other ways, also, the personnel manager has been actively assisting the employee representatives to make a success of their jobs, and has also helped in the preparation of material which will make employees better acquainted with their rights under the plan and more inclined to use it.

The union, which has been trying to obtain adherence of these employees, has charged that this is undue interference with employees' self-organization and wants the employer to be made to desist from such practices.

Questions:

1. Which of these practices, if any, constitute unjustifiable exercise of the employer's power? If any are so considered, formulate principles which might be used as a basis for forbidding the employer to show his preference for particular types of organizations against others.

2. What laws of Federal or state governments in operation in recent years have attempted such curbs? In your answer comment fully on the advisability and adequacy of the legislation or of its administration.

PROBLEM 52. WHAT CONSTITUTES "RECOGNITION" AND COLLECTIVE BARGAINING?

There have been many strikes on the issue of "recognition" of the union in which the employer has asserted that according to his ideas he has "recognized" it, while the union has asserted that his actions did not amount to "recognition" at all. The public has at times been confused over these opposing contentions. Mediating and arbitrating agencies have had similar difficulty. The kinds of situations are illustrated in the following accounts of disputes on this issue.

Case A. Denial of Representation by Outsiders

A woolen mill has had a request from a committee of five, representing the workers but containing two members who are not employed at the plant, for a meeting at which to discuss a contract. The committee was informed by the management that it would meet with an employee committee but not with any representative of the employees who was not an employee of the mill.

Case B. Dealing with Union but Not by Name

In an automobile strike one of the concerns stated: "We are willing upon proof of the authority of any employee organization to negotiate for specified persons in our employ to meet with their representatives, whether in our employ or not, and to discuss questions of hours of employment and wages. We are not, however, willing to recognize these representatives as constituting a union, and we will deal with their representatives only as representing the workers in our employ who selected them, not as representatives of their union." The union, in turn, said that this was a denial of recognition and that the strike would continue until recognition as a union was granted.

Case C. Do Conferences with Union Representatives Constitute Collective Bargaining?

A hosiery mill's attitude towards a union committee is expressed as follows: "We will meet with the employees or their representatives at any time, on any subject of their own choosing; if they want to bargain some more, we will talk to them; we have agreed to some of the union's demands but not to all; from time to time in the future, if anything comes up that we can agree to, we will be glad to do it."

The union agent says that this has been a dodge for several months. Always the committee was received and talked with. However, "always some obstacle arose which made it impossible to get anywhere." The employment manager would say he would have to consult the general manager. The general manager would either be out of town, or would have to write to the president in New York, or would make some counter proposal which would deflect the point. The employer said he was engaging in collective bargaining, but the union asserts that it finds itself, at the end of several months, "just about where it started."

Case D. Do Protracted Negotiations Constitute Collective Bargaining?

A small auto company and a local of the machinists' union have been negotiating an agreement. The union would submit one proposal, and the employer would counter with another proposal. According to the union, negotiations on this basis might be dragged out indefinitely and actual collective bargaining agreements be a mirage. All that the employer need do is to propose terms making an agreement impossible.

The employer contends that he has a right to make any kind of counter proposal he desires, since "the normal process of bargaining often starts from something you did not expect to get, even though it is absurd, in order to win a point that might otherwise not be granted." He maintains that he is negotiating in good faith.

Case E. Employer's Memorandum of Conference Held with Union Representatives

A paper mill regards the union agents as persons to consult with when it makes its own decisions on matters affecting the workers. It has issued a memorandum outlining working conditions throughout the mill, in which the following paragraphs indicate the procedure followed.

> The above memoranda of working conditions were arrived at through conferences with committees and officers of the Papermakers Union and affiliated organizations and other A.F. of L. organizations represented in the mill. The company, through its foremen, superintendents, managers, and officials, will be glad at any time to meet with individuals or committees of its employees or representatives of the above organizations to consider any grievances that may arise.
>
> Believing that earnest employees are often aware of improvements that could be made in manufacturing conditions, the management will be glad to receive suggestions of changes that might be of mutual advantage.

The union says that recognition means collective bargaining and that this is not collective bargaining but arbitrary condescension; and that only a mutual agreement definitely establishes such collective bargaining.

Case F. Do Oral Agreements Constitute Collective Bargaining?

A chemical company has at all times received a committee from a union, listened to their demands and, where they seemed reasonable, assented to their requests. The union has gone further and asked that the employer sign an agreement so that all these understandings would not be on a purely oral basis and also that there should be some definite period of time during which the agreement shall be considered to hold.

The union maintains that if an employer assents to proposals concerning wages, hours, and a variety of working conditions involving detailed provision, the agreement, unless reduced to writing, will be impractical of enforcement and fruitful of disputes. The insistence of an employer that he will go no further than to enter into an oral agreement is asserted to be really a denial of collective bargaining.

Case G. Does Recognition Imply Bargaining Regarding Wages and Hours?

A dispute arose between a union organized in a harvester plant and the management over a question as to whether its employee council, which had already been in force for about a decade, constituted collective bargaining. A report on the activities of the council for the previous year, as shown by the minutes of the meetings, was used as an illustration by the union to show that the council dealt only with minor aspects of working conditions in and around the plant. The union showed that in each of the twelve meetings there was a discussion of such matters as safety, athletics, loans to workers, vacations, solicitation for the community chest, grievances against foremen, traffic conditions near the plant, explanation of the Social Security Act, addresses by different officers on the functions of the various departments, an address by the chief metallurgist on the manufacture of steel, and among other things, the reading of a poem by Edgar A. Guest.

The union asserted that in the matter of wages there had been practically no discussion, wages having been decreased or increased by the management with or without explanation to the council. In only one instance, according to the union, was there anything resembling wage bargaining, and this occurred when an employee representative requested a 15% wage increase, and the employer, after some discussion, offered a 5%

wage increase, which was accepted. On the matter of hours, when the Automobile Chamber of Commerce recommended that hours be reduced from forty to thirty-six, the employer discussed in the council the manner of putting this into effect, treating the reduction as an accomplished fact.

The union has therefore asked a government board arbitrating the issue to rule that any such plan which does not give an opportunity for independent negotiation and bargaining with regard to wages and hours should not be considered as collective bargaining.

Case H. **Does "Recognition" Imply Exclusive Contract?**

A union in a plant employing 1000 workers stated that it represented 600 employees and desired to enter into an agreement concerning wages, hours, and working conditions. The company stated that the union was exaggerating its membership and probably had only about half that number, but that as far as it was concerned it did not make any difference. It maintained that a written agreement was unnecessary, since it had already posted a statement of its labor policy on its bulletin board, and had stated that it would continue to deal with the union, with individuals, and with other groups of employees. In protest against this attitude, the members of the union voted to strike, stating that this did not constitute recognition of collective bargaining.

Questions:

1. Define in clear terms the conditions which may be regarded as constituting "recognition of the union" and collective bargaining. (The answer does not involve consideration of whether such "recognition" or collective bargaining is desirable or not, but merely provides a standard to show what in a given case has, in fact, been denied or granted, as an aid to understanding the issues involved in the controversy.)

2. Apply your definition to the given cases.

PROBLEM 53. ASCERTAINING WORKERS' CHOICE OF ORGANIZATIONS

Case A. Selection of Company Plan through Open Petition

A letter sent to the employees of a company stated that some workmen had proposed having a committee of fellow employees bargain for them and that a simple way of doing it would be for those who desired this particular plan to sign a petition to that effect, and then to vote secretly by departments for representatives who would serve for a period of one year. This board of representatives was later called the Employees' Council.

The power in the plant was then turned off, the workmen given prepared petitions to sign, and 571 out of 693 employees signed for the company's plan within three hours. Election of representatives immediately followed. After that, work was resumed.

A union which has been trying to organize the employees asserts that this method was a repressive procedure, since "the employees took what was offered, and without a reasonable opportunity to talk it over outside the plant. Those who accepted it were known to the company, and those who did not could be easily ascertained by reference to the payroll."

Case B. Elements of a Proper Election Procedure

In a company manufacturing farm implements the president was anxious to forestall a union organization. One morning the power in the plant was shut off, and every workman was required by his foreman and superintendent to attend a meeting. The president of the company addressed the men for an hour. He stated that organized labor unions were of very little value to workers and extolled the advantages to be obtained from company unions. He concluded his remarks by stating that he might shut the plant down or move it away.

He then conducted a ballot as to whether or not the employees desired a representation plan; and a company official counted the ballots, stating that over three-fourths of the men had approved the plan. The day after this balloting, each employee of the company found in his time card slot a printed constitution of the company union.

Later that day the power was again shut off in the various departments, and the men, without prior notice, were again asked by their foremen to attend a meeting where they were instructed to vote for the purpose of nominating candidates to represent them under the company union plan. In one department, the men, after arrival at the meeting place and being told the purpose of their presence, refused to vote and returned to their work. The power was shut off in their department and they were forced back to the meeting place to vote.

On the next day the power was again shut off throughout the plant, and all the men were forced to select from those nominated on the preceding day the ones whom they desired as their representatives. The marked ballots were deposited in a ballot box and the men checked off by a company official against a payroll list as they left the ballot. A notice was then posted stating that 80% of the men had approved the plan. The company testified that the tabulation of the ballots was made by an outside accountant employed for the purpose.

The union contends that no such procedure of election should have any validity since it lends itself to possible abuses. It desires a new election either under joint auspices or a government board.

Case C. **Failure to Mention Alternative Organizations**

In a rubber company an employee organization was started at the instance of several employees who went to the management and asked their advice as to what the terms of such plans were. Two days later the employment manager handed the chairman of the committee a complete draft of what, in his opinion, a desirable plan was. The plan was then put to a vote of the employees. The ballot conducted by this employees' association did not contain any alternative organization, but merely the question as to whether or not they favored this plan. A majority of the employees favored it.

The union contends that no election is valid that does not provide for names of alternative organizations which may be in the field. The company not only denies the validity of the position of the union but states that in any event there is no basis for considering the subject until the term of these representatives expires, eleven months later. The union says that the employee organization was just a trick to delay their collective bargaining and discourage their union following.

It asks that immediate elections be held to determine the basic question whether the employees would have preferred a union to the sole plan proposed.

Case D. A Complicated Task for an Arbitrator

Maritime unions in the San Francisco Bay area are attempting to conclude a collective agreement that would involve all of the seafaring men whose ships call in that district. It is not known exactly how many companies would be concerned, but the number is believed to be several score.

Some of the local shipping companies are opposing the contract in a statement which includes the following:

> The shipping companies are willing to meet their employees for the purpose of collective bargaining, but they do insist that they must deal with representatives chosen by their employees and not merely with unions who claim to be such representatives and yet who will not or cannot present credentials.

There is a conflict between the unions themselves as to who represents the men. For instance, both of the following unions have been claiming to represent the licensed deck officers: (1) Masters, Mates and Pilots Association; (2) United Licensed Officers Association. Each of the following unions claim to represent the licensed engineers: (1) Marine Engineers Beneficial Association; (2) United Licensed Officers Association. Each of the following claim to represent the unlicensed personnel: (1) International Seamen's Union; (2) Marine Workers Industrial Union.

The first and essential step is for the unions to show their credentials. The steamship companies will cooperate in the elections necessary to establish the facts of representation, but their employees cannot be deprived of the right of freely selecting whom they desire to represent them.

The union, which has called a strike, asserts that such elections could not be held because many boats will not return to shore for weeks or months, and that the offer of shipowners to hold "free and untrammelled" elections on vessels on the seven seas would mean that the preponderance of influence would pass to the steamship captains and owners in determining the result of elections.

Questions:

1. What procedures may be considered adequate to determine the workers' choice of organizations in a disputed case?

2. What procedures have been used in such cases by government boards under recent or existing legislation?

3. What would be a method helpful in settling the issues of representation in Case D?

PROBLEM 54. MAJORITY VS. PROPORTIONAL RULE

The question of what to do when neither a union nor an employee representation plan has a large enough following among the workers to justify its representing them all, or when the employer refuses to accept a particular group as the exclusive bargaining agency, has caused endless difficulties in labor relations. The kinds of cases which have arisen under Federal administration of labor relations are illustrated below.

Case A. Feasibility of Competing Employee Associations

For several years prior to the advent of a union in a company manufacturing automobile parts, athletic events among the men had been promoted by a loose-knit association which consisted simply of a treasurer and a chairman in charge of athletics. When the union started, the association was given the name of the Welfare and Athletic Association and a definite structure and form, with members, officers, and a grievance committee for the purpose of negotiating with the company.

Shortly after the Association had been reshaped, a request of the union representatives for recognition was denied, while at about the same time a wage increase sponsored by the Association was granted by the company to all employees. Later another general wage increase was granted to the employees as a result of requests by the Association. The company thereafter refused to treat with the union representatives unless they would disclose the union membership list.

Ultimately, after hearings on the complaint of the union before a government labor board, an election was ordered to be held in the plant. The election resulted in 1105 ballots for the union and 647 for the Association, with about 400 not voting.

Thus the union was established beyond question as representing the majority, not merely of those voting, but of all the employees.

Since the election, the company's practice has been to meet every week or two on Saturday mornings, first with the Association's committee and then with the union committee, or vice versa. One thing of general importance, however, was not discussed with the union committee. There had been previously some talk of group insurance. The proposal was now taken up by the company with the Association's committee. Nearly all of the employees agreed to take the insurance, and the Association received credit for its part in making the insurance available.

The union brought the case before a government board which, on studying the situation, made the following observations:

> In the first place, the company's policy inevitably produced a certain amount of rivalry, suspicion, and friction between the leaders of the committees.
>
> Secondly, the company's policy, by enabling it to favor one organization at the expense of the other, and thus to check at will the growth of either organization, was calculated to confuse the employees, to make them uncertain which organization they should from time to time adhere to, and to maintain a permanent and artificial division in the ranks.
>
> At the hearing the company suggested that it might bargain collectively and enter into a collective agreement with a composite committee made up of representatives of the union and the Association, in proportions corresponding to the votes cast in the election.
>
> In the end whatever collective agreement might be reached would have to be satisfactory to the majority within the committee. Hence the majority representatives would still control, and the only difference between this and the traditional method of bargaining with the majority alone would be that the suggestions of the minority would be advanced in the presence of the majority. The

employer would ordinarily gain nothing from this arrangement if the two groups were united, and if they were not united he would gain only what he has no right to ask for, namely, dissension and rivalry within the ranks of the collective bargaining agency.

We have concluded, therefore, that the representatives of the majority should constitute the exclusive agency for collective bargaining with the employer.

The National Association of Manufacturers, in advising employers to oppose the principle of majority rule, contended:

This prohibits any minority group of workers from making mutually satisfactory wage and working agreements with employers. Employers should negotiate with authorized representatives of any groups of their employees. Many individual workers prefer to negotiate directly with their employers regarding their own employment conditions, and their wishes must be respected. This is particularly important since over 75% of all employers employ not over twenty workers each.

Case B. **Pluralities and Proportional Representation**

In a plant of 600 workers an election was held to determine which of the competing groups was entitled to represent the workers. The result was as follows: 140 voted for a local branch of a national union connected with the A.F. of L.; 120 voted for a competing radical, perhaps a Communist, union hostile to the A.F. of L. union; 160 voted for the employee representation plan which the employer had tacitly favored. The rest of the votes were either scattered, ruled out or, in a great majority of cases, blank. The question arises as to what form of representation to work out in this concern.

A counsel for the employer maintains that the only consistent principle is proportional representation because it is not always certain that a majority of workers will favor any particular form of organization. The way in which collective bargaining could be conducted in any such situation, he stated, is by representatives elected by the employees irrespective of affiliation, and given power in accordance with their individual constituencies.

He thereupon argues that the principle which should be made prevalent in all plants is representation irrespective of affiliation, and that if there happen to be competing groups which do not have a majority, they should learn to "live with each other." He maintains that whether a group has a majority or a minority, it should be willing to accept power in the degree of its strength and ask for no more. He therefore urges a consistent principle of proportional representation.

Case C. An Election in Which a Minority Voted

A serious strike in an electrical products plant ended in an arrangement for an election to determine whether the United Electrical and Radio Workers or a rival plant organization known as the Employees' Committee was to represent the employees. Nevertheless, at the appointed time, circulars and radio broadcasts originating with the Employees' Committee warned that the forthcoming election would mean "rioting, street fighting and general disorder" and discouraged participation in the rioting.

The result of the balloting was that of 9752 employees eligible to vote, only 3163 ballots were cast, of which over 3000 were for the United Electrical and Radio Workers. Certification of the union for collective bargaining was, however, objected to by the company on the ground that the union had failed to secure the affirmative votes of a majority of the eligible voters.

The discussion brought out that the selection of representatives "by a majority of the employees" is susceptible to three interpretations: (1) an affirmative majority of those eligible; (2) the victor in an election where at least a majority participated; (3) a majority of the eligible employees voting. The company urged that the first interpretation was the most logical one.

The union argued that certification was proper to the group casting a majority vote in any election on the ground that "those not voting are presumed to acquiesce in the choice of the majority who do vote." It asserted that if majority rule does not mean majority in an open election, "minority organizations merely by peacefully refraining from voting could prevent certification of organizations which they could not defeat in an election. Even where their strength was insufficient to make a peaceful boycott effective, such minority organizations by waging a campaign of terrorism and intimidation could keep enough employees from participating to thwart certification. Employers could adopt a similar strategy and thereby deprive their employees of representation for collective bargaining."

Case D. **The "Appropriate Unit" for Majority Rule**

1. A company running a small line of vessels employs sixteen deck officers engaged in the navigation of the boats and sixteen licensed engineers engaged in the maintenance of the mechanical equipment of the boats. An organization known as the United Licensed Officers entered into a collective agreement with the company for the thirty-two licensed engineers and licensed deck officers, on the ground that they were all the higher licensed personnel.

An organization known as the Marine Engineers Beneficial Association thereupon filed a petition before a government board that most of the engineers were actually members of its organization and that the sixteen engineers should be regarded as an "appropriate unit" for collective bargaining, separate from the deck officers. The Association contended that marine engineers form a homogeneous group, quite distinct in their training, required qualifications, responsibilities, duties, and interests from licensed officers, and that traditionally they have always been members of and bargained through their own separate organizations.

2. In a tobacco plant of 1000 employees, the tobacco workers constitute the mass of the employees. About a score of machine adjusters are also employed. When a union campaign

of tobacco workers won them the right to an employee election certifying who should represent the workers in collective bargaining, the machinists petitioned the government board arbitrating the dispute that the machine adjusters, most of whom were its members, should not be included among those expected to participate in the voting. Instead, it was urged that the board designate as the "appropriate unit" for the election all employees not engaged in machine adjusting, and that it recognize the small group of machine adjusters as another "appropriate unit," and let the machinists' union represent it.

Case E. **Objection to Granting Majority Rule to Communists**

In a fur dressing company there were two rival unions, one of which, led by radical leaders, was obtaining the most support from the workers. It finally became evident that in any election these radical union members were in the majority. This union insisted upon having such an election so that it would bargain for the whole group. When the issue came before a government board, the employer pointed out that the group was definitely Communist and led by Communist leaders. He said that any rule which would force him to deal with a Communist union was wrong and that he ought to have the choice of opposing any group which was bad for the industry.

Counsel for the union stated that Communist groups rarely had a majority; that when they did, the employer would have to deal with them anyhow; and that when they did not, the majority rule was the best defense against them.

Case F. **Majority Dominated by Racketeers**

An employer of a large number of truck drivers has refused to deal with the group which, apparently, has a majority because, according to evidence he has submitted, the union is nothing but a "racket" in which some ex-criminals and corrupt political leaders have "muscled in." He denies the justice of majority rule, or any other rule, which would force him to deal with a union of this wholly objectionable character.

Questions:

1. Arbitrate each case, supporting your decision with adequate reasoning.

2. Summarize your conclusions regarding the principles which should apply to such situations, preparing a covering statement which might be issued to industry in general.

PROBLEM 55. PRACTICES IN COMBATTING UNIONS

Case A. Spying on Unions

Among the 400 production and maintenance employees of an automobile trailer factory, a union sprang up which included 177 active members and about 100 members who at one time or another paid dues but did not usually attend meetings.

To get rid of the union the plant, through a detective agency, hired a Mr. Smith. The company's vice-president testified that Smith was "a personnel man, as we considered him." It was Smith's duty, as the vice-president himself admitted, "to ferret out the union activities of the men, and to keep us informed of what was going on." He wanted this information because, as stated in his testimony: "We did not want trouble of any kind started in the plant. We wanted to keep a steady flow of business."

In order to make him eligible for membership in the union, the company gave Smith employment in the plant. He thereafter joined the union and eventually became its treasurer. He was thus able to procure a list of all its members. He made reports more than once a week to the company, and the lists of members which he furnished were given to the superintendent. With these lists in his hand, the superintendent went about the factory from time to time and warned various employees against union activities. He summarily discharged nine men and threatened three others with discharge.

As the result of these discharges and the resentment on the part of the members of the union, a special meeting was held at which about 100 men were present to discuss a strike. Smith, who was now treasurer of the union, was one of those speaking against a strike. The influence which he exerted on behalf of the respondent affected the result of the strike vote. Of the 67 votes cast, 35 were in favor of a strike. Because of the rule of the union requiring a two-thirds vote, a strike was not ordered.

Case B. Bribing of Union Officials

A granite corporation was faced with a strike over hours and wages. In order to keep things running smoothly the manager agreed "to pay the labor union agent a bribe of $200 to use his influence to prevent the occurrence of the strike and to pull the right wires." The national union desires a government board to discipline employers who interfere by this method with their activities.

Case C. Repression with Aid of Private Police

In a community of 30,000 inhabitants, 10,000 are employed by a steel corporation which owns the street railway system, a motor coach system, the water supply system, and 674 dwellings occupied by employees all located in and about the town. The company also has its own police force.

A government agency which investigated a labor dispute existing there reported the following situation:

> When a union tried to organize the men in the steel works, its efforts were countered by systematic repression. Officers of the union and organizers who came into the town were followed about by the private police. The more important union officers were honored by the respondent with permanent shadows and were followed even into the neighboring town. The house of the financial secretary, at which an organization meeting had been held, was surrounded day and night by the company police, and the employment agent of the respondent sat near the doorway noting down the names of those who entered the house. Persons coming out of the house were questioned. Some were mysteriously beaten and hit on the head while walking in the streets.

A year earlier a union organizer had come to the town and distributed union pamphlets. As he went along the street he was set upon by two persons who beat him severely. He was then taken before a Justice of Police, fined $5, and refused a transcript of record for purposes of appeal. Until he left town he was trailed by automobiles owned by the respondent.

The officers and organizers found it impossible to secure a public place in the town for a union meeting. They were refused the Italian Hall, the Slovak Hall, the Serbian Hall; they were refused the use of open lots. It was necessary to hold their meetings in an open lot in a town across the river.

Case D. Eviction from Company-Owned Homes

A paper mill is located in a secluded spot about five miles from the nearest town, at a point convenient both for receiving logs floated down stream and for water power. In order to make it possible for the employees to live there, the plant has built attractive houses and has rented them at low cost. No other houses are near it on the road for perhaps four miles.

The attempt of the workers to establish collective bargaining resulted in a strike. After this had lasted some weeks, the company decided to collect back rent, and threatened to evict about a score of the most active men in the union. Its bulletin to that effect, giving two weeks' notice, has come before a government board which is trying to adjust the strike. The union claims that eviction from homes during such a strike is an attempt at intimidation preventing workers from attaining collective bargaining. The company says the houses are its own and as landlord it has the right to select its tenants as it pleases.

Case E. Control through Company-Owned Towns

Certain industries, among which mining and lumbering are important illustrations, sometimes conduct their operations in localities so isolated that it becomes necessary to lay out a whole community. The company owns or controls not only the land and the houses but the schools, the churches and other facilities needed, and naturally becomes the dominant force in the education, recreation, and civic life of the inhabitants. Entry to the community may be denied to anyone of whom the company does not approve.

Company settlements, although essential to production, have been under fire for a long while for their unfavorable social characteristics. Among prominent public utterances of this sort was the attack reported in the press on December 20, 1936, by Governor George H. Earle of Pennsylvania, who asserted that company towns must be abolished. He said:

> In some of these towns, chiefly in Western Pennsylvania, men and women are brought into this world by company doctors, live in company towns, buy their food and clothing from company stores, work in company mines or mills, die in company hospitals and finally are buried in company cemeteries. Such conditions are symbolic of a feudalism of the dark ages, which has no place in our modern life.

The executive committee of the United Mine Workers, only a few weeks before, had adopted a set of resolutions concerning needed legislation, one of which read:

> An act eliminating unincorporated communities of the kind and character of Weirton, W. Va. This city having a population of 20,000 is unincorporated and thus completely controlled by the Weirton Steel Corporation. It operates to the detriment of civil liberties and is used as an instrument to prevent all independent labor organization.

What would be substituted for company towns and what practical plan can lessen the oppressive features complained about have, however, yet to be made clear. The question has interested the public but has remained as one in which the answer has proved complicated and difficult.

Questions:

1. Which, if any, of the practices described should be subject to a regulatory law? If it were decided to attempt such legislation what should be its chief terms and the general procedure it should provide?

2. What present laws, if any, tend to curb such practices? Comment fully on their suitability and value.

PROBLEM 56. NATURE OF "INTERFERENCE" WITH UNION CAMPAIGNS

Unions have charged that certain activities of employers constitute intimidation and undue interference with their right to organize. The instances which follow are cases in which a government agency has been asked to intercede.

Case A. Employer's Expression of Views against Unionism

A manufacturer does not like to see his workers organize, and in the small town in which he lives, he has frequent occasion to meet with workers outside the plant, whether it be at the street corner, the paper store, or elsewhere. In many such contacts the organizational activities of the union come up, and he expresses himself quite vigorously on what he thinks about "their invasion." He has spoken scathingly of the union officers and of the harm they have done in other places. The union wants a government board to order him to desist in the public expression of these views to his employees.

Case B. Employees Forced to Listen to Anti-Union Speaker

When a union attempted to organize the workers in a small Massachusetts town, the employer asked all of the employees to quit work at eleven o'clock in order to hear a speaker whom he had invited. This was the industrial secretary of the local chamber of commerce, who spoke for approximately an hour. In his talk he suggested a company union, giving his vigorous opinions concerning unionism in general and the harm that might come from the union that was trying to get into the town. The employees were paid their usual rate for this hour.

The union states that this is an unjustifiable act on the part of the employer, amounting to intimidation. The employer states that just as the union has a right to present its views outside the plant, he has a right to bring his point of view to them inside the plant.

Case C. Invitation to Other Meetings on Nights of Union Meetings

In an Oklahoma community a set of revival meetings lasting two weeks was being held at the Methodist Church. The local superintendent of production of an oil company personally asked each man under his supervision to attend this revival on two successive Thursday nights. These being nights for union meetings, the attendance naturally interfered with the men's listening to the speakers whom the union had provided.

Many of the employees felt that their failure to accept this personal invitation to attend the revival meeting would indicate that they were going to the union meeting, and therefore that such an invitation was a form of intimidation. The union wants such invitations forbidden.

Case D. Intra-Plant Membership Canvass by Company Union

1. In a plumbing factory the organizing committee of the company union has been permitted freely to canvass the plant for members, while no such privilege of solicitation has ever been extended to the union. The company permits the workers' committee to display posters, signed by the organizing committee, and in other ways makes it clear which of the two sides is favored. The union wishes an absolute prohibition of any such privileges to the rival organization unless both sides are given equal space and equal time.

2. In a plant in which solicitation of membership in a labor organization during working hours is forbidden, the workers on the "employees' conference committee," known as the rival of a labor union, have, in fact, engaged in the solicitation of members during working hours. Union officials are prohibited from

doing this on the ground that it would interfere with production and is against rules; but this rule is, in practice, overlooked in the case of the conference committee members. The union has protested that such enforcement of the rule is interfering with their freedom of organization and should be barred.

Case E. **Questioning of Workers concerning Affiliation**

In an oil company two assistant superintendents of production inquired from time to time of their employees as to whether or not they belonged to the union. Representatives of the union contend that no employer has a right to ask an employee whether or not he is a member of the union; and that no employer should ever be permitted to question an employee concerning what was going on in the union or to ask names of fellow members.

Case F. **Shutdowns and Threats of Shutdown as Intimidation**

1. A government board ordered an election in a clothing plant to determine whether or not the employees wanted to form a local of the Amalgamated Clothing Workers of America. Before the election the manager made a public statement that "if the vote is in my favor, I will give you employment until next January. If not, I will close down the plant, discharge all employees and later on rehire only the loyal ones."

2. The president of a firearms company gave the employees facts to show that the rules and regulations of the union in the trade could not be obeyed in this plant without sacrificing a competitive advantage; that he could not compete with other plants on the union scale and that he would have to shut down the plant and they would lose their jobs if they voted for the union form of organization. As a result the union has been unable to interest more than a small minority of the plant.

3. An election was held in a paper company to determine whether the paper workers' union or an employee association was to be the approved form of employee organization. The

majority voted for the union. The government board received a letter of thanks from the paper company for the way in which it had supervised the election. A day later, however, the company shut down its mill on the ground of lack of orders. The employees felt that this was a sort of punishment for the union activities and petitioned for a reopening. They formed an employees' association, made overtures and gave assurances to the company. Thereupon the plant reopened and continued operations, aiming toward capacity production.

The unions in all these cases state that the shutdowns were designed and used by employers to destroy their unions. They ask that all such threats should be regarded as undue interference, and that collective bargaining should be granted by the government board as a balancing factor.

Case G. A "Yellow-Dog" Arrangement by Petition

A lumber plant which was shut down during a strike reopened after a large number of employees had signed applications for employment which contained a clause that the employee agreed "to renounce any and all affiliation with any labor organization." The company contended that it did not initiate these applications but that they were signed voluntarily by the men, and that therefore its hands were clean with regard to the whole matter. The union contends that this is another version of the "yellow dog" contract and is an unwarranted interference with collective bargaining.

Questions:

1. Assume that in the matters of public policy involved in these issues you are asked to outline your views. In such a statement indicate which of these activities you would curb, if any, and how, defending whatever position you take.

2. To what extent have such activities been curbed in recent years by legislation or governmental administration? Comment on such legislation, indicating its good points, evils, and deficiencies.

PROBLEM 57. LAY-OFFS AND DISMISSALS FOR UNION ACTIVITY

Demands for the curb or regulation of the power of employers to discharge workers as a means of enforcing anti-union policies have been an important source of labor controversy in recent years. Illustrations of questioned discharges are presented in the following cases.

Case A. Discharge for Interest in Unionism

1. A union agent attempted to organize the employees of a coke and chemical company and invited fifteen of its eighty workers to attend an organization meeting a week later. One of the company's foremen walked back and forth in front of the hall where the meeting was being held and observed which of the men attended. Eleven of these employees who were invited to attend the organization meeting were discharged during the week, no others having been similarly treated during that period.

The union asks reinstatement of all these men and an order prohibiting such tactics on the part of the employer.

2. An employee of an oil company has been very much interested in unionism and has made statements to his baker and other merchants from whom he purchases his supplies that he would not patronize them unless they offered him union-made products. He was discharged for these activities, and he is protesting this action as having no relation to his right to a job.

Case B. Employee Who Contradicted Employer at Anti-Union Rally

When the employees in a fiber box company were being solicited by union agents, the employer held a meeting at which he discussed the whole subject. He told them that they had the right to freedom of self-organization and that he would not interfere with it, but expressed the company's low estimate of labor unions in general, and those affiliated with the American Federation of Labor in particular. At this, one of the employees got up and stated that this was giving out a lot of "salve" and in general criticized the whole procedure. The employer resented this interference and later discharged the employee.

Case C. Discharge for Solicitation of Members

1. A company made a rule prohibiting during working hours the solicitation of fellow workers to join a labor union. In certain of the departments employees normally talked with each other while at work, without interfering with their operations. A worker was overheard giving some strong reasons why he had joined the union and stating to a fellow worker that "If I were you, I'd get on the right side." Although he had been an employee of the firm for nine years he was discharged for this violation of the rules.

2. An employee of a furniture plant had been employed by the company continuously for six years and, with the exception of one other man, was the oldest employee in his department. There had been no complaint about the nature of his work. However, he had become interested in a furniture workers' union and in the process of arousing interest among workers distributed literature to them during lunch hour, on the way to work and at other times, but not in the plant itself. The employer stated that such literature would then be read during working hours, would lead to discussions among the workers during working time, and that therefore he had discharged the employee as a troublemaker.

The union demands reinstatement in these cases on the ground that what an employee says in private conversation or does outside of working hours in relation to his fellow workers is entirely within his own rights and should not be the subject of discharge.

Case D. **Discharge for Complaint to a Government Board**

A master mechanic employed by a radio company who engaged in union activity was transferred to a new department. The day following his transfer, work in that department was curtailed and he was laid off. His competency and the seniority rights to which his period of service was held to entitle him were ignored in his lay-off.

He tried to get reinstated, but being unsuccessful, complained to a regional labor board. At the hearings held, he proved that his union activity was the cause of his discharge. On the ground that "any man who would complain to a government board and attempt to make trouble of that sort was not worthy of employment," the president of the company instructed the manager that the man should not be rehired. His prior lay-off status was definitely registered as a discharge.

Case E. **Discharges Alleged to Be "Victimization"**

1. A worker in a coke plant, steadily employed for fourteen years, was the only Negro worker of the union among the Negroes employed at the plant. One day he and two non-union employees were discovered by the department superintendent in a little old shanty. For many years it had been the custom for the men, when their work permitted, to rest in that shanty. The company had not issued any warning that this custom would no longer be tolerated. He was accused of sleeping on duty and, despite his long service with the company, was summarily discharged. The other two were retained in employ.

2. An employee was discharged on the ground that his domestic and related personal behavior rendered him an undesirable employee. The union pointed out, however, that most of the instances of faulty behavior had taken place before the

employee had voluntarily left the company, two years before. Thereafter, with full knowledge of these instances, the company reemployed him and later promoted him to a position which carried with it certain responsibilities not shared by his fellow workers.

The union contends "that acts or statements of an employee which, under some circumstances, might properly warrant disciplinary action, may not properly be so classified when, as we think is the case here, they find their origin to a substantial extent in a justified resentment against the employer's apparent opposition to the self-organization of his employees." It asks that all such cases should be subject to review by an impartial government authority, in order that subterfuges should not sanction cases of victimization for union activities.

Questions:

1. *By reference to the contested points of view, indicate whether the employer's use of discharge for union interest or activity should be curbed or left unimpaired, and apply your principles to each of the cases.*

2. *To what extent, if any, have employees been protected against such discharge under recent or existing legislation? Answer with comment on value, feasibility, and limitations of such governmental action.*

PROBLEM 58. DISPUTED FAIRNESS AND LEGALITY OF CERTAIN TYPES OF STRIKES, BOYCOTTS, AND PICKETING

Case A. Picketing of Ball Park Because of Anti-Union Activities of Ballplayer's Wife

When baseball fans came to Sportsman's Park in St. Louis on May 18, 1935, to see the Cardinals play the Boston Braves, they were surprised to find three different unions picketing the entrance. Two of these unions, the Bartenders' Benevolent and Protective League and the Ticket-Takers and Ushers Union, had a direct grievance because of the desire to unionize the bartenders, ticket-takers, and ushers. The third union picketing, however, was the International Ladies' Garment Workers Union. Their grievance was against the wife of the Cardinal's shortstop, because she was working in a shop where the union workers were on strike. She had apparently taken part in anti-union activities. The intention of the picketing was evidently to get people to stay away, and thus to put pressure on the owners of Sportsman's Park to have the shortstop persuade his wife to cease aiding the anti-union employer with whom she had made business arrangements.

Case B. Strike and Boycott of Unionized Company to Enforce Unionization of Affiliated Concern

Three creameries were consolidated into a creamery product corporation. One of the three concerns, Company A, had been a union shop employing only union men, while the others had been operated on the open shop plan. The local union of milk drivers and creamery workers, in order to secure contracts with these other two shops, declared a strike in Company A.

This company thereupon hired other workers in an endeavor to conduct its business. The strikers followed the teams, however, and tried to induce prospective customers by persuasion and alleged intimidation not to trade with the A Company. Many people thought the strike unjustified, but those who might not otherwise be induced by argument were scared away by the strikers' activities.

The company took the case to court, showing its extra expenses in keeping going and its losses, stated that the strike was illegal, and sought a judgment for the amounts involved against the union.

Case C. **Sympathetic Picketing of Newspaper by Outside Groups**

In July, 1936, a newspaper located on the Pacific Coast dismissed its chief of photography and its dramatic critic. It stated that this was done in the first case on grounds of inefficient management of the department, and in the second case for gross insubordination. The American Newspaper Guild, the union of editorial and news employees then seeking a contract with that newspaper, charged that both had been dismissed for Guild activity, and its unit voted to authorize the Seattle chapter to negotiate with the management of the paper for their reinstatement. The management refused to reinstate the two men, asserting that they had been discharged for cause.

The Guild placed the paper on its "unfair list"—that is, listed it as unfair to organized labor in dismissing men for alleged union activity—and requested the Central Labor Council of the city to do likewise. This was done at a meeting of the Council on August 12. The Guild at the same time asked the paper to agree to bargain collectively through a Guild contract on wages, hours, and working conditions, and on being denied this demand, voted a strike effective at 8 o'clock the next morning, August 13th.

The Guild pickets by themselves were unable to prevent any

non-Guild employee from entering the newspaper building. Beginning at 11 A.M., however, hundreds of other union men began to appear on the picket line and soon surrounded the building with mass picketing, while large details of police looked on. The new pickets included teamsters, longshoremen, sailors, metal workers, and boiler makers.

At noon the first large shift of printers appeared for work on the "green edition," which has a 5 P.M. deadline. The printers looked at the picket line, listened to the "advice" of the pickets (as the Guild has it) or their "threats" (according to the management) and then walked away. Most of the photo-engravers, stereotypers, pressmen, and mailers followed the printers. All the mechanical unions had contracts obligating them not to go out on "sympathy strikes," but the contracts also obligated the management to provide them with a "safe" place to work.

The management of the paper suspended publication, but called for "law and order enforcement" to insure safety to members of mechanical unions who were not on strike, in passing through the picket line established by "a mob of wrecking crews from unions of teamsters, maritime workers, timber workers, and other radical groups."

A labor leader, in reply, insisted that the waterfront employees and other workers not connected with the newspaper industry were justified in showing their sympathy with the strikers by taking that action. He said:

> If the newspaper receives help from organized business men who have no direct connection with the newspaper industry, why should not the Guild receive similar help from organized labor? The Industrial Council is raising an anti-union fund from the various business and industrial concerns in the city as a result of the Guild strike. They are trying to crush organized labor. Every time a union is in a strike, the Industrial Council is back of the opposition. If industry is going to pile its resources into the fight, what else is there for organized labor to do?

Case D. **Refusal to Work on Non-Union Materials**

Justices of the Supreme Court of the United States divided sharply on the legality of strikes called by the Journeymen Stone Cutters' Association, the workers' organization, on jobs in which limestone cut by the Bedford Cut Stone Company was supplied. The majority decision relates that until 1921 the company had carried on its work under agreement with the union, but when it refused to continue its contract with the union the latter issued a notice to all its locals directing its members not to work on stone "that has been started—planed, turned, cut, or semi-finished—by men working in opposition to our organization." As a consequence, any local contractor who supplied such stone on a construction job found that the men would refuse to work it.

Mr. Justice Sutherland, who on April 11, 1927, delivered the opinion of the Supreme Court, emphasized the fact that the cause of strikes against any one contractor was solely to reach a third party, the company from whom he purchased the stone, and therefore that the purpose was to coerce or induce local employers to refrain from purchasing that company's product. He then stated:

> The present combination deliberately adopted a course of conduct which directly and substantially curtailed, or threatened . . . to curtail, the natural flow in interstate commerce of a very large proportion of the building limestone production of the entire country, to the gravely probable disadvantage of producers, purchasers, and the public; and it must be held to be a combination in undue and unreasonable restraint of such commerce within the meaning of the Anti-Trust Act as interpreted by this Court. (274 U.S. 54.)

Mr. Justice Brandeis, in delivering the dissenting opinion, concurred in by Mr. Justice Holmes, included the following:

> The manner in which these individual stone cutters exercised their asserted right to perform their union duty by refusing to finish stone "cut by men working in opposition to" the Association

was confessedly legal. They were innocent alike of trespass and of breach of contract. They did not picket. They refrained from violence, intimidation, fraud, and threats. They refrained from obstructing otherwise either the plaintiffs or their customers in attempts to secure other help. They did not plan a boycott against any of the plaintiffs or against builders who used the plaintiffs' product. On the contrary, they expressed entire willingness to cut and finish anywhere any stone quarried by any of the plaintiffs, except such stone as had been partially "cut by men working in opposition to" the Association. . . .

The manner in which the Journeymen's unions acted was also clearly legal. The combination complained of is the cooperation of persons wholly of the same craft, united in a national union, solely for self-protection. No outsider—be he quarrier, dealer, builder or laborer—was a party to the combination. . . .

The contention that earlier decisions of this Court compel the conclusion that it is illegal seems to me unfounded. The cases may support the claim that, by such local abstention from work, interstate trade is restrained. But examination of the facts in those cases makes clear that they have no tendency whatsoever to establish that the restraint imposed by the unions in the case at bar is unreasonable. (274 U.S. 59–61.)

Case E. **Refusal of Longshoremen to Handle "Hot Cargo"**

The arbitrator of the agreements in force between the San Francisco Waterfront Employers Association and the Longshoremen's Union wrote a letter to the two parties on April 20, 1936, in which he stated that he would continue as arbitrator only under certain conditions. Referring to "hot cargo," viz., cargo affected by some controversy involving labor disputes in other industries, he protested that: "The rulings of the arbitrator on this question have not been accepted and the Union and its members have maintained their position that they will not handle such cargo so long as it remains under the ban imposed by other labor organizations."

The employers involved, and others, condemn this form of refusal as being a sympathetic strike having nothing to do with waterfront work. They state that longshoremen do not ask why some other labor organization is striking, but refuse to handle cargo when notified that a union involved in its production is on strike, thus becoming an ally of every striking organization, no matter how unfair or how far distant. They do not, of course, let any non-union labor handle it, so that if the waterfront employer tried to get anyone else to move the cargo a strike would extend to all cargo. A public group points out that such action on the part of the longshoremen, teamsters, or similar service unions, handling the products of a variety of industries makes them a party to every labor dispute in which goods may be moved. That the union remain neutral in regard to outside disputes is the policy favored by this public group.

The union leaders appear to think otherwise. In the official publication of the union in that district, a vigorous article has appeared which reads in part: "There are some things of more importance than awards or agreements, and one is the defense of our own organization and its cooperation with the rest of the labor movement. If one local is to set against another local and one district against another district, what have we an organization for?"

Case F. A One-Man Strike and Picket Line

The mayor of Seattle, in citing what he called "the extremes of sympathetic strikes," stated on August 28, 1936: "Recently, one radio operator on a ship at Longview, Wash., struck for more money. He made himself an oilcloth sign declaring the ship unfair to organized labor and started walking up and down the dock in a one-man picket line. The longshoremen saw him and refused to load the ship because they could not 'pass through a picket line.' "

Case G. Public Policy regarding "Sit-Down" Strikes

In various parts of the country groups of workers have within recent years adopted a new and radical form of strike which involves simply the refusal to leave the work place. The strike conducted for past centuries meant merely a refusal to enter the plant, or refusal to let others enter the plant, but did not involve trespass on the property of those owning the building or forcible seizure of the equipment. Is the sit-down strike a valid weapon in industrial disputes? A newspaper editorial states:

> The public is not likely to tolerate forcible ejection of the strikers, or the use of armed force for "protection" or otherwise, by the companies themselves. But does it follow that the public authorities must simply keep hands off? If they do, what are likely to be some of the consequences? A union that controlled only a minority of the men at a plant, particularly if that minority were at key positions, could force the shutdown of the plant. Under such circumstances labor unions, even if they represented only minorities, could ask almost any terms and win almost any strike they pleased.

Questions:

1. In which of these cases, if any, do you believe that labor is engaging in unjustifiable and improper activity with relation to innocent parties? Defend your answer whichever view you take.

2. What are the laws and legal precedents applying if a party affected adversely by these actions were to seek a remedy at law:

a. in most jurisdictions?

b. in your state?

3. Comment on the defects or inadequacies, if any, of such legislation, suggesting necessary provisions or changes which you may regard as desirable.

4. What do you believe to be the consequences, favorable and unfavorable, of sit-down strikes, and what, if anything, should be done about them through government intervention?

PROBLEM 59. DEMOCRACY IN LABOR UNIONS

Case A. Attempt at "Pure Democracy" through Meetings

A well-known union leader with long experience in directing labor organizations has been accused of being an autocrat. He retorts that those who make this charge are either naïve theorists or inspired by malice. He writes:

> The theoretical outsider talks of "democracy" in unionism as glibly as if the failure on the part of leaders is due solely to a desire for autocracy. On the contrary, many union leaders would prefer democracy if they could make it work. What they find is that to a certain extent democracy of management is unworkable and often detrimental to the interests of the workers. Starting with a realization that democratic methods won't function quite as planned, they gradually get to rely more and more on independent initiative and perhaps in time acquire an aggressive autocracy in a manner that seems compatible with efficiency as they conceive it.

He then describes what he states is a typical experience which occurred earlier in his career and which illustrates the difficulties of handling the union membership. A two-year contract with the employers is about to expire. The union leaders draw up terms that the members want and have these demands approved at a mass meeting. They then begin negotiations with the committee of employers of the trade, and three weeks or more are consumed in conferences. But the situation is at a standstill because apparently the employers won't yield. A strike may have to be called after all.

The union committee feels that the best thing to do is to continue negotiations for several weeks more so that eventually a compromise will be reached. On the other hand, it may be impossible to agree, and a strike call may have to be issued at any time "for its moral effect." Now the question is whether the officers should continue their negotiations in secret, leaving the union wondering what is going on, or call a mass meeting and explain the situation. He writes:

We call a mass meeting. The following occurs:

1. The meeting is announced for the best time, 5:30 P.M., a half-hour after work. Most of the workers arrive late and the meeting does not begin until 6:30.

2. The hall secured, the best available, is long and narrow. One officer of the union, a former politician with a loud voice, makes himself heard. But the speakers who rise from the audience insist upon talking inaudibly, and the room becomes noisy with the buzz of conversation.

3. Neurotic types of workers get up to voice their opinions on things foreign to the subject at hand. The chairman is almost exhausted with constant poundings of the gavel and his attempts to get order. He begs, cajoles, threatens, insults the crowd, but the noise continues.

4. Some of the impractical, uncompromising, Communist workers, who believe only in fighting, assail the officers, declaim against the employers and raise trouble, without sticking to the point at issue.

5. Most speakers berate the committee for having come to them with nothing but talk and no special issues to decide or no actual strike to engineer.

6. Straw votes on various issues are asked for, but by this time the crowd becomes impatient and more than half of the 2000 workers present have left.

7. The demagoguish types of workers use the time for oratory and for urging an immediate strike.

8. After four hours of terrible wrangling the meeting breaks up in disorder.

The union leader's letter concludes as follows: "At the end of that meeting I decided that the bunch could go to hell before I would call another meeting to report to them or to get their advice. I decided then that when I called on them again I would have some definite proposition I wanted ratified. Instead of exhausting myself trying to hold that mob of hyenas in check and giving the wild ones a chance to rouse the crowd, I will have my own speakers planted and I will recognize chiefly those who I think will talk common sense. Instead of wasting time and energy in such impractical procedures, however, we run the union from headquarters as far as we can."

Case B. **Attitude of Union Leaders toward Members**

A student of labor unionism makes the assertion that "many union leaders despise the mob they are working for, because they find them unwieldy, unthinking, uncooperative, disloyal, hard to deal with and hard to control, and stupidly blind to their own interests." He also states that most of the members "haven't a grain of interest in the duties which make real self-government possible. If we trusted the crowd too much we should only be shifting tyranny harder to fight than the old tyrannies because it would continually slip from one bunch to another." He then relates difficulties because of the apathy and indifference of the average union member, and how this encourages bureaucracy as "the most effective way of running a union."

Questions:

1. What are the essentials of a democratic form of government?

2. What procedures in the management of unions or provisions of typical union constitutions may be listed as

a. unnecessarily undemocratic?

b. wisely fulfilling the standards of effective democratic control?

3. After visiting two or three labor union meetings in your locality and talking with their members and officers, indicate what conditions tend to foster apathy and which encourage intelligent interest on the part of members in the affairs of the union.

PROBLEM 60. JURISDICTIONAL CLAIMS AND DISPUTES

Case A. Civil War over Metal Trim on Doors

The making of doors has always constituted an important part of the work of carpenters, while the making of various kinds of tin and metal covers has been within the jurisdiction of the sheet metal workers' union. When fire regulations and other considerations led to the use of doors encased in tin and other metals, the fact that the interior was wood and that doors had always been put up by carpenters led to a continuous dispute between them and the sheet metal workers as to who was entitled to jobs of this kind. For decades the issue between the two unions flared up in strikes called by one or the other and held up building or caused losses which some students have calculated to be in the tens of millions of dollars.

As to the actual relative competence for the job there has been considerable difference of opinion. Many contractors feel that the hanging of a metal door is better done by a man trained as a carpenter and skilled in the use of a square and level, because the doors must be centered and must be hung accurately. Others believe that the work should go to the sheet metal workers. The latter was the decision of a voluntary board of jurisdictional awards in which architects, contractors, and engineers and others were represented, as well as building trades unions.

When this decision was made, the carpenters refused to abide by it, and being one of the largest and most powerful unions in the country, it enforced its demand for this work. As the sheet metal workers' union is a relatively small one and has less of a place in the building industry, contractors were inclined to favor the more powerful union, but it was never certain whether they could "get away with it," or would have a strike on their hands.

Case B. Delay in Huge Construction over Trifle

In 1933 the building projects of the Federal government included the construction of two large new buildings in Washington, D.C., to house the headquarters of the U.S. Department of Commerce and the Interstate Commerce Commission. These huge construction jobs involved an item of 1300 radiator covers. When about 1100 had already been installed by the carpenters, the iron workers pointed out to the contractor that it was really their work, and got him to promise to put them on the rest.

When the iron workers were assigned to install the radiator covers the carpenters' union ordered its men to strike. As a consequence the contractor was soon unable to continue on the building and had to close down, throwing a thousand men out of work, and completely tying up two jobs whose contract price was about $10,000,000. Thus, although a total of not more than $800 in wages was involved in the disputed work itself, the wage loss per day was $8000, or $40,000 per week, for the fortnight or more during which the strike lasted.

Case C. Boundary Lines of Plasterers' Work

1. Among the unions chartered by the A.F. of L. are the bricklayers and the plasterers. The full name of the former is The Bricklayers, Masons, and Plasterers International Union, and one paragraph in its charter permits it to include "all exterior or interior plastering, plain or ornamental, when done with stucco, cement, and lime mortars, or patent materials, . . . etc., etc." The other union is called the Operative Plasterers and Cement Finishers International Association and its charter gives it a right to "all interior or exterior plastering of cement, stucco, stone, imitation, or any patent material when cast, . . . etc., etc." While much of the work is different, there

is an opportunity in various jobs for keen rivalry concerning who shall do certain plastering work.

Bricklayers are everywhere much more numerous in the building industry than are plasterers. In many small towns there are no local unions of plasterers, and the latter are permitted to join the bricklayers' union. By an agreement between the two unions made in 1911, the bricklayers agreed to permit a vote of two-thirds of the plasterers in any bricklayers' union to decide whether a separate local of the plasterers' union should be formed. If the plasterers decided to have a separate organization, the bricklayers agreed to take no steps to prevent the plasterers' international from granting their craftsmen a charter.

This agreement worked amicably until the Florida building boom. Plasterers from other parts of the country went South and formed a local union. The bricklayers objected, saying that the agreement of 1911 provided that only resident plasterers might vote on the formation of locals of the plasterers' international union.

The Executive Council of the A.F. of L. could not reconcile the two conflicting groups and when one large New York contracting concern let its plastering contract in Miami to a company which employed bricklayers to do the work, the plasterers called strikes on $22,000,000 worth of that company's building operations in New York, Philadelphia, and Chicago. This brought stoppages in various other trades by preventing electricians, painters, and others from finishing tasks on which they were engaged. The same type of dispute affected $100,000,000 worth of work throughout the country.

2. In the erection of a group of apartment houses in a mid-Western city a few years ago, a controversy arose between the plasterers and the bricklayers as to who should set some ornamental precast mantels. A National Board of Jurisdictional Awards, then in operation, decided that such mantels should be erected by the plasterers. The bricklayers struck. The contractor tried to substitute wooden mantels and that made both

unions angry and a strike ensued. The National Board of Jurisdictional Awards then decided that it would make an exception of these particular mantels and that the bricklayers should erect them. Then the plasterers struck. In all, over thirty-five days of work were lost as a direct result. As there was a shortage of housing, the extra cost was included by the owners in the overhead and figured in the rental charged to the tenants.

Case D. Jurisdictional Differences and Wasteful Production

1. Hoisting engineers claim the right to run engines. A contractor on one small job had a small gas-driven pump which required no skill and little attention. Any one of the building workers could have given it the incidental time required. But to avoid a strike the contractor had to hire a union engineer at $8.00 per day simply to start the pump in the morning, oil it occasionally, and stop it at night.

2. A metal door manufacturer put a finish on his doors at the factory, instead of on the erection job, by a new baked enamel process. After he erected the doors he needed only common laborers or scrub women to wipe off the dust. He states: "Since rubbing off requires no skill it would for that job ordinarily cost not more than $1,000. But the painters' union threatened to strike against the contractor who had ordered the doors from us on the ground that he was passing over to the laborers work that belonged to painters. The only way to avert this was to employ skilled painters to rub off the dust. Owing to the threat, and to help the contractor we were forced to pay the painters $13,000 for rubbing off the dust—the equivalent of what it would cost to paint all the doors and trim in the building."

3. A committee of the Federated American Engineering Societies published an impartial study on waste in industry, ascribing to various elements in the productive process the aspects of waste which it believed should be eliminated. Concerning the unions in the printing industry it stated:

Perhaps their most trying practice is the insistence that members of one craft union shall not encroach upon the work of another. In as simple a matter as printing the names of individual firms on catalogue covers, where the imprints are all set up in slugs, after each imprint is run off the pressroom workers have been known to insist that a compositor be brought from the composing room to make the change to the next imprint, while they stand idly by. In a case of this kind, where the runs are short, it amounts practically to requiring two persons to do the work of one. Similarly with paper handlers, sheet straighteners, feeders, and pressmen, it is not at all uncommon to be forced to have men from several different unions participate in a simple piece of work which could be performed more easily and economically by one person.

Case E. Questioned Solutions for Jurisdictional Disputes

The construction of the Philadelphia Post Office in 1934 involved a jurisdictional dispute between three unions, the International Union of Elevator Constructors, the International Bridge and Structural Iron Workers Union, and the Brotherhood of Carpenters and Joiners, over the installation of a conveyor system for the carrying of mail. The dispute resulted in a strike which retarded the construction of the entire building.

At that time a National Labor Board, of the N.R.A., mediated between the parties. It urged direct negotiations or reference to an impartial tribunal, but made no headway. It then asserted that it was clearly a function of the A.F. of L. to adjust jurisdictional disputes. The head of the building trades department of the A.F. of L. stepped forward, stating that if the dispute could be referred to him, it would be "quickly and satisfactorily settled."

Objection to this was raised by one of the smaller unions, on grounds not openly stated, but indicated by a private memorandum presented by a spokesman who feared to speak frankly. In his communication he stated:

> The official appointed to adjudicate jurisdictional disputes in the A.F. of L. and having most power outside of the Convention itself,

is an appointee owing his place to a combination of a few of the largest unions controlling the majority vote. Therefore he plays ball with these unions, and a record of his decisions indicates that in almost every case the small unions opposing these other unions have the decision against them. This indicates the hopelessness of the situation as far as justice is concerned, and we can't submit our case to that tribunal.

The Board then ruled that in view of the failure of the various unions to agree upon a proper method of assigning the work, the contractor should be free to award the task as he saw fit. The Board said that this was the course to be followed on all other government buildings in which a jurisdictional dispute had arisen over the installation of conveyors until a settlement of the controversy was reached, either directly by the unions, or by an impartial tribunal, or by the American Federation of Labor.

This at once aroused vigorous opposition. The representative of the Elevator Constructors told the Board the decision was "thoroughly unwarranted," because his organization had been traditionally invested with this work through its charter in 1901 and by former jurisdictional decisions "by proper agencies" since that time. The representative of the Bridge and Structural Iron Workers stated that the contractor had made the decision to the "disadvantage of elevator constructors and iron workers and to the advantage of millwrights who receive a lower wage scale." The carpenters' union would not budge in its position. Their general representative stuck to his point that the carpenters did this kind of work long before the elevator constructors came into the labor movement.

The representative of the elevator company likewise objected to the decision. He stated that the company "would be unable to function under the Board's decision, since when an employer starts to settle a union jurisdictional dispute it is like entering a domestic quarrel." He favored decision by the A.F. of L., but one union spokesman stated that this was because he recognized that he would have less trouble if the big unions, even though merely obstinate and unjustified in their position, were held in line.

Questions:

1. Assume that the situations described regarding jurisdictional claims remain for adjustment. On the basis of research, indicate:

a. What have been the chief types of former efforts at adjustment, and their sources of strength and weakness.

b. What are the wisest and most practicable courses to be followed in the immediate future to minimize or adjust such disputes by (1) organized labor; (2) the government; and (3) employers. Apply to each case.

2. Submit a paper, based on further research, regarding charters and jurisdictional disputes, presenting a classification of the main national and international unions of the A.F. of L. into the following three groups:

a. Unions with so definite and limited a field as to involve no likelihood of jurisdictional disputes.

b. Industries in which amalgamation of two or more related crafts would be a simple and practical solution of jurisdictional questions involving friction or waste.

c. Unions whose conflicting jurisdictional claims seem most difficult to adjust and which raise the fundamental questions and major practical issues of future inter-union relations.

PROBLEM 61. SOME HARD QUESTIONS FOR INDUSTRIAL UNIONISTS

INTRODUCTORY NOTE: For some years one of the foremost problems facing unions has been the question of the readjustment of their structure to meet new conditions. Shall the mass production industries, such as automobiles, steel, rubber, oil, and radio, be organized on a "horizontal" (craft union) basis, or in "vertical" (industrial) unions? This struggle is several decades old, but was forced to the front through the aggressive tactics of the industrial group within the American Federation of Labor. The point of view and the reasons for desiring such a change may be illustrated by the following declaration of John L. Lewis, President of the United Mine Workers:

> The form under which most labor is now organized is obsolete. Years ago there were craftsmen. Years ago it was all right for men in the same trades to band together. Today the machine has so changed conditions as to make that kind of organization impractical.
>
> In the old days most industrial operations were carried on in small plants, in which often the man who employed labor was himself a craftsman. Then most of the employees in factories were skilled workers who had served their apprenticeships in learning their trades. The unskilled workers did not have to be considered because there were very few of them.
>
> But in the last half-century a great change has taken place. Mechanization, technological improvements, and mass production have rendered skillful manual operations obsolete. Trained craftsmen have been driven out by arms of steel, and cog wheels have taken the place of brains. A few pattern makers and machine-maintenance operators are all the skilled men required in a large factory today; for the most part, skilled operators have been replaced by unskilled ones.

It has become more and more evident, therefore, that any organized labor movement composed exclusively of craft unions is not the voice of labor. Today there are more than 30,000,000 workers in the United States and a trifle over 10 per cent of them are members of the American Federation of Labor. There are millions of workers who have not been able to join a union and those who have, except in one or two industries, have been split into small groups.

We mine workers belong to one union. If we have trouble with our employers we are all united. In most of the other industries the workers in each craft belong to separate unions, though they are employed in the same industry, so that hostile employers can deal singly with each. Skilled trades have obtained advantages, but it has always been at the expense of unskilled workers who in their unorganized state have been helpless.

This point of view has become widely familiar to the general public but it is generally assumed that the question of craft vs. industrial unionism presents a one-sided issue. Difficulties pointed to by craft unionists which should properly be taken into account in the type of industrial unions and the kind of inter-union relationships advocated tend to be overlooked. The purpose of the present problem is merely to provide a corrective.

For this reason *this problem frankly takes the form of presenting only the practical objections and difficulties asserted by craft unionists.* It is expected that this challenge to keener thinking on the part of industrial unionists will have the result of assuring a more realistic and mature understanding of the structural readjustments in unionism required, without necessarily gainsaying the place or superiority of industrial unionism.

Case A. Assertion of Unsuitability of One Skilled Branch to Represent Another

A tobacco company has for some years dealt with the Tobacco Workers' Union, an affiliate of the A.F. of L., under a closed shop agreement. In this plant 2450 of the workers are members of the union, and the remaining 232 employees are actual or potential members of fourteen different craft unions. The largest of these craft groups consists of 138 skilled machinists, oilers, knife grinders, machine fixers, and apprentices, who are claimed as members by the machinists' union, which has asked for a separate agreement with the company.

The spokesman for the machinists' union argues that the machinists are a separate craft by occupation, payroll classification and supervision, and that it is absurd to have a wholly different union as guardian for men in a highly skilled craft. He states that whatever might be the possibilities of an industrial union in a metal working plant, there is no basis whatever for such unionism where the nature of the work of the great majority of the workers is tobacco manufacture.

Case B. **Impaired Mobility of Craft Workers**

In a large brewery there are a number of electrical workers whom the brewery workers' union—an industrial union—claims as members. The local agent of the electrical workers' union, however, points out that an electrical worker, unlike a brewery worker, is employed in various industries. Should the electrical worker want to go into the building trades or into other plants, he would find himself limited by the fact that he is a member of the brewery workers rather than the electrical workers' union.

The metal trades department of the American Federation of Labor, in commenting on situations of this character, put its objections to industrial unionism as follows:

> If the attempt to organize these so-called vertical unions is carried to its logical conclusion it would result in the dismemberment of a number of our affiliated international unions. Draftsmen, patternmakers, moulders, machinists, boiler-makers, sheet metal workers, blacksmiths, electrical workers, plumbers and steam fitters, engineers, in fact all of the skilled mechanics represented in the metal trades department would be divided among the membership of the vertical unions.

Skilled mechanics going from place to place in search of work would face the problem of becoming members of a number of vertical unions in order to protect their welfare.

Case C. **"Wage Chaos" for Craft Workers**

The Carpenters' Union states that at present it is able to establish standard wage scales in communities or areas, whereas if the competitors were members of industrial unions every union might permit a different scale for competitors in the agreements. Thus one doing the same work might receive $8 a day in an automobile factory, $9 a day in a rubber factory, and $10 in a brewery. It is also stated that officers of vertical unions will never be intimately familiar with the craft conditions of employment and methods of production in other establishments. The result will be a multiplicity of wage scales which will unsettle the market and cause trouble.

Case D. **Difficulty of Maintaining Craft Organizations**

The supporters of craft unions in the metal trades state that even if craft unions were to limit themselves to a small sphere it would be almost impossible to maintain a strong and efficient organization. A report on the subject states:

> To break down existing international unions and merge their members into separate vertical unions without cohesion or the capacity to plan adequately with other separate vertical groups would be to remove the foundation and the framework upon which the American trade-union structure has been erected and to expect the shell which remains to stand firm, dependable and without collapse when the stress and storm of industrial friction blackens the sky.

An editorial in a weekly periodical called *Labor*, which is the official organ of the railroad labor organizations of the country, makes the following assertions:

> Mr. Lewis would have us believe that industrial unionism—that is, one union for all employees in each industry—is the salva-

tion of the American workers. There is nothing in the record of the last fifty years to sustain that claim.

Mr. Lewis' own union, the United Mine Workers, is an industrial union, and it has had the advantage of Mr. Lewis' leadership for fifteen or sixteen years. Surely, if industrial unionism is a panacea for the ills that beset American workers, then Mr. Lewis' union will furnish a shining example.

But less than three years ago the United Mine Workers were practically "on the rocks." It was saved by the labor provisions of the N.R.A., and those labor provisions were adopted by Congress at the suggestion of the American Federation of Labor and the railroad brotherhoods.

In other words, after it had been butted by the depression for three years, Mr. Lewis' industrial union was saved by the craft unions, which had succeeded in holding their ranks intact during the most trying period in our country's history.

Case E. "Martyrdom" Required of Skilled Workers

The union official of a highly skilled group of workers in the railroad industry states that these men are in a particularly favorable position to bargain with their employers because, although they constitute only about one-tenth of the workers in the industry, if they go on strike, trains cannot run. They have a strong union organization and are satisfied with the terms and conditions which their contract specifies. They say, therefore, that for them to become part of an industrial union would be to sacrifice their technical position in behalf of workers who have not taken pains to acquire a skilled occupation and who have not been loyal enough to unionism to stand by their organization during periods of sporadic leadership.

The union official says, therefore, that the outcome would in all probability be that the unskilled and other workers, constituting 90% of those in the trade, "would engulf us, would dominate in wage negotiations, and would perhaps insist upon radical changes in the seniority arrangement and privileges which we now enjoy and which have always marked our industry."

Case F. **Fear of Unmanageable Size of Industrial Unions**

A union officer in the building trades opposed to industrial unions states that if they combined their workers into one big union they would probably enroll a million workers. This, he states, would put the top official way out of the reach of the other workers and would create much the same kind of problems as over-expansion and excessive size in our large corporations. Unions and officers "would lose the personal touch and the intimate knowledge of particular group conditions which are so valuable a part of craft unions."

Case G. **Prophesy of Internal Struggles**

An officer of one of the unions in the printing industry takes issue with Charles P. Howard, president of the International Typographical Union, who is one of the chief protagonists for the movement for industrial unions. Mr. Howard had made the statement that

> Let us take an actual condition to make the point clear. Here is a plant that employs 6,000 workers. They compose all classes, and groups of various members are engaged upon different skilled work. It is impossible to organize these workers upon craft lines and draw jurisdictional limits. In a single day some of these workers are engaged upon classes of work that fall within the jurisdictional claims of more than one craft union. If organized upon craft lines they would become involved in jurisdictional controversy, or compelled to join more than one craft union, to have regular employment. And no group by itself would have sufficient economic strength to secure satisfactory settlement of its grievances in dealing with the management.

In answer to Mr. Howard the union officer points out that "when you put together a lot of miscellaneous crafts into one union, there will be clashes of interest and opinion leading to internal struggles, secession, unsanctioned strikes and other consequences, with the possible result also of making it impossible for an industrial union to maintain its contract." He also asserts that the United Mine Workers, as an example, has had a continuous series of difficulties with rival and insurgent groups. He further draws attention to the fact that "The International Typographical Union at one time had under its jurisdiction and as part of the organization the compositors, proofreaders, pressmen, bookbinders, stereotypers and electrotypers, mailers, news writers, photo-engravers. By agreement the bookbinders, stereotypers and electrotypers, and photo-engravers have formed separate organizations from the International Typographical Union."

Questions:

1. How far are these opposing contentions valid and what corrections in theory or principle may be made of them in the light of past experience, present needs, and future trends?

2. In what way can the structure of craft and industrial unions take into account the obstacles mentioned and adjust the forms of unionism to meet the difficulties?

PROBLEM 62. THE CLOSED SHOP AND THE CHECK-OFF

Case A. The Open Shop in Unionized Plants

An employer who has been opposing a collective contract with a union has finally become willing to accept all terms offered except the union's demand that every worker should either be a union member when hired or should at once become such. The terms of this closed shop clause as proposed by the union read as follows:

> The employer agrees to employ none but members in good standing of the union to do all work that may be required. The employer agrees that whenever he may be in need of additional workers, he shall first make application to the union for the same, specifying the number and kind of workers needed. The union shall be given 48 hours to supply the specified help. If the union is unable to furnish the required help the employer shall have the right to secure his help from elsewhere, and the union agrees to give a working card to such workers upon application for affiliation, which must take place within one week.
>
> A member in good standing is one who is fully paid up or who is in arrears for not more than four weeks of dues and assessments in the union, and who carries the union membership card and who has not for any cause been suspended from the union.

The employer insists upon an open shop, which he defines as one in which a worker may be a union member or not, and promises that no question will be raised in hiring or in lay-off concerning such affiliation. He states that a closed shop would give the union a monopoly of the labor market and soon would make it impossible for him to hire anyone, however efficient he might be, who did not want to join the union.

The union counters that since the terms of the collective agreement it won will be enjoyed equally by members and by those who do not pay dues, workers will be inclined to forget the need for solidarity and it will be difficult to maintain the organization. The union points out that since an employer is normally opposed to a union he is likely to hire non-union individuals as a matter of course, and that in any event, without a closed shop, every hiring of a non-union man and every lay-off of a union man while there are non-union members in the plant, will seem an act of hostility and will keep the organization in a suspicious mood.

The employer thereupon states that inasmuch as the union has only about 85% of the workers in its ranks, he is willing to agree to a stipulation that he will not reduce this ratio during the life of the agreement.

Case B. **Open Shop Involving Friction among Employees**

A clothing concern made an agreement with the union which retains the principle of the open shop. About 10% of the workers did not join the union. But soon after the agreement was signed, fellow employees of these non-members began a systematic campaign of intimidation. They called these workers "scabs." They played pranks on their clothes, poured water into their lunch boxes, and made these men so uncomfortable that some of them have quit, with only a comparatively few sullenly holding out. This has lasted four weeks.

As it is only a matter of time before the concern will become a closed shop, the employer has been doing what he could to retain the workers who had stood for the open shop. It is believed that he is secretly paying them extra wages to make up for their extra trouble. In hiring new workers he is in the main favoring non-union employees, pointing out to the union agents that by doing this he is really retaining a semblance of the status quo and that his action is not interfering with the life or organization of the union nor with the non-union quota.

The employer states that the situation is causing him "a lot of grief," and he is uncertain whether to hold out for the principle of the open shop, submit to a completely closed shop, or propose some modified principle which will prove more satisfactory to both sides.

Case C. Closed Shop against Rival Labor Union

A struggle is being waged in a plant between two rival unions of shoe workers. The company, a few months ago, entered into a closed shop agreement with that union which beyond all doubt represented a majority of the men in the plant. We shall call this Union A. Some workers who at that time joined the union also retained their membership in the other union, which we shall call Union B.

Sometime later Union A notified the workers that they were violating a provision in its constitution that no member could belong to any other organization in the trade. They were given an opportunity to resign from Union B, which they refused. As a result, they were tried in a trade union tribunal, fined and suspended. The employer was thereupon notified that they were no longer members of Union A in good standing, and under the terms of the closed shop agreement they were discharged. They therefore have asked a government board to rule that such action has deprived them of the right to belong to any organization which they choose.

Union B is not sought by the workers as a bargaining agency, and it could not serve as such in the company if it were desirous of so doing, because it is in the minority. The complaining employees are bent upon retaining their membership in Union B in order, it would seem, to keep certain extraneous benefits, and are at the same time desirous of belonging to Union A.

The officers of Union A contend that such employees in effect ask that the union be compelled to surrender the advantages gained in an agreement reached as a result of collective bargaining. It asserts that by requesting and accepting membership at a time when it had already adopted the constitution, they assented to it, and ratified the closed shop agreement.

Case D. Closed Shop by Company Union against Labor Union

A cotton mill has been very strongly opposing the organization of a union. As a result of its attitude and with its encouragement a "Friendship Association" was formed among the employees which obtained the adherence, at least outwardly, of a majority of the employees. It may be true that in any case the majority actually do prefer this association to an outside labor union.

The mill has made a collective agreement with the Friendship Association, as representing a majority of the workers, which provides for a closed shop for one year. The terms of this agreement may be seen in the following notice posted in the shop.

> Pursuant to a contract this day entered into by and between the C—— Cotton Mills and the C—— Friendship Association, only members of the Friendship Association will be employed in said Mills after this date. All seeking employment in said Mills will be required to exhibit membership cards in said Association, unless he or she shall exhibit a power of attorney authorizing said Association to represent him or her in all matters pertaining to collective bargaining.

Membership in the Association excluded participation in any other labor organization, as the by-laws provide that "any member hereof wishing to join any other labor organization may do so but the joining of any other labor organization shall be considered his resignation from this Association. No member of any labor organization shall be eligible to membership in this Association."

When the mill opened, the Friendship Association officers and members turned away all applicants who did not have the requisite membership card or power of attorney. About 130 employees on the first shift and about 137 on the second were thus refused admission. By resolution of the Association later adopted, and as stated in a notice then posted, such employees were given a week to become members or sign powers of attorney. About 133 employees took advantage of the opportunity, became members or were reinstated to membership in the Association, and were given employment. Ninety-six persons regularly employed when the mill closed and who still desire employment at the mill have not been reinstated because they refused to join the Association or to sign the power of attorney.

The union opposes a closed shop agreement made with this Association on two grounds, first, that the Association is really a creation of the management and second, that a closed shop agreement of this character forbids genuine collective bargaining, and should not be permitted.

Case E. Discharge of Members "Not in Good Standing" with Union

1. A theater chain made an agreement with a union of stage employees providing for the closed shop. Not long after the agreement had been in operation the union notified the theater management that three men who were in its employ were not in good standing with the union. They were refused membership because in years gone by they had taken the place of its members out on strike. The union asks the employer to discharge these workers as not being members of the union.

The employer contends that this is not a valid interpretation of the closed shop, since these men are now willing to join the union.

2. A local shoe union fell into the hands of several officers who, it was believed by the workers, used their positions merely to draw salaries and live on expense accounts. Several workers of the more aggressive sort attacked the officers at an open union meeting, demanded an accounting of dues and assessments, and then formed a voluntary committee to turn senti-

ment against the officers. The latter therefore appointed a membership committee to consider the actions of these dissatisfied elements, and on the ground that they were trying to disrupt the union and were a menace to the organization they were expelled. The union officers have asked the plants in the locality to discharge these workers as being not in good standing with the union.

Since there is a possibility that these actions may precipitate a strike of fellow sympathizers, the employers involved are raising objection to closed shop practices which force them to discharge the workers who are willing to remain members of the union but who happen not to be in favor with its officers.

3. A union operating under a closed shop agreement has suspended several workers for delinquency in paying certain assessments for the aid of a general labor movement or for not paying fines. The union has demanded that the employers lay off these workers until the suspensions are lifted. The employer retorts that matters of suspension are union business and not company business and that it will not become an instrument of the union in its administrative relationships.

Case F. Plight of Employees Who Work during a Strike

A group of longshoremen formerly employed on the San Francisco waterfront have written an appeal to the U.S. Department of Labor and to the Mayor of San Francisco, asking what might be done to enable them to be permitted to do longshore work in or anywhere near San Francisco. They state that at the time of the longshoremen's strike in the summer of 1934 they had had no grievance against their employer and had assisted him in moving some goods, instead of going on strike. They were at once called "scabs." When the strike was settled, the union did not readmit to membership those who, whether formerly union men or not, had worked during the strike.

An official familiar with the situation states:

> Many of the longshoremen didn't know what to do in the particular emergency and were torn between loyalty to particular bosses who had always treated them right and the call of a strike in which they didn't happen to believe. Others had had their personal differences with union officials. Most of them would have gone on strike immediately if they had foreseen the consequences.
>
> The settlement of the strike required that men who had been in longshore work at any time during the previous three years were to be registered for assignment of work through the dispatching halls. As a matter of practice the union has been dead set against any man who happened to work at any time during the strike. It is over two years now, and not one of them has been allowed back. The union has been harder on the men than employers ever have been on strikers, for no matter how much of a bad actor a worker has been, an employer will relent after a time and let him come back if he seems to be in the right spirit. About 400 or 500 men have completely lost their livelihood in the longshore work on the Pacific Coast, but some have shifted to certain Eastern and Lake ports.
>
> A solution for this would be easier if we didn't have an absolutely "closed" San Francisco Bay area and for that matter on the whole Coast. We could get a man a job in that case, and that is why I am against a rigidly closed shop unless some responsibility over union policies and practices can be exercised.

Case G. Union Demand for "Check-off" of Dues

A coal union has made a collective contract with a steel company operating eleven isolated bituminous collieries distributed over several large counties of a Southern state. The union has demanded that the dues payable by the workers, which are expensive to collect because of the distances involved, should be deducted by the employer from the weekly wage. The colliery refuses to do this. It states that it will abide by the closed shop agreement, hire only those who are union members, and discharge those who are not in good standing, provided that adequate notice is given and this practice is not abused. It refuses to assist the union in its organizing activities by the "check-off" of dues and assessments.

The union responds that its contracts in the anthracite field uniformly call for the check-off of union dues and assessments, the first not to exceed $1 per man per month and the latter not to exceed $2 per man per year. The union asserts that failure to grant such a privilege is evidence of hostility, and that the company is not genuinely accepting collective bargaining but only making it harder for the union to maintain itself.

Case H. **A Tacit Closed Shop**

While the contracts of the railroads with the four Railroad Brotherhoods of conductors, brakemen, engineers, and firemen are on an open shop basis, these unions exclude Negroes from membership in their organizations through specific provisions of their union constitutions. Negroes are thus in practice barred from four of the best paying jobs in the trade. A Negro organization protests bitterly against this exclusion, stating that this unwritten practice is, in effect, a tacit closed shop, and that the Federal government should enforce a liberal racial policy upon unions controlling interstate carriers.

See also:

Problem 47, Case D. Labor Union Contract Involving Discharge of Negro Craftsmen

Questions:

1. Evaluate the pros and cons of the closed shop and the check-off, in terms of the advantages and disadvantages under practical conditions to the employer, to unions, to the workers, and to the general public.

2. If the closed shop in some form is to prevail in a given agreement, what arrangements and stipulations, if any, might be made to prevent possible injustices?

PROBLEM 63. EMPLOYEE DISCHARGES UNDER UNION AGREEMENTS

A joint union agreement in a shoe factory and one in a hosiery mill have almost identical provisions, reading as follows: "All controversies between the parties to this agreement shall be subject to adjustment and arbitration as herein provided. The discharge of any employee which the union claims to be unjustifiable shall be arbitrated." The following illustrate the types of cases which the impartial arbitrator, provided for in the agreements, is called upon to arbitrate.

Case A. Dismissals on Ground of Inefficiency

1. In a shoe company a patent leather repairer was discharged for low production. The company makes other complaints against the operative, such as inaccuracies in reports and unsatisfactory quality of work, but these it considers less serious than the alleged low production.

The foreman who discharged the repairer testified to the amount of patent repairing which he considers a fair day's work, asserting that others of his crew do it. The union, in defending the worker, replied that the foreman has an exceptionally good crew. The discharged repairer frankly admitted that she doubted her ability to do satisfactorily the volume of work which the foreman stated that he expects, although she has had about four years' experience in three other factories in the city.

The arbitrator asked two other foremen for whom the repairer has worked about the quantity and quality of her work. Each of these foremen stated that the discharged repairer is fully competent. She asks reinstatement both to avoid discharge and to preserve her reputation as a good worker.

2. A hosiery mill discharged a seamer for bad work. The employer alleges that an unusually large number of the stockings she had made had been defectively seamed and that some of them could not even be properly repaired.

The union replies that the whole average work of the department in which she was engaged is low, that there was an insufficient number of individual checks on the seamers' work in general to permit a fair comparison with the average performance, and that the penalty of discharge was too drastic. The union contends, further, that discharge should be an exceptional penalty for extraordinary reasons and that there is no more justification for a company to discharge a worker for ordinary inefficiency than for the union to try to throw an employer out of business because he runs his factory poorly.

The employer replies that this means that once an employee is hired, it is a marriage with no divorce permitted; that poor workers will share equally in work with good ones; and that aside from other disadvantages, the interference with the foreman's power would impair discipline to the point of permitting employees to be lax and uncooperative.

Case B. **Dismissals on Ground of Carelessness**

1. A knitter in a hosiery company permitted a machine under his supervision to do "double-dipping," resulting in a smash of the machine. The company discharged him for this on the grounds of carelessness and incompetence. Among his several shortcomings, as presented by the company in this case, was that he failed to notice the difficulty with his machine as evidenced by the sound of its operation.

The union protests that such an accident might occur to any knitter having supervision over several machines, that he was at the time engaged in fixing an adjoining machine, and that this had required considerable concentration which had made it less easy for him to notice the peculiar noise of the other machine.

The company replies that a skilled knitter has the judgment and the alertness required to prevent unnecessary damage, and that the company alone is the one to judge whether a man who has permitted a damage as unprofessional as this is competent enough to be kept on the job.

2. A fitting room bench operative was suspended for putting stain on the edges of three cases of light colored kid saddles on which no stain of any kind should have been put, thus making them unsalable.

The suspended operative has been in the company's employ over a year. She has performed different bench operations, including staining edges. Prior to the present difficulty she had, however, stained edges of black leather only and thus had not had direct opportunity to become familiar with the fact that edges of colored leather, except tan calf, were not stained. The operative involved is conscientious, distressed by her mistake, frank in admitting it, offers no excuses, gives the most straightforward statement of fact, and is eager to retain her job.

Case C. **Dismissals on Ground of Discipline**

1. The union asks reinstatement with pay for lost time of a worker discharged for leaving the factory without permission of the foreman. The manufacturers' association asks confirmation of the discharge.

Testimony indicates that the discharged employee waited several hours for work on three consecutive mornings. On the first two, she eventually received work; on the third, she went home after waiting several hours without being given any work. The following morning, the worker asserts, she reported to the foreman that she was kept waiting an excessive length of time for work. She said she would take it up with the union. The foreman and the worker each made remarks bound to anger the other. The foreman told this worker that no employee gained anything by going over his head to the boss with a complaint and that she would not gain anything if she went to the union. The worker retorted by charging the foreman with favoritism. She was thereupon discharged.

2. Two men were discharged by a hosiery concern. Immediately this became a matter of interest to other workers in the department. Thirty-seven of them became excited and went on strike. They refused to go back to work although their union shop chairman and the outside union officials made every effort to have them resume operation of their machines. After a stoppage of several hours these men were discharged by the management because of their refusal to work. The union protests the discharge as being too severe a penalty.

Questions:

1. What are the advantages and disadvantages of such restriction of the employer's power of discharge? In your answer indicate what provisions and procedures would protect the parties concerned, not only from possible abuses of the power of discharge but also from the disadvantages of interference with the right of management to discipline and, when necessary, to discharge.

2. What would you be inclined to rule, as arbitrator, in the given cases?

PROBLEM 64. ADMINISTRATION OF UNION WAGE AGREEMENTS

Case A. Refund of Part of Wages by Employees

A company belongs to a manufacturers' association which has signed a collective agreement with a union. This company is located at a part of town in which the workers live, and its officers are very much liked by these workers. The factory is a large, modern structure built, unfortunately, in 1929, at the peak of building prices. At that time there was no union contract. Now, according to the management, costs are too high to meet competition. It has done all it can, and the next step requires a wage cut.

The head of the company recently called a meeting of the workers and explained the situation clearly, saying that it was a choice between a wage reduction of at least 25% from union scales or enforced part-time work for a while, with probably the eventual closing of the factory. He said that he would accept a voluntary offering of a 25% refund of wages to keep the factory going. Cards were distributed permitting such agreements, and the majority of the workers signed them as an apparently willing act.

The union contends that this procedure is contrary to the letter and the spirit of a wage agreement and that the employer should not be allowed to request or receive such rebates.

Case B. Right of Employer to Pay a Higher Wage

1. A company which has signed a market agreement with a union concerning wages, hours, and other conditions has been paying higher rates than those specified to certain classifications

of skilled workers. The fellow members of the manufacturers' association assert this to be a violation of the union agreement. These manufacturers state that for this concern to pay a higher rate under such circumstances encourages similar demands, demoralizes the wage agreement, and makes it impossible to have a standard contract.

The company replies that a union contract should set minimum rates but should not prohibit paying more than the minimum. It maintains that it has always paid more than the minimum and wants to continue to get the cream of the workers.

The other companies retort that while in an exceptional case a concern may, as in this case, actually prefer to pay a scale higher than agreed upon, normally such a situation represents a higher wage forced by some group under threat of strike. They say that even if such a higher wage is granted by the employer freely, it puts ideas into the head of militant groups of workers which would "unsettle the agreement."

2. A contract was signed in the building trades in an Eastern city which gave a new high wage rate of $1.25 an hour to bricklayers and carpenters. It was to go into effect on October 1st. Pay day was on October 3d. On the morning of October 3d, with no warning, the Laborers' Union, which had received 12¢ an hour less in the agreement, reached a large number of contractors and forced some of them into signing a contract for the payment of the $1.25 rate, on the penalty of having a strike called immediately on their jobs. By the time payrolls were to be ready, around noon, the rumor around town was that the higher wage was being paid everywhere, and so, to avoid strikes, employers paid it on demand. Concerns which had contracts on their hands at the agreed-upon rates had losses, and charged the union officers with bad faith. The latter retorted that if employers paid higher wages than the agreement called for, the union could not do anything about it.

Case C. Deductions for Breakages and Spoiled Work

1. The handle of a machine used by a knitter in a hosiery concern was broken during its operation. The company maintains that this damage must have been caused by gross carelessness of the knitter, since such a break of a slacker handle has been rarely experienced in the hosiery industry. The company found no casting flaw in the broken handle. The company feels that it is justified in holding the knitter responsible for one-half the amount of the damage.

2. A clothing cutter has ruined a large bolt of cloth by cutting it up wrongly. The employer has arranged with him for payment out of his weekly wages for the value of the cloth, and for deductions of wages for the time he spent in cutting it. The union protests any private arrangements of this kind, asserting that such reimbursements shall be given only for willful negligence and in all cases shall be reported to the union so that it may take a protest, if necessary, to the impartial chairman.

Case D. Special Concessions to Meet Non-Union Competition

In 1931 a coal operator in the Illinois area was appointed by his fellow employers as the spokesman to meet a union committee of the district to urge a radical reduction in the wage rates. He pointed out that the average earnings of the miner in Illinois were over two dollars a day more than in Kentucky, and showed that a substantial proportion of the business of the local operators had been taken away by Southern non-union mines. He asserted that the higher wage in the union areas would merely serve to ruin the mines which had collective bargaining, and thus would help the non-union mines.

The union agent of the district opposed any reduction. He maintained that there was no use in trying to compete by reducing low wages, for the non-union mines would always be able to go the union one better. The union would merely be losing one of its chief talking points to the non-union men, viz., the great difference between union mines and non-union mines in the wage rates paid.

Case E. **Special Rates on Particular Orders**

A shoe concern requests specified lower piece-rates to apply only on specified orders taken at lower prices to fill in during a slack period. It points out that a selling policy which will accomplish steadier operation is greatly to the benefit of both operatives and manufacturers, and that to reduce wages temporarily in order to enable the manufacturer to carry out such a selling policy would give employment to many people.

Case F. **Specifications concerning Number of Helpers**

A contract being negotiated in the pocketbook industry requires different wage scales for the experienced workers, the helpers, and the apprentices. A helper has previously been defined as one who "has worked on pocketbook work for at least 18 months, is capable of performing all pocketbook work, except turning in of corners, chopping, creasing, trimming and edging and is working with a teamer in the capacity of a helper."

The union states that manufacturers have tended to use the more skilled and experienced workers as helpers too long, and that by allowing a skilled worker several such helpers, the wage scales will, in fact, be reduced. It therefore demands as a part of the agreement a clause to the effect that "No pocketbook maker shall work with more than two helpers," and desires control over the number, rate of advancement, and definition of apprentices who wish to be helpers.

Case G. **Right of Access to Employer's Payrolls**

In a complicated agreement being negotiated, piece-rate scales for various grades of workers, and other detailed arrangements regarding wages and hours, have been agreed upon, but the union states that such an agreement is of value only if faithfully adhered to by the manufacturers. It has therefore insisted that the agreement signed should include the following clause: "A duly authorized officer or representative of the Union shall have access to the employer's factory payroll books for the purpose of ascertaining the correct earnings of the workers employed in the employer's shop."

Case H. **Protection against Secret Violations of Agreements**

A building contractor paying the union rates of wages finds that some contractors within the locality who had formally agreed to the new union wage scale appear not to be paying the full wage and are thus able to underbid the legitimate employers on new work by wide margins. As the labor item in estimating a contracting job usually outweighs the material and overhead items heavily, it is practically impossible to take a job in open bidding from one of these contractors, whose shop is ostensibly a union one but which is really working for less than union wages. Thus, one union is believed to permit its men to work for 90¢ and $1.00 per hour instead of the rate of $1.25 called for in the contract. The business agents of the union seem to be in collusion with these competitors, so that the evidence is difficult to get.

Questions:

1. Discuss the appropriate action to be taken with regard to the terms and administration of the collective agreement in each of the cases presented, indicating what concessions or adjustments could properly be made by either the employer or the union to meet the needs of the situation.

2. What features of an agreement are possible means of protection of employers who obey its terms, against collusion between unscrupulous manufacturers and dishonest union officials?

PROBLEM 65. ATTACKS UPON UNION WAGE POLICIES

Case A. "Fair" Wage or Monopoly Scale?

An official of an employers' waterfront association on the Pacific Coast states that a union introduces mass action "whose economic intelligence is like that shown in the Townsend plan," and therefore its members are remunerated "way out of line with economic possibilities. Their leaders, if they know better, must take an unreasoning attitude in order to hold their following." He says further:

Unions may sometimes say that they are merely interested in a "fair" wage, but in their actual practice they are trying to get all they possibly can without reference to what a "fair" wage might be. They will not only admit that this is so, but actually publish it.

A fair wage policy would be one which would at least take into account the general consumer. Leave profits, if you will, at the very minimum, yet every increase obtained by any union which has a monopoly over wages is paid for by other workers through higher prices, directly or indirectly forced upon the product.

A fair wage policy would take into account fellow workers. Do you find that a strong printing union or railroad union or any other monopoly group in a craft, or part of an industry, worries about what the other workers are getting? They look out for themselves and say, "Let the other fellows organize and get theirs."

A fair wage policy requires some economic sense, and some willingness to consider the whole picture. Could you possibly get that out of a wild meeting of longshoremen, or get them to follow any leader who counselled moderateness and a consideration for other people?

Case B. "Impossibility and Futility" of Union Wage Demands

A manufacturer of women's garments complains that under the industry's agreement, the coat, reefer, and dress operators are paid a piece-rate to yield them an average of $1.50 an hour, or an equivalent weekly rate of $50 (aside from overtime), and that on the same way of figuring, the contract yields machine pressers $57 per week, shirt operators $48 per week, and coat finishers $41 per week. It is his belief that the union in his industry has forced an exorbitant scale on the trade. He argues that if every industry were organized on a collective bargaining basis, and if every employer yielded, or had to yield to such wage demands, the wages demanded would in all probability exceed enormously the total income of the country, even including salaries, profits, dividends, and all other forms. He writes:

> Since the increase in national income required would make more efficient production indispensable, even this would be impossible because unions tend to curb demands from the employer for output or discipline, so that with unions in power everywhere we could not even produce the extra income to pay the wage bill. Under these conditions the demands would be impossible to meet and would fall of their own weight. They would be futile because they would merely mean spiral increases in cost and prices, which would leave the real wages about where they were.
>
> The only basis on which wage increases demanded by unions may be given is when only a few trades are organized. These unions are then able to obtain for their members higher incomes at the expense of others who are unorganized.

Case C. Effect of Union Wages on Demand for Products

A printing establishment which specializes in color plates believes that paintings reproduced in color, rather than in black and white, could have a large popular appeal if put out at a low price. The owner states that if the workers would be willing to accept $30 or $35 a week, instead of demanding contracts stipulating $60, $70 and more, he could produce these plates far more cheaply and could expand his business enormously, so that in time plants in the industry could give employment to many times the number of people now in this kind of work. He says:

> The result of union wage policy, instead of increasing purchasing power, actually restricts industrial expansion, penalizes the consumer, reduces the opportunities for labor, makes it possible for foreign concerns, at least in our trade, to leap over the highest tariff wall, and benefits a few against the many.

Case D. **Economics of Union Wages in Building**

Building contractors object that wage rates of $10, $12, and $15 a day, plus bonuses, keep many people from building or engaging in repairs, and greatly restrict the amount of construction work. Real estate, house, and hotel owners blame the building trades workers, in part, for the inadequate amount of housing available for the masses of people, and for the high rents necessarily enforced by the high initial cost of building.

The recurrent complaints from economists and others who have no direct relationship to building or construction, but who regard the construction industry as the leverage raising or lowering business prosperity as a whole, are often in the same tenor. A statistician who has made a study of the subject writes:

> An expansion of housing and construction is, as you know, regarded by many authorities as the chief way out of a depression. Whatever may have been the cause of the last depression, the fact remains that in residential construction alone, as gauged by contracts awarded, there was a decline from 1929 to 1932 of approximately 80%. Union labor realized the conditions by granting some reductions without recognizing it in their contracts. But government construction soon stiffened the laborleaders, and the minute recovery got under way, the monopoly of union workers began to get its usual preference in employment, so that they tightened up on wage rates.
>
> In 1935, for example, almost 20% of all skilled building workers in the country, under union scales, were paid at a rate of $1.50 or

more per hour. As the average rate of even helpers and laborers was 81¢, the scale for union workers in the various building trades averaged $1.20 per hour both in 1934 and 1935. These are some of the conditions which slowed up what might have been a big housing boom for the masses.

Everyone urged upon the government that it finance and undertake a housing program, and this might have carried us far except for the insistence of the building unions upon having wage rates corresponding to union scales charged to private contractors. This re-introduced the issue of artificially high costs. Partly as a result, it was the automobile industry, which was not at all controlled by union labor, which got the jump and helped to pull us out of the depression. If the building trades had not had a strangle hold through excessive wages and arbitrary restrictions on the construction industry, we might have had a boom in housing too, recovered quicker and left a few million better homes for the people to live in during our next depression instead of cars.

The building trades union reply is that if wages are figured on an annual basis their rates are not excessive, and that the chief remedy required for housing is to reduce the monopoly prices charged by the makers of building materials, mortgage companies, and land speculators. Some economists reply that undoubtedly everything should be done to break up the rings which boost the prices of building materials and to remove the other obstacles of a financial nature which interfere with building. They point out, however, that in building costs the labor factor is 50% and often 60% of the total, and that the principle they are urging applies in either case. They say that there would be less irregular work in building and more stability if wage rates were more flexible and corresponded to economic conditions.

Case E. Allegation that Excessive Wage Demands Can Be Curbed Only by Dictatorship

A student of public affairs who terms himself a "cynical believer" in the value of collective bargaining states that society owes capitalism a debt for the opposition that it puts up to union wage demands. He states that too harmonious relationships with unions usually mean that both sides are taking it out on the public. He further states that even good socialists and liberals, if they are clear thinking, will admit this. He cites the following excerpt from a book by John A. Hobson, a liberal English economist:

> In some trades organization of labour is half-consciously directed to getting for the employees a share in the plunder obtained by charging "monopoly" or semi-monopoly prices to other trades, or the private consumer, for the goods or services which they supply. As organization becomes more effective in the fundamental and pivotal trades, it must be expected that the mutual recognition on the part of the capitalists, managers, and workers of the waste from a conflict between these factors will bring them into closer and more harmonious cooperation in seeking a common gain out of the public at large by sharing the gains from high prices. (*Incentives in the New Industrial Order*, New York, Thomas Seltzer, 1925, p. 20.)

This "cynical believer" asserts further: "No form of capitalism or socialism could curb the excessive demands of unions if the balance of power veered sharply towards labor. The outcome would be fascism or Communism, in both of which the curb comes through dictatorship, subordinating unions drastically through arbitrary power."

Questions:

1. What would constitute, in principle, a fair level of wages for which a union is justified in striving?

2. By reference to typical wage rates in strongly organized trades in your community, or elsewhere, indicate whether there appears to be any tangible basis for the assertions that unions are exacting monopoly scales.

3. Comment on the validity of union wage policies from economic and sociological standpoints, paying special attention to the serious charge made in Case E.

PROBLEM 66. DISPUTED VALUE OF UNIONS IN PRODUCTION

Case A. Leaders' Reluctance to Support Unpopular Changes

In a coal company in Illinois, the management a few years ago desired to introduce a change from room and pillar work to the long wall system. The latter permits taking out practically all the coal, instead of leaving about half of it underground. It requires fewer maintenance men to lay and repair tracks, fewer timbermen, and fewer people to clean up falls of roofs. The company urged this system upon the men because it anticipated lower costs of production that would enable it to compete with lower cost non-union mines then operating down South, which were already using the long wall system.

As part of this new plan, the company planned to subdivide the miner's work somewhat, so that drilling and blasting would be done by special men, as well as the handling of the empty cars and timbering. Thus the miner would have less idle time and waiting, and would be able to dig coal more steadily. The plan did not involve more or harder work but a different organization of work. By using these men continuously during their eight hours of work, instead of intermittently, as was then the case, the company expected to get twenty-four tons of coal per digger daily, as against twelve tons under the existing system. Instead of paying per ton mined, it would pay a flat day rate specified in the union agreement for day men, equivalent to the average former earnings of tonnage men in this area.

The three main officials of the local union were an intelligent and friendly group, but they said that the miners would see the plan as a way for the employers to get more work for less pay. It would seem to double efficiency and thus to enable the work to be done with fewer men, either in this mine or in the industry as a whole. They felt they would lose their influence with the union membership and with higher officers of the union if they permitted this plan.

Under the terms of agreement with the employers, the union had no right to specify any particular method of operating a mine. But the tonnage rate of pay had been specified, and if this basis was not changed, the actual earnings of the miners would have been doubled under the newer, more continuous system of work and thus have made the plan impossible. Hence the introduction of the plan was, in effect, stopped because the union officials held out for the tonnage rate.

Case B. **Compatibility of Unions with Scientific Management**

An intelligent textile employer, who has been a liberal leader in his field and a supporter of unions in the trade, describes himself as a turncoat against his former ideals and an opponent of unionism in his own plants. He asserts that unions are masses, with the intelligence of masses, and "they see short cuts to higher wages where none exist." He says ironically that "unions would be a good thing in the trade for me only if my competitors alone would have them," and writes as follows:

> As one who studied his labor relations under Professor Robert F. Hoxie before the War, I find myself forced by experience to admit that he was right and I am wrong. For a while I thought that with proper nursing I could get a union group to see our joint interest in greater production and efficient operation. The union cooperated for a couple of years, and I thought everything lovely. But the end result is that I find that workers as a whole are incapable of understanding the economics of efficient operation and are hostile. If given power, unions try to solve complicated industrial difficulties by reducing the hours of work, putting a curb on technical developments, as they did in our trade for a while under the N.R.A. textile code, and resisting all the things our highly competent industrial engineer is trying to work out to reduce costs. I find that the only way to put such changes across is to avoid giving a union group much power.

Professor Hoxie, who was a labor enthusiast, always recognized that unions and efficiency are at opposite poles. In his book *Trade Unionism in the United States,* he makes much of the point that there is an essential incompatibility between the basic ideals of scientific management and those of the dominant type of trade unionism. Scientific management, he says, can function well only on the basis of constant and indefinite change of industrial conditions; trade unionism of the dominant type can function successfully only through the maintenance of fixed industrial situations and conditions, and the establishment of definite rules and restraints governing the adoption of new processes and methods of production.

The letter then emphasized that labor unions are defensive and protective in nature, that scientific management has to be imposed upon labor, and that it is impossible to expect to be able to introduce it with their understanding and cooperation.

Case C. **Union-Management Cooperation Which Went Wrong**

(The material in this case consists of excerpts from a first-hand study made by Professors R. C. Nyman and E. D. Smith of the Institute of Human Relations, Yale University. The first part of the case is taken from a summary by Professor Nyman on "Labor Extension in a Cotton Mill," in the *Personnel Journal* of February, 1934, pp. 269–271. The last three paragraphs are taken from their joint book, *Union-Management Co-operation in the "Stretch Out,"* published by the Yale University Press, 1934, 210 pp.)

At the Pequot Mills the management, in 1928, proposed to introduce the "extended labor" or "stretch out" system as an emergency cost reduction measure. Working conditions at the Pequot Mills were exceptionally good, and wages had long been much above the level of the industry. The mill officials were singularly sincere and sympathetic in their attitude toward labor problems. The workers were represented by a fully recognized and long established trade union. Despite these conditions, fear of unemployment, demotion, and excessive job burdens led the workers to oppose the introduction of the "stretch out" system, even though wage increases had been promised the workers to be "extended." Not until the management consented to base increased job assignments upon joint factual analysis rather than upon executive judgment as to what constituted a fair job burden would the workers agree to the development.

As a result the trade union not only fully participated in and to some extent controlled the development, but also brought about the employment of an industrial engineer and the establishment of a joint research organization to supervise.

The results were unsatisfactory to the management because the officials of the company were of the opinion that the degree of extension achieved was not as large as it might have been. The workers on their part were dissatisfied because 350 of their number, including some permanent workers, had been eliminated, because as many more had been demoted at reduced wages, and because they soon came to believe that the new job assignments had created excessive job burdens.

Though wage rates and earnings continued to be much above the level of the industry as a whole, the "stretch out" system consequently came to be regarded with increasing hostility, and the trade union officials with animosity, because they had agreed to its introduction and the wage reductions which followed it. Because of this attitude and because the development was largely completed, the industrial engineer in charge was released and the joint research organization disbanded. "Joint research" and "stretch out" had apparently become things of the past.

The increasingly adverse effects of the depression and continued pressure for cost reduction, however, led the mill officials early in 1933 reluctantly to propose a resumption of joint research and further "stretch outs." When the union officials agreed to this proposal, the workers rose in rebellion. In defiance both of the company and the officials of the union the workers remained away from their jobs for ten weeks.

Since the union officials had refused to sanction the strike, regarding it as a violation of contract, the workers, within a week after it was settled, resigned in a body and formed an independent organization.

This left the mill officials to deal with three antagonistic labor organizations—the new independent union, the remnant of the old union, and a small but well-knit loomfixers' union which had been in existence for many years, and which had refused consistently to participate in the technological development. It also left the company unable to conduct any research tending to increase job assignments or change working methods for a period of two years, regardless of a continued need for cost reduction.

Since the provisions for communication between the management and the workers for joint discussion of mutual problems had ceased to reach below the union officials, the employee body as a whole was neither fully aware of nor understood the reasons for the new changes. These appeared unreasonable to them and created in their minds a conviction that only by preventing further "stretch outs" could they preserve their security and well-being.

The experience of Pequot raises important questions to which the answers are speculative. Could a more effective means of keeping the workers and operating executives in constant touch with management and labor problems and with the safeguarding aspects of "joint research" and union-management cooperation have been devised? And would such an arrangement have brought them the same understanding that enabled the small group of mill and union officials to work in harmony?

Above all, would the position of "joint research" have been made sufficiently clear to have been understood and supported by workers and lesser management if the management had undertaken full responsibility for determining, establishing, and maintaining all methods and conditions relating to the change? Should it have left to "joint research" the sole task of indicating these conditions, how well they were being maintained, in what ways they were defective, and what extension of labor they justified, thus placing "joint research" unequivocally in a position of safeguarding labor, not administering a "stretch out"?

Could any or all of these have enabled the partnership of management and union to carry through the difficult adjustments to technological change in an unprecedentedly long and severe depression, with labor extension following labor extension and with repeated disruptions of the status quo?

Case D. **A Successful Case of Union-Management Cooperation**

One of the best known examples of union-management cooperation is that which began on the Baltimore & Ohio Railroad and spread to other roads. Its guiding spirit from the standpoint of the unions was Otto S. Beyer, Jr., a consulting engineer, employed by them for the purpose. Mr. Beyer, in an article describing the success of the plan, stated:

> Strange as it may seem, it is by virtue of the very fact that labor is organized that it has been able to develop a constructive instead of a negative or destructive policy toward the introduction of new machinery into industry. For when workers are organized and their unions are entitled to negotiate with management, the means become available to find a solution to the problems precipitated by improved machine methods.
>
> Agreement between employers and employees to a revised set of working rules which had due regard for the earnings and the stability of employment of the workers affected in the revised agreement heeded the inherent right of the worker not to suffer temporary unemployment and reduction in wage income because of the use of improved machinery.

An account of what the plan involves may perhaps be better illustrated by showing the success reported by one of the other railroads. The material which follows is the statement of an official of the Canadian National Railways.

> The policy of union management or industrial representation was experimentally tried out on one of the larger American railroad systems in 1923 with success. President Sir Henry Thornton decided to give the co-operation plan a fair trial on the Canadian National Railways. Since that time the Joint Co-Operative Committees have been organized at all the major car and locomotive repair shops. To date, thirteen shops are operating successfully under this plan.
>
> Under the plan as formulated by the officials of the Federated Shop Crafts and accepted by the management of the Canadian National Railways, it was agreed that, as economies were effected as a result of cooperation, the management would be in a position to further stabilize employment, giving the shop employees participating in the plan some assurance of steadier employment. The principal incentive then to increased efficiency was the company's guarantee that the expected improvements in production would not result in greater irregularity of employment but, on the contrary, would bring about a progressive increase in the amount of work available, thus increasing the yearly earnings of all men employed in C.N.R. shops. The guarantee of more stable employment has thus far proved a sufficient incentive to make the plan a success.
>
> The machinery for putting the plan into force is comparatively simple and consists of joint meetings held bi-weekly between the local federated shop committees, representing the employees, and the local supervising officials, representing the management. The committee representing the management is usually made up of the shop superintendent and heads of the various departments. The committee representing the men is the regular trade union shop committee, made up of one representative for each craft.
>
> These committees in their regular joint meetings discuss and act upon all questions of shop policy and operation affecting their local shops. Questions affecting more than one shop or the entire system are passed on to a committee known as the Joint System Co-Operative Committee which meets at regular intervals.

At these local and system meetings, proposals for improvement in shop practice and operation may be brought forward by either side for full discussion. All proposals found to be practicable and which do not require large capital outlay are put into operation at once. The management reserves the right, however, to postpone the application of improvements requiring large expenditures until such funds are available.

It might be interesting to note that to date thousands of recommendations have been submitted, and 71% of which have been adopted, materially increasing the morale of the plants, adding substantially to the efficiency of the shops and creating a spirit of good will and cooperation between employees and management.

The following partial list of the subjects discussed in local meetings was selected from a voluminous compilation of all suggestions offered since the inauguration of the plan: job analysis and standardization; better tools and equipment; care and distribution of tools; storage of materials; economical use of materials; rearrangement of machine tools; balancing of forces and work in shops; condition of shops, heating, lighting, ventilation, etc.; installation of safety devices; improvement in quality of work; introduction of output records; improvements in technical training for apprentices; co-ordination and scheduling of work through shops; getting business for the road; recruiting and building up of competent, responsible, working forces.

The union management cooperation plan makes no change in the established trade union method of negotiating wage agreements by collective bargaining and adjusting grievances arising under working rules in conference between representatives of the unions and of the management. These subjects are excluded from consideration in the cooperation meetings in order to eliminate criticism and fault finding and permit the development of a spirit of mutual helpfulness.

While grievances are not discussed in the joint committee conference, the agreements reached in these conferences have tended to prevent disputes and the total number of grievances has been reduced by more than 75% since the cooperation plan has been in effect.

One of the most interesting developments in connection with the cooperative plan has been the discussion in trade union meetings of methods of getting new business for the road. Night meetings with business men in the shops have been held at many points for the purpose of pointing out the importance to the town of continued activity in the shops and the connection between the volume of traffic hauled by the road and the amount of repair work available. A considerable amount of new traffic, both freight and passenger, has been secured in this way.

Questions:

1. Analyze and outline the economic and social factors which create resistance between organized workers and management in the use of efficient methods of operation. Discuss the conditions and techniques which might give promise of a better basis of relationship in this respect, indicating what should be the function and responsibility of a workers' organization in the introduction and administration of technical changes.

2. What types of cooperation from union officers is a management justified in asking or expecting concerning technical changes likely to prove unpopular with the membership; and what might the management do in an industry in which union officers have not shown a cooperative interest, or in which they fear to oppose the sentiment of their workers?

PROBLEM 67. REEMPLOYMENT OF STRIKERS AFTER STRIKES

Case A. Are Striking Employees Still Employees?

An issue arose between a New York pocketbook concern and the union, and the workers called a strike. The employer asserts that the union made impossible demands. He takes the position that the inability to obtain any reasonable concessions from the union, or to settle the strike, had terminated all relationships of the company with its employees and that as they were no longer its employees there was no further obligation to them.

The opposing contention, made by the union, was that striking workers are still the employees of a concern, that a strike can hardly be considered a permanent abandonment by the striking employees of their jobs, and that it is a temporary and collective withdrawal of work as a means of exerting legitimate pressure in support of pending negotiations.

Case B. Preferential Treatment for Substitutes or for Strikers?

1. During a strike lasting three weeks the employer hired substitutes. When the strike came before a mediation authority, the employer stated that it would be unjust to those men who had worked for him during that period, and who happened to be non-union men, to displace them.

The union contends, however, that any such procedure is just a subterfuge for using non-union men. All an employer has to do is to precipitate a strike, hire non-union workers, and then assert a sense of responsibility for these workers. The union states that the prior responsibility is to the workers who had previously been employed. They demand that all "scabs" hired should be immediately dismissed, and the places given to the men who had struck.

2. A conflict which arose between the workers of an enameling mill and the management lasted almost seven months before it came before a board of arbitration. This authority found the employees in the right on the issue involved, and the employer unfair in his policy and practices. This decision was made in the middle of February. The strike had lasted since the previous July and the plant had been operating with substitutes during that time.

The workers insisted that the only possible value of such arbitration would be to apply the remedy of giving back the jobs which they had lost. This meant that they wanted the mill to drop all the employees who were not on the payroll the day the strike was declared, and to reinstate in such vacancies all individuals employed on that day who still wanted their jobs in the plant, with possible exceptions among those employees who were receiving substantially equivalent employment elsewhere.

3. A wallpaper company which engaged in collective bargaining with a union for several decades found it could not accept the terms of a new agreement, and a strike ensued. To fill the vacancies, the company was able to hire several men by guaranteeing them that they should work a full year. Naturally, these were non-union men, for no union man would take a job under these circumstances. The company and the union, after several weeks, formulated all the terms of an agreement except the discharge of these men, and the case came to arbitration.

Case C. Choice of Workers Reemployed after a Strike

1. A strike lasted for about seven weeks. When the issues were about to be settled, a seasonal slack arrived and the employer had no occasion to rehire any of the workers. He said he did not see the likelihood of reemploying most of them for

an indefinite time. The union contended that if business conditions prevented an employer from reinstating them then, a preferential list should be drawn up and, as rapidly as increased production permitted, men should be hired from that list only. It demanded that this be on the basis of seniority.

2. In a strike settlement the union asked that all those on the payroll at the time of the strike be given preference in rehiring. The company called attention, however, to the fact that it had been laying off workers for a couple of years, and that those previously laid off should be the first to be rehired.

The union contends that this is just a trick procedure by which the employer may select workers who, having been unemployed, did not participate in the strike or join the union. It demands that all workers who had been employed at the time of the strike should be rehired first.

Case D. **Strike in Which Violence Occurred**

A protracted strike led to violence in several instances on the part of certain workers whom the union could not easily control. The union contended that, since the employer had been at fault in infuriating the workers, it was to be expected that some of them would lose their tempers. Therefore the union argued that the incidents of the strike should be forgotten and all the strikers rehired.

Questions:

1. What decisions would you make in each of these cases if you were arbitrator? Summarize the main points of these decisions as principles which should apply to the settlement of such issues.

2. What laws have been passed in recent years regarding the status of strikers and of strike-breakers in collective bargaining, and what decisions have been rendered under these laws by administrative bodies?

PROBLEM 68. LEGAL REMEDIES FOR LABOR UNION ABUSES

Case A. Violence in Organization Activities

1. Window cleaners have wanted to organize the industry and find that here and there employers are using non-union workers. In an organizing campaign, groups of union workers have attacked such non-union employees, pushed away the ladders on which they were at work, beaten them up, and in some cases broken the windows of the building on which they were engaged.

2. Building unions are making a "clean-up drive" in a large city to discover the use of non-union employees. A series of fires in apartment houses under construction has been noted, the fire department reporting that in each of nine such isolated cases over a period of a few weeks the jobs on which the damage was done were all of non-union construction.

3. Fur workers engaged in a strike against their employers invaded shops in various places, threw acid on the fur coats, broke the furniture, and inflicted bruises and severe injuries on employers and workers present.

Case B. An Irreconcilable Minority

The leader of a radical group representing less than 20% of the employees of a plant has been attempting to obtain a collective agreement for the personnel of the whole company. He has made no progress with the great mass of the workers because of misrepresentation, poor strategy, impossible demands upon the company, and other faults. The employer has in no way opposed him, and has announced publicly on several occasions that he is willing to make a collective contract with any organization of his employees which can poll a majority membership in an election held under government or other neutral auspices. He denounces the strike which the minority group has called and which is interfering with the work of the 80% opposed to the stoppage.

The union leader has asked a government board which has attempted to take jurisdiction of the strike to "stay out" of the situation. He asserts that the way for a union to achieve power is by converting a minority into a majority; that a strike can be successfully conducted through a minority; and that when a militant minority forces the employer to give wage increases and other terms to the workers, the minority will become a majority.

The strike is ruining the employer and causing great misery among the workers forced to be idle by the action of this minority. Both the employer and a delegation of non-union workers have asked for government intervention.

Case C. **A Destructive Factional Dispute**

A group of anthracite coal miners who were dissatisfied with the management of the United Mine Workers Union in the anthracite district decided to organize their own group, the United Anthracite Miners. These insurgents forced a contract with certain coal companies in the neighborhood, but could not obtain the adherence of others who had contracts with or leanings toward the United Mine Workers. As a result they called a strike in these collieries. An article in *The Nation* of April 17, 1935, described the conflict that ensued, as follows:

> The contract between the operators and the U.M.W. will expire one year from this month. The insurgents realize that they must be strong enough to demand their signatures on the new contract if they are to survive. For the next year the new union must recruit thousands of new members and keep morale at fever heat. To do this, it must have strikes.
>
> The United Mine Workers are also aware of the approach of April, 1936. This winter they began an intensive campaign for

the extermination of the new union. Committees of the old union guarded the mine entrances and allowed only men wearing the U.M.W. buttons to work. Violence and fighting ensued, groups of several hundred miners rushed each other. Scores of men were carried off to hospitals or their homes with cracked heads and broken bones.

Threatening notes tied around bricks were hurled through kitchen windows, warning members to quit their jobs. Effigies of scabs and unpopular officials dangled from telegraph poles. Bombs exploded almost nightly, not only in miners' homes but in tenements housing many families.

This lasted over a period of months, flaring up here and there in accordance with provocation or the activities of rival factions. No official in the state or Federal government was able to get them to resolve their difficulties peaceably. In the process scores of people were injured, including innocent bystanders, and some members of the rival factions were killed.

Case D. **Oppressive and Vindictive Control**

1. In a large city an investigation was made of monopoly practices, including those alleged to be practiced by unions. One such instance reported was of a bakery union whose workers controlled a large number of small shops making bread purchased by its foreign-born population. The investigator stated:

These bakery workers have much higher pay and much shorter hours than their brethren in other bakeries, but not content with this situation, the officials of the union try to prevent employers from organizing for the purpose of collective bargaining. They do not deal with the employers' organization. Among other things they have required the bakeries to sign individual contracts with the union.

The form of contract which they have been requiring in this way from the employer is one of the most amazing documents I have ever seen. If lazy, incompetent, impudent, or discipline-destroying men are sent him by the union, he cannot discharge them. He must employ a given number of men regardless of whether he needs them; he is not permitted to work in his own business more than a given number of hours prescribed by the union. If he has a grievance he is not allowed to ask for its arbitration by an outsider but only by the executive committee of the union itself.

If he should get into trouble with the union they not only picket his place, but spend the union's money in establishing competition next door to him, buying bread in the open market and selling it to his customers at less than it cost them—in order to destroy the recalcitrant employer.

2. An industrial commission of an Eastern state conducted hearings concerning labor conflicts. Among its witnesses was a gray-haired contractor who told how for seven years he had been "hounded" by the union of marble workers and had his prosperous marble and tile business ruined. In describing his despair over his inability to obtain legal relief, the witness, for thirty years a marble contractor, stated that his troubles began when he withdrew from the Marble Employers Association when the Association sought to compel him to have all his bids approved by the secretary. He testified before an investigating committee that the Association and the union were in league to fix prices, and as a result the Association was disbanded.

From that time on the union would not furnish him with men. He named the president of the building trades council and two business agents of the marble workers' unions as having told him they would ruin him. They followed up the general contractors from whom he got business so that the other crafts would walk out in sympathy and refuse to return until the general contractor cancelled his agreement.

Case E. Exploitation of Members by Union Officers

1. A certain union controls the union labor in its industry and is thereby aided in making contracts with employers whose products go to the types of stores patronized by union labor

and its sympathizers. In the area in which its membership is largely concentrated, the vast majority of the members are dissatisfied with the national officers, who, they feel, are feathering their own nest rather than trying to improve conditions generally for the workers. One writes that "it seems impossible to get these officers off our backs."

The court of final authority in the union is its annual convention. Under the union's constitution each local union, no matter of what size, has one delegate, and there are additional delegates for the additional membership which the local may have above the first 200 members. Each delegate has one vote. In order for a local to be started, it needs to have only seven members. On this basis an isolated local with seven members has as much power in the convention as a local in which there are 195 members, and five locals, with 35 or 40 members in all, have as much power as a large local with nearly a thousand members. All that the international officers have to do is to charter a lot of little locals throughout New England and even the mid-Western states, pay handsomely the expenses of one of the seven members as a delegate to the convention, and so have a packed convention in which 100 locals with a total membership of only 700 have more delegates and therefore more power than 10,000 members in the hostile area. A worker states:

> Members of the opposition soon find themselves unemployed because one who attacks the administration may be suspended or expelled from the union and lose his means of livelihood. Innumerable pretexts are used, such as "creating or attempting to create dissatisfaction or dissension," "disturbing the harmony of meetings," "using profane language in the property of the local union," or "revealing the business of the union to outsiders." When a man is thrown out of the union he cannot get a job with any of the factories in the area who have a union contract, since that would be hiring someone not in good standing.

2. In 1932 fifteen members of the Local 3 of the International Brotherhood of Electrical Workers alleged in affidavits

that the officers had failed to account for $7,500,000 of union funds in the last five years, that much of the money had been used illegitimately, and that members who sought an accounting had been barred from union meetings, discharged from jobs, fined large sums, suspended from the union or beaten. Their complaint made the following charges:

> That the regime of the president does not permit an electrician to accept a job unless approved by the union, "thus putting the livelihood of every member subject to the dictation of his regime."
>
> That the union officials, working with a combination of favored contractors composing the Electrical Contractors Association of New York, form a "ring" which uses the union to harass competitors and so parcel out the most profitable contracts among themselves.
>
> That the union local has 8,000 members and the International Union 40,000. For three years, according to the affidavits, the present regime has held on by force and the income of the union in recent years has increased tremendously, while all checks on expenditures have been removed, with union members unable to obtain an accounting. Dues were increased from $28.80 to $108 a year per person; initiation fees from $150 to $300; and heavy fines for trivial offences account for an additional total of $200,000 a year.

One man's affidavit alleged that the funds have been used to fasten on the people of the City of New York a racket participated in by certain favored contractors and certain favored members of the union. He stated:

> It is my belief that the large amounts of money from this enormous fund have been used for political purposes to stifle threatened investigations, to obtain favorable decisions in cases that might be brought, to prevent prosecutions of instances of violence that are resorted to by the emissaries of the regime, and generally to put the favored contractors and the favored members of the union above and beyond the reach of the law.

Other affidavits asserted that the signers had been dismissed from jobs shortly after they had taken part in an effort to amend the by-laws to deprive the union officials of considerable power. One of the affiants swore that since he had taken part in the move to amend the by-laws, he had been unable to gain admittance to the employment room of the union, where men receive notification of jobs. Another, a member of the union since 1915, said he was not permitted to attend union meetings, but was stopped at the door.

Case F. When Is It "Racketeering?"

The district attorney in a mid-Western city who has been making a study of labor racketeering states that he is puzzled as to what actions to take and what recommendations to make, because it is often so hard to distinguish technically between racketeering properly named and aggressive or selfish union activities which are merely called racketeering. He says that there are "three levels of racketeering," which he describes as follows:

> The first type of racketeering is that which is genuinely run by gangs and racketeers who have no record as labor leaders, but who fasten themselves on an organization because it is a dues-paying proposition and because they can levy tribute on employers. For example, in Chicago a notorious ex-convict got hold of the Newspaper Wagon Drivers' Union and thirteen other unions. The workers were forced to pay high dues, and the employers and others were forced to pay money to prevent strikes from being called. Al Capone in his time got hold of a large number of the unions through terroristic methods. As an example of how far this kind of thing may go, the president of one union was kidnapped and ransomed for $50,000, and the secretary-treasurer of the Truck Drivers' Union, who refused to sell his secretaryship for a good round sum, was taken for a ride and shot to death.
>
> In the second level of racketeering are the union leaders who have risen to power from the ranks but have succumbed to the numerous temptations of their office. The easy money gets them, and there are politicians and corrupt employers who are willing to spread them with plenty of it in return for "advice."

A third type is the alleged racketeering of the aggressive, hard-boiled labor union leader who is unscrupulous in his methods of attaining the purposes of his organization, but who himself does not get any illicit profits. Such a labor union official may be getting a high salary, in five figures, from the union, freely granted to him by the majority. On behalf of his organization he may obtain for the workers very high wages and other conditions and, at the same time, aid employers against competitors who do not observe certain monopoly or trade agreements, whichever you would call them.

In a great many cases our aid is asked when all that appears to be occurring is that the union employers and union officers are together trying to get the non-union chiseler into line, so as not to penalize the employer who believes in decent conditions and is willing to do his share in maintaining collective bargaining. Just how to separate this third type of racketeering from legitimate union efforts to get the best industrial conditions for the workers is one of those economic and social problems where knowledge of the law does not help one much.

Questions:

1. By reference to the particular kinds of evils described, what are the legal measures available to those needing protection, as: (1) employers, (2) workers, (3) the general public, under the ordinances, laws, court decisions and the administration of justice in (a) your community, (b) your state, (c) the United States.

2. Comment on the adequacy and suitability of these legal provisions, and the dangers of the abuse of such legal powers in repressing vigorous efforts of workers to organize. With these points in mind, indicate the chief reforms or changes needed, if any, in the law applying to the abuses of which unions might be guilty.

PROBLEM 69. COMPULSORY ARBITRATION OF LABOR DISPUTES

Case A. Dictum that "All Strikes Are Justified"

On February 2, 1934, Emma Goldman, the well-known anarchist, came back to the United States on her first visit since her deportation in 1919. She happened to arrive when there was a taxi strike in New York. According to the newspapers, in greeting reporters, she said she was delighted "to be welcomed by a taxi strike; that is as it should be with me." Asked whether she knew the issues, she said that she did not, "but I consider every strike on the part of the workers justified."

Case B. Refusals to Arbitrate

1. When a labor dispute on the Interborough Rapid Transit Company in New York some years ago resulted in tying up traffic, literally millions of people were temporarily put to great discomfort or stopped from going to work. The city authorities tried to effect a compromise, but the company, refusing to deal with the striking motormen until they returned to work and rejoined the so-called company union, unconditionally rejected a proposal from the Mayor for arbitration of the questions involved in the strike.

2. In the same year there was a coal strike, and the United Mine Workers refused to arbitrate. A labor publication, the *Metal Trades Department Bulletin*, commenting on the pending negotiations, wrote editorially:

> The coal workers will not arbitrate a wage scale any more than a clothing dealer or a coal retailer would consent that outside parties arbitrate the price of a suit of clothes or a ton of coal. The coal miner sells his labor power, and he does not propose to allow outsiders to dictate the kind of a living he shall get, or how he

shall educate his children, or the kind of food he shall eat—for that is what a wage arbitration amounts to. After a wage scale is signed and in force, the miner is willing to arbitrate disputed points in the agreement but not the original pact.

3. An important officer in a longshoremen's association states that he has no use for arbitration and would never agree to it. "It means that we give up everything we have been fighting for just when we have a chance to get the terms we want. When labor is in power there is no need for compulsory arbitration. Only when it is weak and cannot make headway would that be an aid to it."

Case C. **Right to Strike in Public Utilities**

1. The employees of an electric light and power company of a large city are dissatisfied with the conditions of their employment and have threatened to strike. A good part of the city—its offices, factories, homes, water supply, and other vital needs—are dependent solely on the use of electricity. If the strike were called, there would be no light, no heat, no refrigeration, and many other conveniences would be unavailable to a large part of the city.

The local civic association has vigorously appealed to the mayor against having any strike in this industry. Within this association are two groups which urge a change in the law of strikes. One group insists on a plan essentially like the Canadian Industrial Disputes Investigation Act, requiring that in all industries affected with a public interest no strike or lockout shall be declared until a board of conciliation and investigation has reported on the dispute, on pain of fine and imprisonment to those violating the law. Another group insists upon outlawing strikes in such industries entirely, and desires a law requiring the two sides to submit all issues to voluntary arbitration, or otherwise, whenever deadlocked.

The commissioner of water supply, gas, and electricity stated that the threatened strike would constitute a health menace, a fire menace, and a crime menace and would justify the use of emergency powers to meet it if there was no authority otherwise.

2. An advocate of regulation of strikes asserts that there is no logical reason for limiting such legislation to public utilities, for many other industries are just as important. He points out that the State of Kansas has a law on its statute books designed to provide compulsory arbitration, which has been the subject of considerable litigation but never repealed, and which reads, in part, as follows:

> The operation of the following named and indicated employments, industries, public utilities, and common carriers is hereby determined and declared to be affected with a public interest.
>
> (1) The manufacture or preparation of food products whereby, in any stage of the process, substances are being converted, either partially or wholly, from their natural state to a condition to be used as food for human beings; (2) the manufacture of clothing and all manner of wearing apparel in common use by the people of this State whereby, in any stage of the process, natural products are converted, either partially or wholly, from their natural state to a condition to be used as such clothing, and wearing apparel; (3) the mining or production of any substance or material in common use as fuel either for domestic, manufacturing, or transportation expenses; (4) the transportation of all food products and articles or substances entering into wearing apparel, or fuel, as aforesaid, from the place where produced to the place of manufacture or consumption; (5) all public utilities.

He says: "Certain phases of this law were declared unconstitutional, but the way forward is to pass amendments to control all strikes, and not by implication to limit such legislation to a few industries."

Case D. Rights of Strikers vs. Rights of Public

In the winter of 1936 there was a 13-day strike of employees in New York which deprived hundreds of office buildings and apartment houses of elevator service. In view of the fact that many of the tenants in these buildings had to walk ten or twenty flights of stairs, some even more, the strike not only caused great hardship to large numbers of people but bore particularly heavily on old persons and weak people, to the danger of their health. Their alternative was to remain almost prisoners in their offices or apartments. An official in the department of health stated:

> The interest of the public should cut both ways. The real estate owners and employers involved should, of course, be made to submit to arbitration. Likewise there should not be any strikes permissible on the part of the workers. It would be less harmful for many people to walk twelve blocks than it would be to climb twelve flights of stairs. Why should a group of unskilled workers be permitted to say that all the rest of us should suffer indefinitely and that they may refuse to arbitrate the question as to whether the wage demand that they are making is excessive under given conditions? To permit this is to give a special privilege to a few at the expense of the general public. This is just as objectionable in the case of a few laborers as it would be in the case of a few business men.

This official is therefore of the opinion that building service employees should be included among those to whom the right to strike should be prohibited, and that some jurisdictional board or optional machinery for adjustment should be their exclusive remedy.

Case E. Denial of Impartiality of Arbitrators

A militant union has refused to accept arbitration for a settlement of its dispute. Among the chief reasons is the allegation that there are no impartial arbitrators. The general organizer of the union states:

> Who is impartial these days? We would have to choose somebody pretty well known to both sides and that means a lawyer, a college professor, or someone who derives his income and has achieved his success through the prevailing system. They are all

unconsciously with the capitalists and find it difficult to support any real change in the workers' condition. They are too much used to the prevailing methods of thought, if not actually affected by their personal interests. If we suggested anyone who was not, the employers would refuse to accept him, so that eventually we would have to agree on someone acceptable to them and therefore likely to have their point of view on vital issues.

Case F. Place of Industrial Codes in Arbitration

A newspaper article on the role of government arbitration makes the contention that "there is no such thing as simple arbitration of disputes. There are only two alternatives: government control of labor conditions as a whole or mere mediation of disputes." The rest of the material in this case consists of excerpts from this article.

The fundamental weakness of arbitration that merely sets up a government arbitrator is that he cannot fall back upon a set of principles recognized as controlling industrial relations. He becomes merely a compromiser on all issues. He is more concerned about stopping strikes than about grievances or injustices.

Laws providing machinery designed to prevent strikes in industry as a whole have been passed at various times, and such interventions have brought together many parties whose relations were at the breaking point or who had already got into dispute. But the Federal government, like the states, has had no set of controlling principles, and therefore its mediators could contribute little but friendly intervention to any strike situation.

In April, 1918, when the National War Labor Board was established through proclamation by President Wilson, it soon had to draw up a set of policies to be promulgated as guiding principles in labor relations. Adherence to these principles was secured through war patriotism, aided in some cases by the refusal of war contracts to those not abiding by the regulations and, in three instances, by the exercise of drastic war emergency powers accorded to the President.

The provision of national principles and methods of adjusting disputes for industry as a whole came in June, 1933, with the NIRA and with the Emergency Railroad Transportation Act, signed at the same time. The latter went much further than the NIRA in recognizing and specifically providing for unions. For example, it definitely forbids a railroad employer to "deny or in any way question the right of the employees . . . to join the labor organization of their choice, . . . to interfere in any way with the organization of employees or to use the funds of the railroad under his jurisdiction in maintaining so-called company unions, or to influence or coerce employees in an effort to induce them to join or remain members of such company unions." The NIRA labor provisions, affecting all other industries, made possible the setting up of machinery for dealing with similar causes of disputes in industry at large.

The Wagner-Connery National Labor Relations Act took the place of these NIRA provisions in an attempt to provide some control which would be held constitutional. But aside from this point of whether we do or do not need constitutional amendments to make such control possible, an enforceable code of principles regarding the industrial rights of the two sides would be a requisite if we instituted compulsory arbitration.

Case G. Objection to Arbitration as Making Economic Progress Impossible

A prominent social worker asserts that to enforce compulsory arbitration, even on a voluntary basis before arbitrators jointly appointed by the two sides, would mean that the workers could not make any real advance in their living standards or make any fundamental changes in the economic institutions under which they live. The reason assigned is that any arbitrators chosen by both sides, to adjust an issue of wages or other conditions, must consider the conditions of the trade or of the industry as well as the demands of the workers. This means that they will give weight to certain customary considerations of rents, profits, royalties, bond interest, real estate values, competition, and other features of the present economic system.

She states:

> For example, if it were a strike of building workers against real estate owners, the arbitrators would consider the investment and profits of the real estate owners and therefore would honor the rights of bondholders, or mortgage holders, and the inflated value of the land. By that time the worker might perhaps be asked to take a reduction of wages instead of an increase. The only way for the working class to break the hold of these repressive customs and to increase the standard of living is to use economic pressure even at the expense of vested interests and the employing class. If not, they will be held down by those who at best represent the status quo.

Case H. Compulsory Arbitration in Practice

An opponent of compulsory arbitration states that it is an impossible thing in a democracy because it would lead to "two horns of a dilemma." One horn would be that in the absence of voluntary arbitration the decision would have to fall on some government official. Therefore an effort would continually be made by one side or the other to "capture" or control this public official. In a state dominated by labor he would be pro-labor and in another jurisdiction he might favor the employers.

The other horn of the dilemma, he states, would be that if a decision was not acceptable to one side or the other it would be unenforceable or lead to a great deal of trouble. If the enterprise refused to abide by it, the only remedy the state would have would be to take the company over, "which means trying to run and probably ruin some complicated business." If, on the other hand, the union refused to abide by it and was determined to resist, it would mean trying to fill the jails with thousands or tens of thousands of ordinarily good citizens who, on the particular issues, are blinded by some grievance or feel heroic and patriotic in their resistance. He gives as one instance the following:

> The system of compulsory arbitration which had been in force in Norway under various provisional acts was tested in 1928 by an unofficial trade union revolt against an award of the court of arbitration providing for a reduction in the wages of building workers. This dispute, which was ultimately settled by a compromise, was generally regarded as definitely discrediting the compulsory arbitration system. An Act was subsequently passed relieving persons from the penalties which had been imposed on them for supporting the strikers by collecting contributions. The Act was allowed to expire without renewal, as both the trade unions and the employers' federation protested against its continuance. The latter argued that unless more stringent penalties could be applied, compulsory arbitration was useless, while the former maintained that it was impossible to enforce penalties that would be effective.

Questions:

1. *Are all strikes justified? If not, when are they unjustified?*
2. *Is a union in an essential industry justified in refusing to submit an issue to impartial arbitration? State your reasoning fully, applying it to Cases B and C.*
3. a. *If there is a divergence between the rights of the public in a situation and the desires of a militant group of workers, how shall the interests of the public be brought to bear upon the situation?*
   b. *Show how this would be applied to the conditions described in Section 2 of Case A.*
4. *Comment upon the validity of the assertions made in Cases E and G.*
5. *What should be the place of compulsory arbitration in the United States? In your answer include comment on the points of view expressed in Cases F and H.*

PROBLEM 70. PROPOSALS TO REGULATE UNIONS

Case A. Registration or Licensing of Unions

From time to time the proposal is made that unions be registered or licensed in some way, so that if they fail to adhere to certain minimum standards of operation they may be deprived of the right to function. An illustration of such a proposal is contained in the following paragraphs appearing in a longer communication sent to a newspaper:

> Laboring groups are too often exploited and used for selfish purposes by their own leaders. The ordinary member of a union has no knowledge of what his money is used for. Some of the leaders receive substantial salaries, but the amount is not always known to the rank and file.
>
> A law compelling all unions to be registered in their respective states, and at Washington, so that an audit can be made of all money collected and expended and a complete list of all their members published annually, might start the ball rolling in the right direction. Salaries of all labor leaders should be public property. Election of officers supervised by the U. S. Labor Department would also protect the rank and file. These laws should in no way curtail the right to strike or to bargain collectively, or otherwise, for better conditions, but they would at least protect union members from racketeers in their own ranks, give the public a fair deal, allow management to know whom they are really dealing with and enable the government to act intelligently.

Case B. Incorporation of Unions

For decades there have been proposals to require unions to incorporate. On September 6, 1936, President Nicholas Murray Butler of Columbia, in a speech widely publicized, included such a recommendation so that unions would be made subject to the same supervision as other corporations. Arguing that this, contrary to frequent contention, would strengthen the position of labor, he stated:

It is of the highest importance that trade unions be given definite rights which can be upheld and defended by the whole power of the state, rather than privileges which rest largely upon sentiment and which can often be upheld only at the cost of economic war. A trade union must not be made a privileged class outside the law in respect to civil liberty.

Every trade union should be registered at a public office and its financial holdings and administration should be open to public inspection. Each trade union which holds property should be incorporated and make the annual report required by law to the appropriate public official. In these respects, the trade union is to be classed with the many other voluntary organizations in the field of liberty which are non-profit-making and which have the public welfare as their aim.

Case C. **Making Labor Agreements Enforceable at Law**

The proposal that a labor union agreement be made enforceable at law on both parties, which has been put before the public at various times, has come to the fore recently as the result of decisions of the courts making certain aspects of such agreements binding. The following editorial, from the New York *Times* of January 1, 1937, illustrates the recommendation:

Two affiliated dress companies in New York City made agreements with garment workers' unions, in one clause of which the companies agreed not to move their factories from the present location to any place beyond the five-cent-fare zone. The companies did, notwithstanding, lock out their union employees in October and move their machinery to Archbald, Pa. The unions brought suit, and Supreme Court Justice Philip J. McCook has found in their favor, ordering the companies to return all the machinery to New York, to re-employ the union workers they locked out and to pay damages to them for their loss of income.

This sweeping decision raises anew some leading questions. Should agreements between unions and employers be merely "gentlemen's agreements," in which each party must rely primarily upon the good faith of the other, or should they be legal contracts? If they are merely the former, then neither side can claim the right of suit. If they are the latter, then suit can be brought by either side. But if there is to be any equity in this arrangement, then the union must be made fully as responsible as the employer. The employer must then have the right to sue for breach of contract, for injury to person or property during strikes, and for other illegal acts. There must be some entity from which he, too, can collect damages.

Whether this is a condition that can be brought about in practice is doubtful. The unions generally have opposed the idea of incorporation, Federal or state, precisely because they have feared that it would mean that they could be sued. It is true that in the Danbury Hatters and in the Coronado Coal cases the courts have ruled that the unions could be sued, even though unincorporated; but such suits in practice have been comparatively rare, because they are likely in any case to prove unprofitable, and because it is often impossible to fix responsibility.

Case D. A National Labor Relations Law with a Code for Unions

The Twentieth Century Fund, Inc., a research foundation, appointed a special committee of prominent authorities on labor, to study and report on the part which the government should play in promoting and controlling labor relations. The committee issued a book *Labor and the Government* (McGraw-Hill Book Company, Inc., New York, 1935, 413 pp.), which recommended legislation and a national commission to grant employees certain rights. The following illustrative paragraphs from the proposed law indicate its purpose and scope:

> Sec. 7—The right of the employees to full freedom of association, self-organization, and designation of representatives of their own choosing for collective bargaining with their employers is hereby recognized and affirmed. It shall be the duty of the Commission to foster that right, and to encourage collective bargaining. . . .

Sec. 8—It shall be an unfair labor practice: (1) For anyone to interfere by fraud or violence with the free exercise by an employee of his right to participate in the formation of a labor organization or with the free exercise of his right to choose representatives for collective bargaining; (2) For an employer to interfere in any way with the free exercise by an employee of his right to participate in the formation and in the activities of a labor organization or with the free exercise of his right to choose representatives for collective bargaining, or to contribute financial or equivalent support to any such labor organization; . . . (3) For an employer to discharge or discriminate against or in favor of an employee for any activity in connection with forming, joining, or assisting any collective bargaining agency of employees, or in connection with the choice of employee representatives for collective bargaining.

These recommendations are, in the main, the same in principle as those embodied in the Wagner-Connery Act, passed in June, 1935, establishing the National Labor Relations Board. The latter contained also a section to the effect that "Nothing in this Act shall be construed so as to interfere with or impede or diminish in any way the right to strike."

Is the committee's proposal the solution of the question of the role of the government in labor relations? Because this is the basic question, one need not take into account the fact that the Wagner-Connery Act in itself was at once attacked in the courts on various grounds, and its constitutionality challenged. If the principle is valid, it can, conceivably, be introduced into the Constitution by the amending process.

One of the important criticisms made of the report and recommendations of the committee of the Twentieth Century Fund was that it imposed on the employer the obligation of dealing with the union without imposing reciprocal obligations on the union to deal fairly with the employer. Among the union practices complained of in a brief opposing the Act were:

1. The unwillingness to submit issues on which the two sides are deadlocked, or complaints of the employer, to impartial arbi-

trators mutually chosen, resulting in protracted strikes or the granting of extortionate terms.

2. Failure of the union to abide by an agreement after it is once signed, resulting in strikes violating its terms.

3. The arbitrariness of some union officials and their lack of cooperativeness, making a union a thorn in the side of industry instead of a mutually helpful agency.

4. The inability of the union factions to agree among themselves, resulting in inter-union strikes and jurisdictional squabbles which penalize the employer.

5. The prevalence of racketeers and grafters in certain unions, protected by the unfair system of elections that they are permitted to engineer, the fines they levy, the blacklists they issue, and the lack of control over the union funds which they handle.

With such grievances against unions as illustrations of the burdens which collective agreements may impose, these critics say that it is wrong for the state to enforce collective bargaining and yet not enforce decent or fair collective bargaining. They say it should not be illegal to refuse to deal with a union which has repeatedly violated its agreements or is dominated by actual racketeers levying graft on the industry.

A witness at hearings held by the Senate Committee on Education and Labor proposed as an amendment to the Wagner-Connery Bill that any union which wished to avail itself of the privileges of the Act should agree to a code of fair labor union practices. His memorandum included the following stipulations:

1. Union officials should be required to keep adequate books and bank accounts, and to give bond for the proper care of money in their custody.

2. Periodic audits of all income and expenditures should be made mandatory. Such audits would become a powerful weapon in helping to eliminate union tribute to underworld racketeers in situations where government agencies hitherto have been powerless.

3. Annual elections by secret ballot under government supervision would eliminate fraudulent elections which sometimes perpetuate faithless union officials in power.

4. It should be a serious offense to take strike money from sick or death benefit funds, except by extraordinary authority from the membership.

5. Since a "closed shop" can become an economic threat to qualified workers who are not union members, a union should be prohibited from imposing inequitable restrictions on members, or on admission to membership, from demanding excessive initiation fees or exorbitant dues, or otherwise from excluding workers who meet reasonable qualifications.

6. Expulsion from a closed-shop union means "economic decapitation." These are the words of Samuel Gompers. Therefore, suspension or expulsion should be prohibited except for traitorous conduct proved after a fair trial.

7. Union members should be protected by law when making complaints, and be assured of swift, impartial and inexpensive redress of grievances. . . .

8. Because the power to call or call off a strike becomes an instrument of oppression and betrayal in the hands of unfaithful union officials, it should be illegal for a labor union to strike, or to call off a strike, until the rank and file have had an opportunity to give the question adequate consideration and to vote on it by secret ballot without interference, restraint or coercion.

The New York *Times*, in an editorial on January 6, 1937, said in effect:

The terms of the Wagner Labor Act itself deal solely with the alleged transgressions of employers. The only unfair practices mentioned in the law are practices by employers. The law provides that the employer cannot "refuse to bargain collectively" with his employees. In order to bargain collectively, must the managers of a company grant some or all of the demands of a union, no matter how extravagant?

But while the employer is compelled to bargain by the act, the employees are not. The right to strike is specifically upheld, and nothing in the law is to be construed "so as to interfere with or impede or diminish" it "in any way." Has the employer any recourse if it can be shown that it is only a minority of his employees that is tying up his works in this fashion? On all this the Wagner act has nothing to say. It does not declare a single act of labor to be an unfair practice.

Questions:

1. Evaluate each of these proposals from the standpoint of their value to labor and to society. Consider these not only in theory but with reference to the probable practical results.

2. If a code such as discussed in Case D were to be imposed, what should it include, and how should it be administered?

APPENDIX A

SOME ELEMENTARY PRINCIPLES OF ANALYSIS AND THEIR APPLICATION IN THE STUDY OF PROBLEMS

Excerpts from a memorandum prepared by the author for distribution to his classes:

This memorandum is designed to point out a few elementary habits of mind which the student should cultivate in order to develop his powers of analysis and expression. It is based on the observation of all too common faults exhibited not merely by untrained persons generally, but by people of education who have missed certain essentials of training and mental discipline.

Part I deals with certain processes of thinking which will be found of general use in analysis and presentation. Part II attempts a specific application of these principles in a procedure for dealing with business situations, in particular with problems in the form presented for class study.

The suggestions herein made are more generally necessary than is usually recognized. Some of these injunctions will seem so simple and obvious that the deceptive effect is produced of leading one to believe that he is, of course, actually applying them in practice. They are like the basic rules of sports, such as "Keep your eye on the ball," or "Keep your mind on the play," which everyone knows to be essential to successful performance, but which all but the accomplished players too frequently neglect.

The purpose of these suggestions is not, however, to supply ready-made maxims but to make one sensitive to standards of thinking and style of presentation, and thus to promote progressive improvement in these through independent reflection.

I. EFFECTIVE THINKING

1. Apprehending the Real Issue

One cannot go far in playing chess unless one understands that the whole point of the game is to protect the king against checkmate. Yet in classroom work there is a comparable fault in the frequent failure of students to devote enough attention to determining the real nature of the question which an issue or problem proposes. It is strange how frequently the one elementary requisite of all effective analysis and thinking is disregarded.

Students sometimes assert that the instructor is at fault in not putting his question in the most explicit and direct way in which it can be stated. When the vagueness is unintentional, this criticism is justified; but it is still true that from a teaching standpoint it may be better purposely to introduce such questions from time to time in order to accustom the student to stop and think. Discrimination is needed because, in actual life, situations are not explained or presented to one in the clearest possible terms and without confusing elements.

In dealing with a question or issue one should, therefore, concentrate at the outset upon analyzing the meaning of the question, on turning it over upside down, on examining its form to see why particular words were used instead of others, and thus to make sure that some incidental aspect of the statement or the wording, hastily read, does not trick him into a misinterpretation.

One excellent way of preventing this, after careful analysis, is to restate the problem or issue in one's own words. To make this process valuable requires that the student do more than reword or repeat what may often seem a perfectly obvious question in the problem. What he really needs to do is to interpret the situation in both its narrow and its broader phases.

As an illustration let us assume that the case presented is that of an organization which has a number of older men whose department and work have to be abandoned and who do not seem to be adapted to other work in the plant. The issue in this situation is more than the immediate disposal of these few men. The question involves the meeting of obligations implied by their long service, and the retention of the morale of the plant. Among the long time objectives are the setting of right precedents, of anticipating similar problems in the future, and of providing some program for others who may soon be in this position.

In any situation, therefore, there are a number of allied considerations which form the combined issue, and which require not merely an interpretation of the question but reflection upon its implications. A terse statement of these would at once indicate whether the student's understanding of the problem involves a command of the full situation.

2. Planning for Comprehensiveness of Treatment

It is not only in the comprehension of the issues involved, but also in the solutions considered that this rounded approach is required. The rush for an "answer" often results in a fragmentary, unimaginative, partial treatment. The human mind is not innately orderly, but it may often be made so. To avoid treating merely the incidental details or going off on a tangent, it is necessary to lay out the major divisions of the subject first and then the subordinate, individual items in their place. This gives one a perspective of the field to be covered.

With the many-sided possibilities before one, it becomes feasible to proceed in any way one chooses. One may decide to discuss systematically the major categories of the problem, in order to treat main aspects before minor ones, or to discuss merely one phase. Even a minor issue may thus be considered alone, to the exclusion of others, because it is done with full knowledge of the whole and does not imply a distortion of emphasis.

3. Seeking the Significant

The elements of any situation provide a choice as to what shall be regarded as important or significant and what may be regarded as irrelevant or relatively unimportant. People differ widely in their capacity to hit upon the essential factors requiring attention. And it is this difficulty which to no small degree marks a distinction between the big, broad-gauged or effective person and the one whose outlook as a whole is limited and whose analysis is inconsequential.

What makes this difference in understanding is, of course, complex, but there is little doubt that much depends upon whether one has given adequate reflection to this problem. A serious attempt to weigh various elements in terms of their relative importance will aid in developing one's sense of discrimination and thus lead to improvement in one's capacity to select the vital or significant factors.

There are two mental processes which are of enormous aid in this respect. One is the acquirement of a habit of properly grouping or classifying data or issues; the other of becoming sensitive to the sequence in which one lists various factors. These two processes, basic to the orderly mind, are discussed in the two succeeding sections.

4. Classifying Data and Ideas

The ability to observe similarities between things is one of the essentials of rational activity, and such an ability is an implicit classification of the things observed. A world of otherwise scattered phenomena thus becomes more intelligible. But many people have not learnt to do this effectively. When a complex situation is presented for diagnosis, a mere listing of all the observed conditions may be supplied, rather than a grouping of allied points. Often the superficial designation "miscellaneous" is used for the items which require more than a moment's analysis, and the others are put under vague titles.

Such a haphazard listing of a host of detailed items is not a thoughtful way of analyzing a problem. It wholly neglects classification, a process of the utmost importance in effective thinking. In dealing with a range of seemingly separate items, one should seek their fundamental similarities and attempt to classify them, first, into broad categories of major significance, clearly defined, and then within a class, into distinctive sub-classes. The whole should be based on an obvious and organic relationship and cover the field.

Classification is helpful in making new knowledge available. This arises because the instances coming within a class are seen as probably a part—perhaps only a small part—of the whole range of instances occurring. As an illustration of how classification can extend knowledge, let us assume that a number of separate accidents in a plant are found by classification to belong in a group, under some such subject head as "Injured from falling object." From this we may infer that there is generally a poor method of piling boxes or objects; that many objects fall down because of improper piling; and that such falls, while not causing injury to workers necessarily, do probably cause breakage and loss. In this way we are able to broaden our concept of a problem and to develop insight into a probable remedy.

What are the elements of a good classification of facts and ideas? The following are among the standards to be borne in mind.

a. *Comprehensiveness of Categories:* A complete analysis of the subject, rather than just jotting down a few items which occur to one's mind, is necessary to bring one's thinking beyond the half-way mark. The main concepts and categories should be examined with the view to seeing whether they cover the whole field under examination.

b. *Significant Basis of Grouping:* If an uneducated domestic were sent into a room and asked to arrange the books on the shelves, she would probably choose some wholly superficial basis, such as size, or color of bindings. A somewhat more literate person would arrange them by alphabet. A research worker or librarian would try to group them by subject matter. The classification of significance for the particular purpose depends, in part, on the purpose in mind, but as long as the person making the classification has a very definite intention of seeing that the basis of his classification is significant, he will in large measure be fulfilling a fundamental principle of good classification. Thus he will be able to learn what is a better basis of classification, viz.: alphabetical classification of books within main sections based on subject.

c. *Unified Basis of Division:* Whatever the basis used, it must be applied uniformly to the phenomena to which it applies. Confusion is likely to result unless the main groupings are all branches of a common tree, and the subordinate groupings are twigs of these branches.

d. *Exclusiveness of Subclasses:* Classification should be mutually exclusive as to content. It is difficult, of course, to group together phenomena which belong under more than one heading. In that event they should be parcelled out with more circumscribed titles, under two or more different headings.

e. *Adequate Breakdown of Classes:* The question as to how many divisions one should aim for when classifying a situation is only partly answered by the purpose. One individual may see a range of phenomena as divisible into two significant groups, with minor subdivisions, while another may want to make a half dozen major divisions and fewer subdivisions.

f. *"Self-selling" Titles of Classes:* It may be that the student who makes a classification has in his own mind a fairly logical basis, but in the terms used to label the classifications it is difficult to see their validity. Thus, in a given case, in discussing the ills of a particular industry, some students enumerated as among the causes of trouble the single word "Executives." This is silly. They probably meant "Absence of executives," or "Too many executives," or "Poor quality of executives." When the validity of a classification is not clearly recognizable, this defect in wording may be an actual lack of preciseness of thought.

5. Employing Conscious Sequence

Some people who enumerate points in a discussion do so in a haphazard, off-hand fashion instead of marshalling these points in a sequence of relationship indicative of a methodical or orderly procedure. A first point mentioned may be a duplication of or closely related to the last, or another point mentioned might better have come first. The mind of the reader or listener finds it hard to grasp the sequence involved. The confusion engenders inertia, if not resistance, where understanding or openness to conviction is required.

It need hardly be urged that the analysis and presentation of a problem involves careful consideration of the order in which various matters should be given attention. The priority of thought and treatment should be purposeful. A sense of sequence is necessary also to make presentation effective. It is necessary, therefore, to choose some suitable basis for determining the sequence of thought. Certainly, in presenting the results of such thought to others, haphazard, slothful enumeration is confusing and tends to impair the interest of the listener or reader.

The choice of priority in presentation may be made with regard to a variety of considerations. For example, among others, are the following bases:

a. *Chronological or "Logical" Relationship:* From a start or beginning which makes a rational sequence and which drives the mind to follow along an established path.

b. *Relative Importance:* From the aspect requiring immediate action, or deserving most importance or constituting the major difficulty, to the minor elements which may be treated only if time permits.

c. *Psychological Advantage:* From the points which will rouse least apprehension, or which will engage attention to the issues regarded as least troublesome, or which will provide previous building-up of background, to the points requiring careful support.

d. *Convenience:* From the simple to the complex, in order to assure oneself of solving what seems possible and of ascending to the complex when the groundwork for concentration of attention has been laid.

6. Reasoning Logically

To know what constitutes an individual fact, and to make a proper summarization of such data, are first steps in the process of reasoning. Much of what is written is not authoritative or deserving of confidence. One who has experience in correcting students' work would exhort them to make more critical evaluation of evidence by taking into account the need for—

a. Watchfulness regarding the possible bias of the sources used, including the overcoming of one's awe of a statement of "fact" because some prominent name is associated with it;

b. Avoiding the pressure of one's own personal bias in the selection of the facts;

c. Using a representative and adequate quantity of evidence;

d. Exercising restraint in making an induction, by the limiting of the statement, in doubtful cases, to a summary of the facts actually assembled, rather than extending it by too broad a generalization to a field not studied.

Avoidance of fallacies in reasoning requires mental alertness and a disciplined mind. As one illustration, the relationship of cause and effect should not be asserted merely because one circumstance follows another in sequence of time. The subject is not pursued further here because mere enumeration of fallacies will not itself suffice to build habits of logical reasoning. Thoughtful analysis from the standpoint of one anxious to see the errors of one's ways of thinking, and the pursuance of a good course in the study of logic, are most desirable and should do much to make one more aware of one's mental tendencies.

7. Exercising Good Judgment in Recommendations

The term "judgment" may be used in many senses, but it is intended to designate here that mental activity which strikes a balance between possible courses of action, then decides and outlines the procedure which seems effective in a given situation. In this sense judgment integrates a variety of knowledge into a form having particular application. This is giving a limited and special meaning to the term, but at least making it manageable.

Is it possible to formulate rules by which one may improve one's judgment? At first thought it may seem too difficult because judgment is so undefinable. However, it may be possible to go a certain distance in learning not to exercise poor judgment, or at least, to be aware of characteristic errors in judgment. The following questions illustrate standards to be considered.

a. Is the decision, though logical up to a certain point, inapplicable because of the disregard of psychological or human difficulties involved?

b. Does the action to be taken unintentionally or unwisely disturb established precedent or set a dangerous new precedent?

c. Are the means to be used inappropriate, because they involve more expense or trouble than would be justified by the ends achieved?

d. Does the course of action suggested fail to take into account pressing problems involved in the immediate situation, and thus have a flavor of a purely academic approach?

e. Is the solution suggested a purely partial, one-sided action which gives insufficient evidence of attention to broad economic, industrial and social considerations?

Thus a recommendation which shows good judgment is one in which the analysis has "followed through" to a balancing of all the important factors which may affect the value of that recommendation. It has taken into consideration the long-time as well as the immediate effects, and the social as well as individual points of view.

8. Sharpening One's Expression

Many people express themselves in words which do not actually say what they mean. The habit of slipshod, fragmentary assertions leads to statements which may be too broad, incomplete, or obviously inaccurate. Students who exhibit such tendencies may also add to the confusion by the use of slang terms having a collegiate vogue but out of place elsewhere. A generous attitude on the part of the reader or listener is needed to interpret the statement in accordance with its intended meaning, with resulting doubt because of the choices presented.

In contrast, a well-written or well-spoken statement can stand by itself as completely intelligible to anyone. Its meaning is not affected by what one thinks the reader or listener takes for granted. An experienced instructor has no reason to take anything for granted, for students who are mentally slothful balk at precise terms and take refuge in vague, general assertions that perpetuate bad habits.

It is desirable to practice choosing one's terms carefully, so that the manner of expression will indicate a keenly functioning mind and the thoughts expressed will be interestingly and precisely stated. This habit requires alertness to one's customary methods of phrasing a thought and concentration on what one wants to say and how one is saying it.

The problem method of study and teaching provides greater opportunity than most other procedures for practice in close analysis, broad thinking and careful statement. An attempt has therefore been made to integrate some of the principles considered in the first part of this memorandum into standards of approach which may be applied generally to the solution of problems. This is the subject of the material which follows.

II. A METHOD OF APPROACH TO PROBLEMS

The case or problem method of instruction is employed as a means of accustoming students to analysis of realistic situations. The problems presented are similar to those which one might meet in some professional responsibility, and they provide an excellent opportunity for training in ways of approach, analysis, and solution.

A "problem" as used in the study of labor relations is a case, or group of cases, presenting an industrial situation for the purpose of having the student make an independent appraisal of the issues involved and the measures required for solution. In some instances the case presented may seem to involve no issue. This may be because the course of action taken by the institution described may seem to be the proper one, or because alternative solutions, also presented, are among those which one might choose as applicable. The problem involved in such situations is for the student to decide whether the course of action taken, even if seemingly the best, was really such in the light of all circumstances and more mature consideration.

Suggested Treatment in Three Stages

In this process are there some basic principles of approach and treatment which may be commonly applied to most problems? What follows is an attempt to outline such a procedure for application, so far as seems feasible, to problems generally.[1] This procedure presents an approach in three separate stages. A short, preparatory description is all that will be necessary, because the outline itself, which follows, is intended to be explicit in its directions.

Stage I is a preparation of the problem for study. This is necessary because the facts of a business problem, as in actual life, may reach one through a biased source or with inadequate data and with confusing details. There may be interspersed inconsequential and unrelated information which is of no moment in dealing with the problem and needs to be discarded or disregarded; or the facts may be chaotic in order and confusing in their existing relationship. There may be palpable errors and misstatements which cannot be accepted as facts in dealing with the problem. There may be vague statements due to the em-

[1] The next few pages are a combination of my own ideas with a liberal use of the material and suggestions available in a much more comprehensive and exacting procedure for dealing with problems which was prepared by Elliott D. Smith, Professor of Industrial Relations at Yale, for his classes, and which he was kind enough to let me adapt to my purposes. (The author.)

ployment of ambiguous terms or to the fact that terms are used in a sense having widely different connotations to different people. There may be marked gaps in the facts essential to further action in the problem. Hence any procedure suggested for dealing with problems inescapably begins with a sorting and organization of the facts.

A second important step in Stage I is that of clarifying the issue, question, or objective of the problem. As indicated in the early part of this memorandum, this primary step should receive special attention in the procedure. With the facts sifted and the question or issue clearer, the problem is prepared for study and a better solution is to be expected.

Stage II embodies the planned application of the solution. In order that the total picture may be seen, this stage prescribes a classified, analytic layout or map of the solution, embodying a statement of the main, all-inclusive divisions of the subject, and indicating an orderly sequence of treatment. The values of this approach are many. It reveals the degree of imagination applied to the problem and, to the extent that the plan is lacking in comprehensiveness, it exposes action based on pure hunch or partial analysis. This "map" also promotes an orderly and systematic division of attention. Without a layout and choice of plan, there is little to protect one from a haphazard sequence which skips about, without good reason, from one item—which may be a major category—to some detail belonging in another category.

Stage III is an attempt to check the validity of the solution, to see whether it really meets the terms of the problem as originally defined. It need only be stated here that such a check will often reveal that the problem has been erroneously interpreted or that the treatment is only a partial solution. The actual character of the solution depends upon the intelligence and judgment of the student. Intuition is required to evaluate the forces at work in any problem, those favorable as well as those definitely opposing, to compare means with ends, and to meet standards such as those discussed in an earlier part of this memorandum.

A recapitulation of this general discussion of the proposed procedure may now be put in more definite form by the following outline of an approach to business problems.

STAGE I. PREPARE THE FACTS AND ISSUES FOR STUDY

A. *The Facts*

The facts given may be already clear, pertinent, adequate, and well organized, or they may be a stumbling block to further analysis. The procedure suggested here is only a preliminary organization of the given facts in order to make the problem more understandable, and does not apply to those facts which will have to be discovered in order to answer the problem. To do this it will be helpful to:

1. *Sift the data*, so that by separating the inconsequential or unrelated information one can concentrate on the significant facts.

2. *Clarify the data* of its errors, misstatements, and vagueness, by noting obvious or easily ascertainable errors, and, where one's general knowledge or specific information is corrective, substituting the true fact; or by taking note of vagueness of terms or data, and where important, defining the terms or concepts considered.

3. *Amplify the data*, by supplementary assumptions.

If there are omissions of essential points without which the problem is not clear or is hard to deal with, it becomes necessary to fill in these factual gaps with assumptions. If a single assumption for a given situation is inadequate, as many alternative assumptions as may be necessary to discuss the problem with reference to these possible contingencies should be made. But the assumptions should be *at a minimum* and must be *labelled as such* in order to distinguish them from a statement of facts.

B. *The Issues or Objectives*

With the debris cleaned away and the content sorted for study, it is now time to analyze the question thoroughly and to restate the issue tersely, in accordance with such considerations as those discussed in Part I of this memorandum.

STAGE II. PLAN AND APPLY THE SOLUTION

A. *The Total Picture*

Before proceeding to a solution of a problem, it is necessary to see the whole range of possible solutions in their proper perspective. Otherwise one may start off on an incidental issue and one's solution may be fragmentary. To guard against this it is necessary to:

1. *Survey* the field of principles or solutions applying to this problem by listing the range of types of approach which have a reasonable bearing on the situation, and to classify these items in a well-knit and orderly structure serving as an outline of the possible scope of the solution.
2. *Select* the items to which major attention is to be given, and determine the sequence of their treatment.

B. *The Extent of Progress*

In a long case, or when the issues are complicated, it may be advisable at one or more points to make certain that the analysis is proceeding along the right course, or at least to make this clear to the reader. Such a consolidation of progress may be effected by indicating from time to time, at appropriate places, the extent of the advance made in solving the problem.

STAGE III. CHECK THE SOLUTION

The whole procedure so far may be evaluated by reference to the original purpose. With this in mind it is desirable to:

A. *Review,* in tersest form, the nature of the issue as conceived at the start, with regard to its immediate and long-time objectives.

B. *Validate* the solution by demonstrating the degree to which it meets the terms of that problem.

C. *Check* the solution reflectively from various angles of business judgment to see whether in the means employed, effects produced, or emphasis given, it runs counter to some important, human, technical, or organizational consideration.

APPENDIX B

REFERENCES AND READING LISTS

The users of this volume have, no doubt, observed that there are no references or suggestions given in connection with these problems, although in many cases the solution would require knowledge which the student cannot be expected to possess. The reasons for omitting these direct references in the text but providing some aid here are accordingly presented.

At the outset it should be made clear that while in all instances it would be better for the student to try to "think out" the main lines of approach before comparing his conclusions with those offered in authoritative treatises, and some problems would be better taught through the enforcement of independent thought entirely, adequate readings and references should be at his disposal. In using these problems in the introductory course, at least one reading reference, representing the most recent and appropriate material available at the time, is usually provided in advance on mimeographed assignment sheets. In the graduate course a problem is often given with the request that no reference should be consulted until at least one session has been devoted to it.

From a pedagogical standpoint, these contentions appear true: that the best training in original thinking is likely to be obtained if the student's first contact with a problem forces him entirely on his own resources; that this stage of blundering will heighten the effect and meaning of a subsequent assignment; that, where time permits, the announcement of the favored reference only in connection with a second or later class hour devoted to the problem will be found a useful expedient in this regard; that very few chapters or even books can be found which will completely cover the field intended by both the broad and the specific questions to which a problem directs attention; and hence, that whatever aid of this kind is given the student, the ultimate aim of this type of teaching is to force the responsibility back upon him to integrate his ideas and knowledge, from whatever source they may have been gathered.

It is clear, therefore, that the student should be taught to find information for himself, without regard to a particular course, textbook, or assortment of books. In the Tuck School, for a decade, one of the steps taken to provide formal training of this character has been a substantial assignment in library research, as one of the first tasks in the course, with the men working in groups under the personal supervision of the author. A *Manual on Research and Reports* (the revised edition of which will be distributed early in 1937 through the McGraw-Hill Book Company), has been issued by the School in this connection, and has proved of aid.

Such training is not in place of guidance from the instructor, and for practical purposes it will be found desirable to provide a reading list of the chief material which should be consulted. The student who uses this book independently will likewise wish such aid. Some instructors may wish to specify exactly what readings, by book and page, should be done in connection with each problem assigned. What these assignments shall be depends, in the main, on the point of view of the instructor, on the size of the group taught, on the resources available to provide reference material, and particularly, on the time at which the subject is treated. A reading which may be the best today may be inferior to one issued a year hence. For this reason the recommendations which follow are intended merely to establish a foundation on which an instructor or student may build, rather than to provide assignments neatly fitting the jigsaw edges which the puzzles in the text provide.

The material which follows includes, first, suggestions concerning the best general reading lists in the field of labor relations; second, a description of the output of some of the principal organizations engaged in publishing material in this field; and third, the list of some of the outstanding books applicable to industrial relations courses.

Available Reading Lists

Two pamphlets published by Princeton University, through its Industrial Relations Section (described below), are the most useful short bibliographies available. These are "The Office Library of an Industrial Relations Executive" (1934, 22 pp.), and its companion, "A Trade Union Library" (1935, 26 pp.). Their virtues include clear typography, excellent classification of material, careful selection of references, annotations for each item, and revision from time to time to bring the pamphlets up to date. In these two lists will be found selected publications issued by all of the organizations listed below, as the field has been well combed, but many items are missing which are necessary to cover the full range of the problems presented.

A reading list with a somewhat different emphasis, but which is part of a book, is the fifty-page "Select Critical Bibliography" included as pages 535–584 of John R. Commons and John B. Andrews, *Principles of Labor Legislation* (New York, Harper & Brothers, 1936). It lists books, documents, reports and other material on labor problems and labor legislation, and is the best available in this field. Its material is classified under the following heads: employment and unemployment; minimum fair wage; hours of labor; safety and health; social insurance; individual bargaining; collective bargaining; administration; the basis of labor law. A pithy descriptive note is given for each item.

Organizations Publishing Labor Literature

From the large number of organizations which are, or have been, active in the publication of literature covering one or more of the aspects of labor relations, certain important agencies now functioning are listed below. Among those not included are the

Rand School, whose valuable publications have lapsed or are now spasmodic, Industrial Relations Counselors, Inc., whose exhaustive studies in the field of unemployment insurance and industrial pensions appear chiefly in books, and the National Safety Council, whose excellent material is specialized within its field.

The U. S. Department of Labor, Washington, D. C., publishes an extensive array of documents, technical and general, representing occasional and continuous studies of a wide variety of labor subjects. Its extensive *Monthly Labor Review* ($3.50 per year), with its semi-annual index, enables one to keep in touch with the progress and current technique of labor relations throughout the world, and its *Labor Information Bulletin* (free) is a brief survey covering a few significant developments in popular summaries each month.

The American Management Association, 330 West 42nd Street, New York City, makes available the reports of committees, as well as the papers and the discussions of its conferences, in pamphlets and in its quarterly magazine, *Personnel*. These are excellent contributions to the applied problems of labor relations and personnel management. Some of the best of this material appearing up to 1931 was reprinted that year, under the editorship of W. J. Donald, in the *Handbook of Business Administration* (McGraw-Hill Book Company, Inc., 1753 pp.).

The Industrial Relations Section, Princeton University, already mentioned above for the two reading lists recommended, prepares helpful mimeographed memoranda and short reports, issued free or at nominal cost, concerning company personnel practices and other subjects of labor relations.

The National Industrial Conference Board, Inc., 247 Park Avenue, New York City, is the chief research agency for employers. It publishes studies based on its own surveys of special phases of labor relations, such as wages and the cost of living, salary policies, incentive plans and personnel programs.

The Metropolitan Life Insurance Company, 1 Madison Avenue, New York City, through its Group Service Division, prepares numerous reports and leaflets of practical value on various problems of personnel administration, and distributes these free to interested persons.

The Personnel Research Federation, 29 West 39th Street, New York City, publishes monthly *The Personnel Journal*, which contains valuable articles on matters of personnel technique, psychological problems of industry, and labor problems in general.

The American Association for Labor Legislation, 131 East 23rd Street, New York City, publishes *The American Labor Legislation Review*, a quarterly publication discussing important developments in protective legislation and administration.

A Selected Reading List

The list here presented was originally prepared to meet requests from students and alumni who might wish to establish a small library for personal reference and study. At the very beginning such a list requires the unfortunate decision to omit many first-rate magazine articles, in some cases of only a few pages, which are among the most valuable references that an instructor has. Moreover, at best the choice of a few books from the many excellent ones written raises difficult questions of judgment. Consolation is found, however, in the fact that while many important articles and volumes have regretfully been omitted, these are in most cases mentioned in the larger reading lists previously recommended.

One of the hardest tasks in preparing a bibliography is the classification of material. The general texts, with which the list begins, cover a wide scope of labor problems, but the other books are listed under only one head when in most cases they might be included under other heads. The defects of classification will, it is hoped, be minimized because of the shortness of the list presented.

GENERAL TEXTS ON LABOR PROBLEMS

Carroll R. Daugherty, *Labor Problems in American Industry*. New York, Houghton Mifflin Company, 1933, 959 pp.

A comprehensive text which treats in an informative way a

wide range of subjects in the field of labor economics, labor conditions, unionism, and labor legislation.

WARREN B. CATLIN, *The Labor Problem.* New York, Harper & Brothers, 1935, 765 pp.

A general textbook covering the chief problems of labor in the United States, with some attention to Great Britain.

ORDWAY TEAD and HENRY C. METCALF, *Personnel Administration: Its Principles and Practice.* New York, McGraw-Hill Book Company, Inc., 1933, 519 pp.

The standard work in this field, combining a broad approach to the subject with concrete material dealing with administrative aspects of successful personnel work.

JOHN R. COMMONS and JOHN B. ANDREWS, *Principles of Labor Legislation.* New York, Harper & Brothers, 1936, 606 pp.

The most authoritative and comprehensive study of labor legislation and administration, brought up to date from time to time.

SIDNEY and BEATRICE WEBB, *Industrial Democracy.* New York, Longmans, Green and Co., 1920, 899 pp.

A thorough treatise, long the classic in its field, on the evolution of labor problems in Great Britain, and their attempted solution by wage-earners' organizations and by social legislation.

JOHN A. FITCH, *The Causes of Industrial Unrest.* New York, Harper & Brothers, 1924, 424 pp.

An interpretation of labor friction and unrest intended to provide the background of the struggle between labor and capital in terms of certain objective conditions.

WAGES AND INCENTIVES

STANLEY B. MATHEWSON, *Restriction of Output among Unorganized Workers.* New York, The Viking Press, 1931, 212 pp.

An inquiry in a wide variety of concerns of restriction of output by workers uninfluenced by trade unions, which is revealing as to the causes, extent, and consequences of such practices.

HERBERT FEIS, *Principles of Wage Settlement.* New York, H. W. Wilson Company, 1924, 452 pp.

A collection of decisions from boards of arbitration, official and unofficial, with the contentions of the opposing sides, forming an extremely interesting body of material concerning points of view regarding various aspects of wage principle and wage practice, with some attention to basic principles.

MAURICE DOBB, *Wages*. Cambridge, England, The University Press, 1928, 169 pp.

A compact review of wage theory and the economics applying to wage problems.

SUMNER H. SLICHTER, *Towards Stability*. New York, Henry Holt and Company, 1934, 211 pp.

An examination of fundamental conditions which must be met in order for the economic system to avoid major crises and to achieve a larger measure of stability, with special reference to flexibility of wage rates.

NATIONAL INDUSTRIAL CONFERENCE BOARD, INC., *Systems of Wage Payment*, 1930, 131 pp., and *Financial Incentives*, 1935, 47 pp. New York. Published by the Board.

These two volumes constitute a compact survey and analysis of different methods of wage payment, accompanied by helpful statistical data.

C. CANBY BALDERSTON, *Group Incentives*. Philadelphia, University of Pennsylvania Press, 1930, 171 pp.

A critical survey of the group incentive types of compensation for employees, showing the differences in methods used, the difficulties encountered and ways of overcoming them.

CHARLES W. LYTLE, *Wage Incentive Methods*. New York, The Ronald Press Company, 1929, 457 pp.

A comprehensive technical treatment of the subject of wage methods, including classification and comparison of the various types of incentive wage plans for direct workers, indirect workers, supervisors and executives.

HERMAN FELDMAN, *A Personnel Program for the Federal Civil Service*. (House Document No. 773, 71st Congress, 3d Session.) Washington, Government Printing Office, 1931, 289 pp.

A comprehensive study of the personnel problems of the Government, but with chapters widely used as reference on wage levels, wage differentials, incentives, salary administration and promotion.

PERSONNEL MANAGEMENT AND LEADERSHIP

C. CANBY BALDERSTON, *Executive Guidance of Industrial Relations*. Philadelphia, University of Pennsylvania Press, 1935, 435 pp.

A most helpful volume which begins with chapters containing separate case studies of the labor policies of prominent concerns and uses these as a basis for thoughtful analysis, comparison, and appraisal.

David R. Craig and W. W. Charters, *Personal Leadership in Industry.* New York, McGraw-Hill Book Company, Inc., 1925, 245 pp.

A survey, for self-training in leadership, of what 110 executives, foremen, and supervisors actually do with regard to such matters as maintaining authority, developing teamwork, training, obtaining quality and quantity of output, and similar problems.

American Management Association, *Personnel Administration and Technological Change.* New York, published by the Association, 1935, 35 pp.

A significant symposium on a subject of great importance in which executives and authorities contributed first-rate material.

Howard L. Davis, *The Young Man in Business.* New York, John Wiley & Sons, Inc., 1931, 172 pp.

Full of wise, practical counsel to the young man in seeking a job, in planning his future, in adjusting himself to his superiors and associates, in acquiring various types of proficiency and in supervising the work of his subordinates.

Erwin H. Schell, *The Technique of Executive Control.* New York, McGraw-Hill Book Company, Inc., 1934, 231 pp.

Illustrates the various types of problems arising in the relationship of an executive with his subordinates.

Sam A. Lewisohn, *The New Leadership in Industry.* New York, E. P. Dutton and Company, 1926, 234 pp.

An interesting formulation, by an enlightened capitalist, of the employer's labor problems and of a modern approach to issues of industrial relations.

Whiting Williams, *Mainsprings of Men.* New York, Charles Scribner's Sons, 1925, 313 pp.

An interpretation of the feelings and desires of workers with regard to various aspects of their work environment, vividly described by an industrial executive who put on overalls to find out.

Herman Feldman, *Racial Factors in American Industry.* New York, Harper & Brothers, 1931, 318 pp.

A study of vexing problems of racial antagonisms and discriminations in industry, with special attention to the policies and techniques of management which may minimize this friction.

F. J. ROETHLISBERGER, *Understanding, a Prerequisite of Leadership.* 1936, 17 pp.

An exceptional contribution made before the Business Executives' Group conducted by Professor Philip Cabot, of the Graduate School of Business Administration, Harvard University, and distributed by him and by the author, also of the School's Faculty.

INDUSTRIAL PSYCHOLOGY

MORRIS S. VITELES, *Industrial Psychology.* New York, W. W. Norton & Company, Inc., 1932, 652 pp.

The most comprehensive picture of the whole field of modern industrial psychology, summarizing recent knowledge in a wide range of special subjects, such as vocational selection, employment tests, safety, training, fatigue, monotony, maladjustment and other human problems of work.

ELLIOTT D. SMITH, *Psychology for Executives.* New York, Harper & Brothers, 1935, 311 pp.

Based on the actual experience of a thoughtful executive and student, this volume combines a sound grasp of psychological principles with first-hand knowledge of human reactions in work relationships. The appendixes contain applied analyses on how to deal with various basic situations.

ORDWAY TEAD, *Human Nature and Management.* New York, McGraw-Hill Book Company, Inc., 1933, 338 pp.

A valuable statement of the function of modern psychology in managerial relations, combining an academic approach with concrete applications.

V. V. ANDERSON, *Psychiatry in Industry.* New York, Harper & Brothers, 1929, 364 pp.

An applied instance of the use of mental hygiene and psychiatry in employment relations in a department store, in an attempt to deal with "problem" employees through physical, mental, and social adjustments.

HARRY W. HEPNER, *Human Relations in Changing Industry.* New York, Prentice-Hall, Inc., 1934, 671 pp.

A popularization of industrial psychology and personnel principles, with interesting practical applications.

OLD AGE, INSECURITY, AND UNEMPLOYMENT

I. M. Rubinow, *The Quest for Security.* New York, Henry Holt and Company, 1934, 638 pp.

The work of a noted authority on social insurance, on the philosophy, practice, and program of insurance against accidents, illness, old age, unemployment and destitution.

C. R. Dooley and Helen L. Washburn, *The Employment and Adjustment of the Older Worker.* New York, American Management Association, 1929, 42 pp.

A special report concerned with the middle-aged worker within industry, rather than with pensioning of the aged. This was delivered at a convention of the Association, and is printed with the discussion from the floor.

Murray W. Latimer, *Industrial Pension Systems in the United States and Canada.* New York, Industrial Relations Counselors, Inc., 1932, Two Vols., 1195 pp.

An exhaustive study of industrial pension plans in their chief phases. It was completed, however, before the Social Security Act, and therefore the modifications this may introduce in aspects of such plans are not discussed.

Barbara N. Armstrong, *Insuring the Essentials.* New York, The Macmillan Company, 1932, 717 pp.

A comprehensive text on social insurance throughout the world. It discusses workmen's compensation, health insurance, old age and invalidity insurance and unemployment insurance, and is excellent in its facts, appraisals and recommendations.

Paul H. Douglas and Aaron Director, *The Problem of Unemployment.* New York, The Macmillan Company, 1931, 505 pp.

An introduction to the general problem of unemployment, its extent, its costs, its causes, and its remedies, including a section on unemployment insurance.

Paul H. Douglas, *Social Security in the United States.* New York, McGraw-Hill Book Company, Inc., 1936, 384 pp.

A readable and informative appraisal of the Federal Social Security Act and the legislation of the various states by a leading expert on the problem.

Eveline M. Burns, *Toward Social Security.* New York, McGraw-Hill Book Company, Inc., 1936, 269 pp.

A meaty explanation of the Social Security Act and a keen survey of the larger issues it presents.

E. Wight Bakke, *Insurance or Dole?* New Haven, Yale University Press, 1935, 280 pp.

A first-hand study of English unemployment insurance designed specifically to aid American students to profit by British experience. A good supplement to the earlier and larger volume by Miss Mary Gilson, *Unemployment Insurance in Great Britain.* New York, Industrial Relations Counselors, Inc., 1931, 560 pp.

Herman Feldman, *The Regularization of Employment.* New York, Harper & Brothers, 1925, 437 pp.

A study of the methods by which the irregularity of operations and of employment may be reduced through improved industrial practice.

GROUP RELATIONS AND LABOR LAW

Ernest R. Burton, *Employee Representation.* Baltimore, The Williams & Wilkins Co., 1926, 283 pp.

A thorough treatment of the principles of employee representation and the conditions of its operation, valuable even though it precedes recent developments in structure and procedure.

Selig Perlman, *A History of Trade Unionism in the United States.* New York, The Macmillan Company, 1922, 313 pp.

The best brief history of the rise and progress of organized labor in this country.

J. L. and Barbara Hammond, *The Rise of Modern Industry.* New York, Harcourt, Brace and Co., 1926, 281 pp.

A brilliant and scholarly analysis of the commercial history of Europe and the evolution of the industrial system as exemplified chiefly by its development in Great Britain. Shows the industrial forces released, the problems of labor relations created, and the factors of social control involved.

Lewis L. Lorwin, *The American Federation of Labor.* Washington, The Brookings Institution, 1933, 573 pp.

A factual review of American labor union history, with especially good chapters covering the period 1925–1932. Its final chapter, "Interpretation and Outlook," and the appendixes containing the status of selected unions in various industries are excellent sources of reference.

J. B. S. HARDMAN, Editor, *American Labor Dynamics in the Light of Post-War Developments.* New York, Harcourt, Brace and Co., 1928, 432 pp.

A compilation by thirty-two different contributors which interprets post-war developments and present-day tendencies in trade-union activity and contains interesting sidelights on various aspects of labor unionism.

GEORGE G. GROAT, *An Introduction to the Study of Organized Labor in America.* New York, The Macmillan Company, 1926, 532 pp.

A valuable study of the structure, activities, policies and problems of the various types of American unions and of the American Federation of Labor.

DAVID J. SAPOSS, *Readings in Trade Unionism.* New York, George H. Doran Company, 1926, 451 pp.

Principles and problems of labor organizations, as discussed by trade-unionists in their official publications and writings.

RICHARD C. NYMAN and ELLIOTT D. SMITH, *Union-Management Cooperation in the "Stretch-Out."* New Haven, Yale University Press, 1934, 210 pp.

This first-hand study of the problems of introducing technological change in a textile mill is a revealing contribution to the general problem of the possibilities, limitations and technique of union-management cooperation in production.

JOHN HILTON, and others, Editors, *Are Trade Unions Obstructive?* London, Victor Gollancz, Ltd., 1935, 349 pp.

This volume, published under the joint editorship of six distinguished Britishers (including N. Seebohm Rowntree, Sir Arthur Salter and Professor John Hilton), is based on a study in the chief industries of Great Britain of the extent to which union rules and practices interfere with industrial efficiency and economic prosperity.

ALBERT R. ELLINGWOOD and WHITNEY COOMBS, *The Government and Labor.* New York, McGraw-Hill Book Company, Inc., 1926, 639 pp.

A compilation of the more important statutes, judicial decisions, administrative orders, and reports bearing upon the relations between the federal and state governments and labor in the United States, with illuminating comments and questions.

INTERNATIONAL LABOUR OFFICE, *Conciliation and Arbitration in Industrial Disputes.* Geneva, International Labour Office, 1933, 696 pp.

A comparative analysis of the legislation of various countries on the conciliation and arbitration procedure adopted for the prevention and settlement of trade disputes concerning the fixing of working conditions.

LEWIS L. LORWIN and ARTHUR WUBNIG, *Labor Relations Boards.* Washington, The Brookings Institution, 1935, 477 pp.

An account of the regulation of collective bargaining under the National Industrial Recovery Act by the various labor relations boards.

TWENTIETH CENTURY FUND, INC., *Labor and the Government.* New York, McGraw-Hill Book Company, 1935, 413 pp.

An investigation of the role of the Government in labor relations which begins with an informative discussion of trade-unions, employers' associations and company unions, and then concentrates on the problem of industrial disputes and their adjustment. It reviews government efforts in mediation and intervention before and during the N.R.A. and ends with recommendations concerning needed types of legislation and administration.

NATIONAL LABOR RELATIONS BOARD, (1) *First Annual Report,* 150 pp., (2) *Decisions and Orders,* 1094 pp., (3) *Governmental Protection of Labor's Right to Organize,* 174 pp. Washington, Government Printing Office, 1936.

The First Annual Report is for the fiscal year ended June 30, 1936, the Decisions for cases decided from Dec. 7, 1935 to July 1, 1936. The third publication, labelled Bulletin No. 1, is by the Board's Division of Economic Research, and contains testimony given in behalf of the National Labor Relations Act by authorities summoned to a hearing held for the purpose by the Board.

NATIONAL MEDIATION BOARD, *First Annual Report,* 1935, 69 pp., *Second Annual Report,* 1936, 46 pp. Washington, Government Printing Office.

These two reports, covering the two fiscal years ending June 30, 1936, summarize the work of the National Mediation Board created to administer general labor relations on the railways, and of the National Railroad Adjustment Board, which administers certain types of railway disputes.

INDEX